# Managing Human Resources
# in the European Tourism
# and Hospitality Industry

# CHAPMAN & HALL SERIES IN TOURISM AND HOSPITALITY MANAGEMENT

Series Editors:  C.L. Jenkins and R.C. Wood
The Scottish Hotel School
University of Strathclyde, UK

**Titles in this series:**

**Behavioural Studies in Hospitality Management**
R. Carmouche and N. Kelly
ISBN 0 412 60850 2, 232 pages

**Business Accounting in Hospitality and Tourism**
H. Atkinson, A. Berry and R. Jarvis
ISBN 0 412 48080 8, 336

**Interpersonal Skills in Hospitality Management**
M.A. Clark
ISBN 0 412 57330 X, 232 pages

**Economics for Hospitality Management**
P. Cullen
ISBN 0 412 60540 6, 224 pages

**Doing Your Dissertation**
**A guide for students in tourism, leisure and hospitality management**
M. Foley
ISBN 0 412 60840 5, 200 pages

Books in the series are available on free inspection for lecturers considering the texts for course adoption. Details of these, and any other Chapman & Hall titles are available by writing to the publishers (2–6 Boundary Row, London, SE1 8HN) or by telephoning the Promotions Department on 0171 865 0066.

# Managing Human Resources

## in the European Tourism and Hospitality Industry

### A strategic approach

## Tom Baum

Professor of International Hotel and Tourism Management

The University of Buckingham, UK

## CHAPMAN & HALL

University and Professional Division

London · Glasgow · Weinheim · New York · Tokyo · Melbourne · Madras

**Published by**
**Chapman & Hall, 2–6 Boundary Row, London SE1 8HN, UK**

Chapman & Hall, 2–6 Boundary Row, London SE1 8HN, UK

Blackie Academic & Professional, Wester Cleddens Road, Bishopbriggs, Glasgow G64 2NZ, UK

Chapman & Hall GmbH, Pappelallee 3, 69469 Weinheim, Germany

Chapman & Hall USA, One Penn Plaza, 41st Floor, New York NY 10119, USA

Chapman & Hall Japan, ITP-Japan, Kyowa Building, 3F, 2-2-1 Hirakawacho, Chiyoda-ku, Tokyo 102, Japan

Chapman & Hall Australia, Thomas Nelson Australia, 102 Dodds Street, South Melbourne, Victoria 3205, Australia

Chapman & Hall India, R. Seshadri, 32 Second Main Road, CIT East, Madras 600 035, India

First edition 1995

©1995 Tom Baum

Typeset in 10.5/12pt Times Ten by Photoprint, Torquay, Devon
Printed in Great Britain by the Alden Press, Osney Mead, Oxford

ISBN 0 412 55630 8

A catalogue record for this book is available from the British Library

Library of Congress Catalog Card Number: 95–67606

∞ Printed on acid-free text paper, manufactured in accordance with ANSI/NISO Z39.48-1992 (Permanence of Paper).

*For Alexander*

# Contents

# Series Editors' Preface

The Chapman & Hall Series in Tourism and Hospitality Management is dedicated to the publication of high quality textbooks and other volumes that will be of benefit to those engaged in hotel, catering and tourism education, especially at degree and postgraduate level. All the authors in the series are experts in their own fields, actively engaged in teaching, research and consultancy in hospitality and tourism. This is a distinctive feature of the series and each book comprises an authoritative blend of subject-relevant theoretical considerations and practical applications and illustrations prepared by experienced writers. Furthermore, a unique quality of the series is that it is student oriented, offering accessible texts that take account of the realities of management and operations in the hospitality and tourism industries, being constructively critical where necessary without losing sight of the overall goal of providing clear accounts of essential concepts, techniques and issues. The tourism and hospitality industries are diverse and dynamic industries and it is the intention of the series to reflect this diversity and dynamism by publishing quality texts that embrace topical subjects without losing sight of enduring themes. In this respect, the Chapman & Hall Series in Tourism and Hospitality Management is an innovative venture committed to quality, accessibility and relevance. The Series Editors are grateful to Chapman & Hall for supporting this philosophy and would particularly like to acknowledge the commitment, expertise and insight of the Commissioning Editor, Steven Reed, whose contribution to the realization of the series has been invaluable.

C.L. Jenkins
R.C. Wood
The Scottish Hotel School
University of Strathclyde

# Preface

The tourism and hospitality industry worldwide is one of the fastest growing economic sectors and claims are frequently quoted that it is about to become or already is the world's largest industry, employing by some estimates over 10 million people. Clearly people are a central resource to the effective operation of this labour intensive industry. The purpose of this book is to explore ways in which the human resources of tourism and hospitality can be utilized to better effect, not solely in terms of productivity and short-term bottom line profitability, but also within the context of a longer-term investment strategy, with the emphasis placed upon human resource practices that are sustainable. Linking this aspect of management to the concept of sustainability is relatively unusual but it is hoped that the force of logic behind the argument that connects human resource management and sustainability will become clearer as the reader progresses through the book.

The book also has a focus on Europe. Much that is written about human resources within the tourism and hospitality industry does not operate within the specific geographical constraints of a region or a continent and it is fair to say that the majority of issues which are considered in this book are generic and do have wider applicability than that provided by the confines of Europe. However, it is also clear that aspects of the management of human resources in tourism and hospitality are greatly influenced by their immediate geographical, social, economic and political environment, and this is certainly true in the context of Europe. That said, Europe is by no means more homogeneous in human resource terms than it is in other respects. Each country has its own traditions and practices which influence factors such as the ways in which people work, the remuneration that they receive, the status that they are accorded and the ways in which education prepares them for careers. There is also a very clear divide between western and eastern parts of Europe. Western Europe, broadly embracing the newly expanded European Union plus remaining 'outsiders' within the former EFTA, provides the main focus for this book because of the relative stability that exists within human resources in the tourism and hospitality industry. By contrast, Eastern Europe is in a state of flux and constant change and it is beyond the scope of this book to predict how the social, economic or political shape of countries in this region will emerge over the next decade. However, reference is made in this book to the human resource challenges and problems faced by countries such as Russia and Romania in order to highlight their current status and likely future direction.

This book combines what are frequently considered two separate concepts into a singular adjective and noun. Tourism and hospitality are used in a unitary context to describe one industry in Europe. This is done advisedly, in the knowledge that for some people the two are clearly distinct and separate. However, hospitality does constitute the main subsector within tourism, and in some countries takes on a wider interpretation in that it subsumes tourism as a generic term in its own right, especially within the context of educational provision. CHRIE (The Council for Hotel, Restaurant and Institutional Education), working on behalf of the United States government, is moving towards a definition of hospitality that has much in common with wider descriptions of tourism in that it embraces all activities concerned with the provision of guest services to the visitor or tripper. There are parts of hospitality which, arguably, fall outside of the remit of tourism – catering in the institutional or industrial context, for example. However, on balance, the unification of the two terms is intended to broaden the scope of the material under consideration without necessarily engaging in the complex theoretical debates which the issue of precise definition normally generates.

This book owes much to the influence and advice of colleagues and friends over a number of years. My former colleagues at CERT in Ireland have contributed to the conceptualization of some of the main ideas behind what follows in this book. Professional and academic colleagues in Europe and beyond have also assisted in assembling material and initiating ideas for this book and are too numerous to mention by name. One I would like to highlight, however, is Michael Conlin of Bermuda College with whom some of the initial ideas relating to sustainability in the human resource domain were discussed and developed. My colleagues in the University of Buckingham have provided support and the source of ideas and guidance. In particular, V.S. Mahesh and Sylvia Brunner have provided wonderful sounding-boards in the preparation of this book. Sylvia also contributed her time by her critical and supportive reading of the manuscript in its early form. My thanks, therefore, are wide ranging. However, without the encouragement and forbearance of my wife, Brelda, this project would still remain an idea rather than a reality.

# Human resources in European tourism and hospitality: an introduction

**1**

## THE SCOPE OF THE CHAPTER

This chapter sets the scene for the book. The first aim of the chapter is to set European tourism and hospitality in its economic and social context by addressing its position within the economies of the countries, both East and West, within the continent. This is an important first step because of the major political, economic and social changes which have affected Central and Eastern Europe since the late 1980s and which continue to impact on the region in a way that makes the prediction of outcomes impossible. Prior to 1989, the commentator on the tourism and hospitality industry in Europe could justifiably divide the continent into two from an economic perspective, and consider the halves without any requirement to compare or relate the characteristics of one to those of the other. Literally; they were two separate worlds, divided by both a divergent understanding of what tourism is and how the industry operates. Superficially, this situation no longer formally pertains and tourism and hospitality can be seen to operate to a common agenda throughout the continent. However, the historic legacy of up to fifty years in Eastern Europe will not disappear overnight so that, in many respects, Europe is now a much more complex entity than in the past, when we attempt to consider it from the point of view of tourism. Burton's (1994) analysis, as a geographer, divides Europe into three physical zones based on the Mediterranean basin, the mountainous east–west spine and the industrialized northwest. This classification, however, fails to reflect political and economic change since 1989, and the reality is that any consideration of tourism and hospitality in Europe must be sensitive to a continually changing political, social and economic environment.

The second theme of this chapter is one that binds much subsequent discussion in this book, and that is the link between the concept of sustainability in tourism, and the position of human resources within this development model. It is a key objective here to demonstrate that an understanding of sustainability in tourism provides the 'cement' through which may be bound what are frequently fragmented and isolated activities or functions within tourism and hospitality – namely product and service development, strategic management and marketing, and managerial and corporate culture – with wider human resource concerns within a tourism and hospitality business or the wider industry. This objective will necessitate some consideration of the concept of sustainability and how it is normally applied in order that its application within the human resource area can be introduced.

It is not our task, here, to consider in detail definitions of tourism and the tourist. Good alternative sources do exist for this purpose, for example Medlik (1988) who explores both quantitative and qualitative approaches to understanding what is, in reality, a fairly amorphous concept. Despite the fluidity which affects attempts at defining tourism in a meaningful way, there is no doubt that it does impact widely upon the social, cultural, environmental, economic and, indeed, psychological makeup of both host and originating locations within what Leiper (1990) calls the tourism system. What is important, in terms of this book about European tourism and hospitality and its human resource context, is to be aware of the problems which are confronted in attempting to define tourism and the consequences that this has, particularly for comparative analysis of data and related qualitative information. Bar-On (1989) points to some of the data collection difficulties which are faced with respect to tourism. If we add to this some of the confusion that exists with regard to defining the scope and understanding the interdependencies which are inherent within tourism, hospitality and their wider environment, then we can understand the need for caution in the interpretation of how the industry operates within Europe. We will face this problem in a number of contexts, for example in considering the range of occupations which can be found within the tourism and hospitality industry (see Chapter 2), as well as when comparisions are made between official data sources from various countries.

## EUROPE AND TOURISM

Tourism and hospitality has a focal point within the economies of most European countries. With the exception of small European states such as Malta and Monaco, dependence is, by no means, at the levels to be found in some Caribbean and Pacific nations. However, tourism is a major contributor to foreign exchange earnings for most Western and, increasingly, Eastern European nations as well. Indeed, tourism and hospitality is being targeted as a major platform within the reconstruction of former planned economies in Bulgaria, the Czech Republic, Hungary, Romania and Slovakia, among other countries in the region. The varied but still significant position of tourism within Western European economies is shown in Table 1.1.

**Table 1.1** International tourism and the national economy in Western Europe, 1986

| Country | GDP | Tourism receipts as % of exports of goods/services | Tourism expenditure as % of imports of goods/services |
|---|---|---|---|
| Austria | 7.4 | 18.1 | 10.5 |
| Belgium/ Luxembourg | 2.0 | 2.2 | 3.0 |
| Denmark | 2.1 | 5.9 | 6.3 |
| Finland | 0.9 | 3.0 | 5.2 |
| France | 1.3 | 5.2 | 3.6 |
| F.R. Germany | 0.7 | 2.1 | 7.4 |
| Greece | 4.6 | 23.2 | 4.1 |
| Ireland | 2.7 | 4.5 | 4.1 |
| Italy | 1.6 | 7.7 | 2.3 |
| Netherlands | 1.3 | 2.2 | 5.1 |
| Norway | 1.5 | 3.7 | 8.1 |
| Portugal | 5.4 | 15.6 | 2.9 |
| Spain | 5.2 | 25.9 | 3.5 |
| Sweden | 1.2 | 3.3 | 6.2 |
| Switzerland | 4.0 | 8.3 | 7.3 |
| UK | 1.5 | 3.8 | 4.2 |

*Source*: OECD (1988) in Williams and Shaw (1991), p. 30.

The picture in Western Europe is by no means homogeneous. Tourism and hospitality varies greatly in significance for the economies and levels of employment within the different countries, reflecting a north–south divide between the industrialized nations of the northwest and the greater dependence on tourism and hospitality of the Mediterranean. Nevertheless, tourism is of sizeable importance to all countries in the region and this situation is likely to remain as easy access and the removal of fiscal and psychological barriers to travel within the European Union take greater effect. In considering the above figures, it is necessary to remember that they relate to international tourism alone. The economic impact of domestic travel and tourism, while rather more difficult to quantify, is very significant in many Western European countries, particularly France, Italy and the United Kingdom.

Comparable information relating to Eastern Europe is not so readily available. Hall (1991) points to the problems of arriving at reliable tourism and hospitality data with respect to this region, highlighting in particular data inconsistency and definitional issues as sources of the problem. It is unlikely that this situation will alter significantly in the short term, despite the considerable level of investment in tourism and hospitality infrastructure – including information systems – in the region, supported by the European Union and other donor agencies. One interesting factor at the micro level (encountered by the author in Romania) is a strong reluctance to be found in the growing private tourism sector to supply information of any sort (financial, employment, visitor profile, etc.) to any central bureaucracy. For this reason and others, tourism information from Eastern Europe is likely to be incomplete or derived through exclusively macroeconomic extrapolation such as input–output analysis (Chapter 9). Where data has been available, Hall notes that:

> Tourism receipts in the region have remained low, only exceeding 3 per cent in the case of Hungary by 1987, and often much lower (0.3 per cent for Romania and 0.2 per cent for Poland in 1986), although data are limited and definitions of national product, especially for comparative purposes are not consistent.    (Hall, 1991, p. 103)

These figures are, at this point, somewhat dated and reflect the situation prior to the major political, economic and social changes after 1989. Subsequent tourism performance has been characterized by major restructuring, with the virtual disappearance of traditional East European markets from some countries (Bulgaria, Hungary, Romania, for example) and highly volatile arrivals figures from Western Europe, influenced by curiosity in the first instance and the subsequent realization that product and service standards do not necessarily warrant further visits. The dramatic post-1989 rise in visitor numbers to Hungary, the low level of spending and the equally marked decline in visitor numbers by 1993 illustrate this point.

The economic dimension is only one consideration in an evaluation of the importance of the tourism and hospitality industry in Europe. Product, market and organizational matters are also of concern with regard to the way in which they impact upon the management of human resources. The main theme of Chapter 2 addresses these considerations.

## SUSTAINABILITY IN TOURISM AND THE HR DIMENSION

No discussion of contemporary issues in international tourism and hospitality would be complete without some consideration of sustainability. The theme of sustainable tourism has, in recent years, generated a significant literature in its own right and at least one specialist publication dedicated to the area (*The Journal of Sustainable Tourism*). A useful definition of the concept is provided by Bramwell and Lane in their introduction to the first edition of that journal:

> Sustainable tourism is a positive approach intended to reduce the tensions and friction created by the complex interactions between the tourism industry, visitors, the environment and the communities which are host to holidaymakers. It is an approach which involves working for the longer quality of both natural and human resources.                    (Bramwell and Lane, 1993, p. 2)

Bramwell and Lane are unusual in addressing the concept of sustainability specifically from the perspective of tourism. Many sources derive their definitions from a wider discussion of sustainability in economic, environmental and cultural terms. Cooper *et al.* (1993), for example, draw on the wider definition used by the World Commission on Environment and Development in 1987 (the Brundtland Report) which defines sustainability as 'meeting the needs of the present without compromising the ability of future generations to meet their own needs' (p. 86).

Without specifically mentioning the word 'sustainability', one of the most refreshing new sources to address the issues facing contemporary tourism, Auliana Poon, implicitly also considers this contrast in her analysis of new and old tourism models. She applies this by comparing the characteristics of travel and tourism during the period up to the 1990s with that of the post 1980s period against a number of key characteristics (Table 1.2).

Sustainable tourism is recognized as a complex and multi-dimensional concept. In this, it draws from the much wider concern for sustainability in all aspects of economic and environmental care and management. The Action Strategy for Sustainable Tourism Development produced at the Globe '90 Conference in Vancouver, Canada, in 1990 pointed to this complexity by saying that:

**Table 1.2** Characteristics of tourism, pre- and post-1990

| Characteristic | Pre-1990s | 1980s/1990s–future |
| --- | --- | --- |
| Production concept | Mass tourism | Flexible travel and tourism options |
| Products | Mass, standardized and rigidly packaged holidays, mass markets | Flexible, segmented, environmentally sound holidays |
| Instruments of production | Packaged tours; charter flights; franchises; holiday branding; offices; hotels; resorts | Yield management; specialized operators; destination competence; independent holidays |
| Organization of production | Scale economics are important; anticipate demand growth; stocks held just in case | Scale and scope economies; flexibility; close to market; diagonal integration |
| Manning and training | Labour is seasonal; high labour turnover; reputation for lowest-paying jobs; low labour flexibility | Human resource strategies for the travel and tourism industry not yet clear |
| Marketing | Mass marketing/advertising | Mass customization |
| Customers | Inexperienced, apparently homogeneous, sun-lust, predictable, motivated by price | Experienced, independent, flexible, changed values, mature, responsible |

*Source*: Poon (1993).

> The concept of sustainable development explicitly recognizes inter-dependencies that exist among environmental and economic issues and policies. Sustainable development is aimed at protecting and enhancing environment, meeting basic human needs, promoting current and integrational equity, improving the quality of life of all peoples.
>
> (Action Strategy, 1990, p. 1)

Examples of non-sustainable tourism development in practice, in terms of physical product, are all too readily identifiable in Europe. Unplanned and uncontrolled development along parts of the Spanish coast provide a good example of building that took place in the name of tourism without serious consideration of its long-term conse-quences, of the needs of the local community or of possible changes in consumer demand and expectations. Similar indictments can be levied against parts of the south coast of England – Folkestone, for example – as well as parts of the coastline of mid and north Wales. Eastern Europe also has a number of monuments to mass and uncontrolled development which are now very out of date and unsuitable for con-temporary customer requirements. The Romanian Black Sea coast and resorts such as Constanta offer a good example. Mass tourism devel-oped in all these locations, as well as in many others, in response to immediate market demand and perceived needs without consideration of the longer-term consequences. The problem with these develop-ments when viewed with the benefit of twenty to thirty years of hind-sight is one of renovation and reconstruction, in many cases an almost impossible challenge. But the issue also relates to the suitability of large-scale resorts and structures, detached physically and culturally from the environments and communities in which they have been built. The island of Majorca, recognizing this issue, is attempting reconstruc-tion in the area of Magaluf but, ultimately, the issue is one of a physical product on a massive scale which has worn itself out in a literal sense and also in terms of its market acceptability.

There are, of course, other dimensions to sustainability. The preser-vation of fragile natural, cultural or historic resources is of equal sig-nificance. In many cases, these are the very reasons why tourists come to a destination in the first place. This is true of coral reefs, rare wild-life, great cathedrals, unique works of fine art as well as mountain walks and delicate seashore cliff tops. Unrestrained tourist access, while possibly commercially attractive in the short term, has the effect of 'killing the goose that laid the golden egg' – in other words it de-stroys by over-use and consumption the very attraction that drew visitors to the site in the first place. The sheer weight of numbers during the high season, detracts from the appeal of cities such as Lon-don, Oxford, Paris and Venice, while in the case of the last of these destinations the fragility of the environment is such that excessive visi-tor numbers are contributing to the actual destruction of parts of the city. The threat to endangered flora and fauna is also widespread, not only in the very visible context of, for example, Kenyan safari parks, but also in many European locations such as Zakynthos, the Greek island famous for its giant sea turtles.

At a sociocultural level, the potentially negative impact of tourism on traditional cultures has been widely discussed, especially with respect to the developing world. Both Guerrier (1993) and Long and Wall (1995) consider this issue in the context of the island of Bali in Indonesia, but other examples can be found within the more remote communities of western Ireland, the Scottish islands and Lapland. The effects of tourism and hospitality on existing communities can be far reaching, involving changes to the employment structure, changes in the availability of traditional agricultural and other products, inflationary increases in the cost of commodities and land and health considerations such as the introduction of new diseases, most dramatically in the form of AIDS but also a wide variety of other infections, as well as changes to traditional beliefs and practices. Sustainability in this context means a tourism and hospitality industry that develops in a way that recognizes its potential to change a community and seeks to minimize that community's perception of its most extreme effects.

A number of locations have taken drastic steps to control unrestricted access because of threats to the sustainability of the physical tourism product. Stonehenge, for example, which allowed virtually unrestricted access to visitors up to the late 1960s when family picnics frequently made use of the large stones for seating, now carefully controls access to the site and is planning further visitor management strategies in order to protect the unique heritage. Such rationing measures have proved insufficient in some locations. Historic sites on the Blasket Islands off the southwest coast of Ireland now cannot be visited except in very limited and controlled circumstances. Price-rationing is one policy to ease demand on some locations, a policy followed by major cathedrals in Britain. An alternative approach is a process of attraction substitution by which tourists are offered audio-visual interpretation and mock-ups as an alternative to the real thing in order to ensure preservation. Stonehenge to a certain degree, York and the recently renovated Waddesden Manor in Buckinghamshire, England, have all adopted this strategy in one form or another. In terms of minimizing the sociocultural impact, a good example of control is provided by the Maldives, where tourist resorts located on small islands are consciously isolated from the main centres of population and there is little direct contact between visitors and the predominantly Muslim population beyond that necessary to provide services to the tourists. The concept of a location's carrying capacity as a measure to control access and ensure preservation is one that has gained considerable currency in contemporary tourism development. Carrying capacity is defined by Mathieson and Wall (1982) as:

> ... the maximum number of people who can use a site without an unacceptable alteration in the physical environment and without an

unacceptable decline in the quality of experience gained by
visitors. (p. 21)

Cooper *et al.* (1993) go beyond what is an excessively physical definition when they talk about carrying capacity as:

... that level of tourist presence which creates impacts on the host
community, environment and economy that are acceptable to both
tourists and hosts, and sustainable over future time periods.

(p. 95)

This latter approach can readily accommodate the concept of sustainable human resource development in tourism, which we will address
later in this chapter.

The concept of sustainability in tourism can be developed and interpreted beyond the tangible impact of visitor numbers and their relationship to physical and sociocultural phenomena within the tourism
destination. Sustainable tourism can be interpreted to mean a form of
tourism which develops in harmony with local community aspirations
and is thus responsive to local democracy with regard to the kind of
development which is accepted and, indeed, the control and ownership
of such development. This is clearly a controversial dimension of sustainability and impinges on, for example, local community influence on
planning processes and relationships with outside investors, especially
from overseas, among other things. Ultimately, a model of sustainability which incorporates this dimension includes the right of the local
community to say 'no' to tourism development and tourists, although
such an extreme reaction may be rare. However, it is a dimension
which has significant implications for any discussion of human resources in the context of sustainable tourism development.

In the ideal world, sustainability is built into the planning and development of a tourism and hospitality project or forms the centrepiece of
tourism policy guidelines at the local or national level. It also reflects,
as has been suggested above, community participation in the planning
process and the application, if appropriate, of a veto on development.
True sustainable tourism and hospitality planning anticipates the needs
of future generations of tourists and thus creates or presents a product
which is protected from over-exploitation and has an in-built capacity
for change and development as demand and expectations alter over
the passage of time. More importantly, sustainable tourism planning
recognizes the rights and needs of the host community, its physical
environment, lifestyle and culture, and also its right to determine the
future of local resources, touristic and otherwise. The problems faced
by EuroDisney in achieving acceptance by the local community may, in
part, illustrate a failure to appreciate this dimension of sustainability.
In this sense, therefore, sustainable tourism development does not just
represent the economic development of a locality but also develop-

ment in and on behalf of the host community. Cooper *et al.* (1993) include an example of such a policy from Centerparcs which features a company commitment to recognize local community needs, to ensure maximum local benefits from the tourism site, to source materials locally where possible, and to maximize local employment. On a larger scale, the recently published tourism policy for Bonaire in the Netherlands Antilles (Pieters and Geevers, 1995) presents similar principles within the context of an island that has both a fragile natural environment as well as a small local population.

What, one may reasonably ask, has this discussion of sustainability in tourism to do with the management of human resources? Sustainability is not a term that has been widely associated with human resource policies and is only addressed in passing in the mainstream of sustainable tourism literature. Lane (1992) touches on the issue when, in his classification, he refers to non-sustainable tourism features, including 'no career structure' and 'employees imported' as opposed to 'career structure' and 'employment according to local potential' within the sustainable tourism paradigm. Poon (1993) also implies this distinction when she refers to old best-practices perceiving labour as a variable cost while, under new best-practice, she refers to labour as human capital. But these references are relatively unusual. Urry (1994), for example, in considering the social and cultural impact of tourism development in Europe and writing very much from within the 'sustainable' camp considers what he calls the main changes in European tourism during the 1990s. These are classified as changes in companies, changes in travel patterns and changes in the types of tourism. Interestingly and significantly no reference is made to changes in employment and the wider human resource agenda. In fact, the theme of sustainable human resource development within tourism is one that has not been fully developed in the literature except in an introductory fashion by Conlin and Baum (1994).

The notion of sustainability within human resources is one that underpins much of the subsequent discussion in this book. It is one that is worth exploring a little further at this point in order that its significance can be fully appreciated later on.

It is widely claimed within the tourism and hospitality literature – and indeed that pertaining to the wider service sector – that people are the industry's most valuable asset. To some extent, as we shall show in Chapter 6, this claim can be described as 'humbug', representing the moral high ground of an industry within which some sectors, especially accommodation and catering, belie the claim in the way that they treat and remunerate their staff. The European Institute of Education and Social Policy (EIESP) (1991) in a wide ranging analysis pinpoints one key problem in this respect. Investment in employees is often not a priority. Indeed, 'employers admit that they are not always willing to provide training programmes – or to pay for the additional skills required' (EIESP, 1991, p. 9). When offered, training is purely a short-term expedient, designed to teach staff to do their current job better and no more. It is arguable – and this may well be a line to which an author such as Wood (1992a) may subscribe – that tourism and hospitality is a people industry only in so far as people are an exploitable resource. Should the unlikely opportunity arise to offer the same standard of hospitality and service without human intervention, the industry would show few qualms in pursuing this route. Indeed, there is considerable evidence that sectors of the tourism and hospitality industry are already edging down this road through technology substitution, productivity maximization, job deskilling and, above all, standardization or, as Ritzer (1993) calls it, 'McDonaldization'.

However, as things currently stand, it is true, as this author has argued elsewhere (Baum, 1993a), that tourism and hospitality can be viewed as a people industry from three perspectives. Firstly, tourism is about people as the guest, and the delivery of the tourism product and service is evaluated on the basis of the frequently illogical demands and expectations of the guest. Secondly, the delivery of a high proportion of the tourism product and service is by people and, while productivity in many sectors may have increased and technology substitution has had an impact on delivery, the labour intensity of much of the tourism industry is inescapable and results in its variability, despite strenuous efforts towards standardization by many companies. Tourism and hospitality employees are also part of the tourism product, as entertainers for example. Finally, people as guests are part of the experience which fellow tourists pay for, whether as fellow guests in restaurants or on stage or on the dancefloor at Butlins or in Sandals.

Applying the concept of sustainability in the context of human resources in tourism necessitates recognizing this three-dimensional people input into the tourism and hospitality transaction. Because of the human element, the delivery of most tourism and hospitality products and services defies standardization (despite the efforts of many companies) and is subject to variability and iconoclastic interpretation. In part because of this but also in order to maximize the benefits of human intervention in the delivery of tourism and hospitality in the long term, sustainable human resource development in tourism results in an approach that contrasts strongly with much traditional practice in the industry of which Wood (1992a) is rightly very critical. It is characterized by, arguably, somewhat idealistic principles.

- Investment in people is a long-term commitment by both parties, employers and employees, and all actions must be guided by the recognition of this.
- Effective human resource management requires a faith in the capacity for good and the potential for enhanced achievement of each and every individual within an organization. At its most positive, this optimistic view is expressed by Mahesh (1994):

The question, 'Is nobility and perfection a natural quality in Man, and cruelty and pettiness an aberration, or vice versa?' is likely to be answered very soon in favour of human nature being intrinsically capable of unfolding its potential for perfection. The reasons for such optimism lie in some significant changes that have taken place globally, which have collectively led to the phenomenon that Alvin Toffler calls the Third Wave.                      (p. 1)

- Companies must demonstrate a faith in the capability of people in the community within which they locate and must invest in enabling these people to achieve their full potential.
- Consequently, employment of those from outside of the community, region or country should be a last resort. Parallel to this necessity should be a commitment to the training and development of local potential to fill positions taken on a temporary basis by those from outside. This may appear somewhat xenophobic, especially in the context of an integrated Europe with its commitment to full labour mobility, but it is a necessary dictum especially in less developed regions, in order to maximize the benefits of development within the community.
- Companies must recognize the impact that they have on the character and balance of the local labour market and utilize its strengths and compensate for its deficiencies in so far as is possible.
- Training is about more than attaining finite skills in order to undertake the immediate task at hand. It is also about providing flexible and transferable capabilities over the full length of a person's working career to enable them to respond to changing work demands and opportunities for new responsibilities as they arise.
- The detailed planning of human resource requirements is an integral part of all tourism development planning and must take place in tandem with the preparation of the physical facilities. The lead-time, in terms of recruiting and training highly skilled personnel, is arguably longer than that which applies with respect to physical product or marketing, especially at the macro level (Baum, 1993a).

These principles introduce themes which feature in subsequent chapters of this book. They are also principles which provide us with a framework within which we may make a comparative analysis of human resource management and development according to the 'traditional' paradigm and on the basis of practices derived from the application of principles of sustainability to the human resource environment. In many respects, this model is an attempt to provide the framework which Poon has already suggested is missing when, as shown earlier in Table 1.2 her response to the new manning and training environment was to suggest that 'human resource strategies for travel and tourism [are] not yet clear' (Poon, 1993). Here we argue that greater clarity is at hand, and the outcome of this analysis is presented in Table 1.3.

**Table 1.3** Traditional and sustainable human resource practices

| Old HR practice | New sustainable HR paradigm |
| --- | --- |
| *Recruitment and staff turnover* | |
| Recruitment undertaken without reference to local community/labour market | Recruitment based on careful analysis of local community and its labour market |
| *Ad hoc*, unplanned recruitment to meet immediate needs | Recruitment of staff based on long-term HR planning |
| Staff recruited on basis of immediate skills needs | Staff recruited on basis of potential development |
| Recruitment/'poaching' of staff from other companies | Staff recruited locally from schools/colleges/ universities |
| Expatriate staff recruited on long-term basis | Expatriate staff only employed to meet short-term needs and to develop local staff |
| High staff turnover seen as inevitable/desirable | High staff turnover seen as problematic/ undesirable |
| No measures to reduce staff turnover | Active company policies designed to minimize staff turnover |
| No interest in why staff leave | Exit interview policy |
| Continuing high staff turnover | Relatively low staff turnover |
| *Promotion and career development* | |
| Few opportunities for promotion/development within company | Career planning/tracking within company |
| No career ladder/unclear criteria for promotion | Clearly defined career ladder/accessible criteria for promotion |
| Promotion to 'plug gaps'/no preparatory training | Planned promotion with preparatory training programme |
| Key staff 'imported' from outside/abroad | Key staff 'grown'/developed within company/ locality |
| Part-time or seasonal staff excluded from training/ development/promotion opportunities | Part-time or seasonal staff integrated into training/ development/promotion system |
| No long-term commitment to seasonal staff | Long-term commitment to key seasonal staff |
| Career mobility seen as disloyal/disruptive | Career mobility recognized as beneficial to the individual |
| Opportunities limited for women, ethnic minorities, disabled | Genuine equal opportunities in employment |
| *Rewards and benefits* | |
| Company offers minimum rewards and benefits | Company offers competitive rewards and benefits |
| Conditions to suit employer needs | Conditions reflect local/individual circumstances and needs |
| Flexibility demanded to suit employer requirements | Flexibility seen as employer–employee partnership with mutual benefits |

**Table 1.3** Continued

| Old HR practice | New sustainable HR paradigm |
| --- | --- |
| Staff attitude to company a matter of indifference | Fostering of commitment and feeling of belonging among employees |

*Education, training and development*

| | |
| --- | --- |
| Training and development not planned | Planned training and development policies and strategies |
| Training compartmentalized with specialist department | Training recognized as the responsibility of all supervisors/management |
| No senior management commitment to training | Full commitment to training from CEO down |
| Training operates in isolation from other HR practices | Training linked to opportunities for promotion etc. |
| Gap between industry and education system | Partnership between industry and education system |
| Education programmes with little industry relevance | Education programmes based on industry research/identified needs |
| Education/training programmes terminal and not integrated | Education/training courses provide for further development and progression |
| Industry-developed skills not recognized by education | Industry-developed skills recognized and certified by education |

*Management culture*

| | |
| --- | --- |
| Staff seen as short-term expedient | Staff seen as key resource |
| Staff perceived as a cost | Staff perceived as an asset |
| Authoritarian, remote management culture | Democractic, participative management culture |
| Authority vested in management alone | Responsibility delegated to all levels of staff – 'empowerment' |
| Staff remote from decision-making | Staff consulted/involved with decisions affecting their area of responsibility |
| Inflexible imposition of corporate culture | Corporate culture responds flexibly to local culture and needs |

*National HR planning for tourism*

| | |
| --- | --- |
| Fragmentation of HR planning for tourism | Integrated approach to HR planning for tourism |
| HR considerations not recognized in tourism policy planning | HR considerations to the fore in tourism planning |
| Quality in tourism seen in exclusively physical product terms | Human resource contribution to quality recognized and nurtured |
| Local population detached from/hostile to tourism | Local population helped and encouraged to recognize their role in tourism |

The comparison in Table 1.3 provides an insight into how human resource practices which are compatible with models of sustainability within the tourism and hospitality industry can be developed. The reality is that few companies adopt policies and practices which are exclusively on one side of the divide or the other. Even within companies, the application of broad principles may result in widely diverging outcomes and, at the micro level, how human resource policies are actually implemented will depend greatly on individual managers and their commitment to principles within the right-hand column. And yet, as we shall argue in Chapter 5 of this book, there is a definite link between how employees at all levels in the tourism and hospitality industry are perceived by their managers, the delivery of quality service to customers and the outcome in terms of profitability. Within the traditional paradigm outlined in the left-hand column of Table 1.3, employees are an afterthought to the main focus of the business. Within the sustainable or integrative organizational model, business functions are designed around people. Schlesinger and Heskett (1991) argue in favour of the approach implicit within the sustainable model which they term the 'cycle of quality service':

> Capable workers who are well trained and fairly compensated, provide better service, require less supervision and [are] more likely to remain on the job. For individual companies, this means enhanced competitiveness. (Schlesinger and Heskett, 1991, p. 72)

One good example of how key aspects of the model of sustainable human resource development has been broadly applied, while not from Europe, comes from Taj Hotels in India (Mahesh, 1993). This relates to the preparation for opening of a new 34-bedroom Gateway Hotel in Chiplun, a rural community halfway between Bombay and Goa. The location was one with no tradition of employment in the tourism sector and considerable social and cultural antagonism to the idea. The hotel's eleven-step human resource development plan is, clearly, very culturally specific, but that is the essence of sustainable human resource development in tourism. The plan is outlined in Table 1.4.

This book addresses the application of the 'right-hand' principles from the model in Table 1.3 in a wide-ranging sense so that the reader will acquire a rather clearer understanding of their implications by the end. The theme of sustainability within the management of human resources is underpinned by assumptions about managerial, corporate and governmental responsibility, depending on which level the sustainable model is applied. Indeed, it draws in essence upon the notion of a social contract between on the one hand businesses and an industry sector, and on the other the community in which they operate and the people that they employ. In this context, this book derives its inspiration from the eighteenth century, from writers like Locke and Rousseau who argued for the notion of responsible coexistence between people, their endeavours and the wider environment. In Chapter 10, we will return to this theme in the light of the discussion in the following chapters.

**Table 1.4** The Gateway Hotel, Chiplun, India: Human Resource Development Plan

1. Manpower requirements for the hotel were finalized a full year before opening.

2. With the exception of the positions of hotel manager, the heads of food production, service and rooms division and a temporary training manager, all other positions were to be filled through recruitment of local personnel, following appropriate training.

3. All schools within the area were visited and graduating students were inducted into what a hotel is all about, and what kinds of jobs and careers were available. Given the orthodox and, primarily, rural background of the local community, the very concept of a hotel was so unfamiliar that this first communication was far more complex than would have been the case in an urbanized, more developed region.

4. After considerable persuasion designed to overcome local prejudices against the hotel and catering industry in general, interviews were set up and a tentative shortlist of candidates was prepared. As most of the candidates could speak only their local dialect and had no knowledge or experience of the hotel industry, the criteria for selection were restricted to personality, ability to smile, the ability to contribute to teamwork (demonstrated through games participation), average intelligence and physical fitness.

5. Among those selected, there were many who had difficulty in communicating to their parents or guardians what they had been selected for; in these cases the hotel manager and the training manager visited the homes in order to help communicate with the parents.

6. Those finally selected were put through a rigorous medical examination to ensure that only those in perfect health were hired. This process also helped to communicate the high priority given to health and hygiene by the hotel company.

7. Commencing with the very simple procedures (in this case, the use of forks and knives as the local population were unfamiliar with these), the very raw and inexperienced recruits were educated and trained in different aspects of hotel work. With the objective of facilitating easy job rotation and mobility, many were trained as multi-skilled employees; for example, a resort attendant could work as a room boy, gardener, waiter or utility assistant.

8. Within 6–8 months of joining, most of the employees were adequately trained for the opening of the hotel; for example, those trained in kitchen work could not only prepare a range of basic dishes but could also complete a portion control format and an itemized cost sheet.

9. In anticipation of possible attrition, a number of supernumerary staff were recruited and trained and, in the event, this provision proved vital as a number of staff did leave before the hotel opened.

10. Internal systems for grievance management and counselling were established, wages formalized and all personnel systems were in place from the outset so that potential causes of labour unrest were anticipated and minimized.

**Table 1.4** Continued

11. The training manager was withdrawn only after all systems had been established and the small management team was in position with a fully trained staff. For the first two years, thereafter, central support was provided in the area of industrial relations and associated personnel concerns but, in all other respects, the hotel was able to function independently in the human resource domain.

---

REVIEW AND DISCUSSION QUESTIONS

1. Consider the importance of the tourism and hospitality industry to the economy of a community, region or country with which you are familiar. In what ways is the importance evident and what strategies are pursued by the public and private sector in support of the industry?
2. In what ways might post-1989 changes affect the tourism and hospitality industry in Eastern Europe?
3. Consider the suggestion that sustainable tourism and hospitality is unrealistic idealism.
4. Based on your own working experience, identify human resource practices that fall within either the traditional model or the sustainable human resource paradigm.
5. Table 1.4 presents an example of human resource planning from India. In what ways and with what modifications might this human resource model be applied to the following new tourism and hospitality developments?
   (a) A beach bar and restaurant in Lindos, Rhodes, Greece.
   (b) A budget hotel and restaurant on the outskirts of Bochum, Germany.
   (c) A five-star resort hotel on the Black Sea in Constantia, Romania, recently renovated and operating under a Western European management contract.
   (d) An international theme park, due to open outside Barcelona, Spain.
   (e) Event caterers contracted to provide for 500 000 visitors to the three public days of the British Grand Prix at Silverstone, England.
   (f) An Oslo, Norway, airline formed to compete on major domestic and international business routes within Scandanavia.
   (g) A duty-free shop in Paris, established to cater exclusively for the Japanese visitor market.
   (h) The first overseas representative office located in London to be operated by the National Tourist Board of a small Pacific nation.

# The European tourism and hospitality industry | 2

## INTRODUCTION

In order to gain an understanding of the major issues that affect the management of human resources within Europe's tourism and hospitality industry, it is important to be familiar with the main features of the industry, from a structural, organizational, cultural and historical point of view. These dimensions, together with the impact of wider socioeconomic and political environmental considerations, provide the backcloth against which human resource considerations need to be evaluated and policies developed. In this chapter and Chapter 3, therefore, we shall consider some of the structural, organizational, cultural and historical characteristics of the tourism and hospitality industry in Europe. This will allow us not only in these chapters but also subsequently to assess the extent and manner of their impact on the management of human resources.

It is easy and very tempting to talk about the European tourism and hospitality industry and this certainly provides a convenient shorthand by which to refer to the facilities, activities and organizations which combine to form tourism and hospitality in Europe. It is also a shorthand which implies homogeneity, an industry that has dominant features in common throughout all constituent parts of Europe. The reality is far from this convenient assumption and this chapter will focus as much on the diversity of tourism and hospitality in Europe as upon the common ground which binds it together.

Even attempting to consider any industry on a Europe-wide basis can be problematic. Physical geographers provide us with a definition which, broadly, sees the boundaries of Europe at the Urals to the east, the Bosporus and the Straits of Gibraltar to the south, the Atlantic Ocean to the west and the Arctic Ocean to the north. These delineations match – but by no means 100% – those which social and political geographers may provide. We are immediately faced with a number of problems at the edges of Europe. A number of countries are part in Europe and part in Asia. European Turkey, to the west of the Bosporus, is just a small proportion of the total country, which is predominantly in Asia. The country, as a whole, aspires to membership of the European Union and, from a tourism and hospitality perspective, the main part of its tourism resources lie in what used to be called Asia Minor, to the east of the Bosporus. Russia also divides in two between Europe and Asia; in land mass terms, the majority is in the latter but the majority of the population are to be found to the west of the Urals. Since the break-up of the Soviet Union, the formation of the independent state of Kazakhstan could be taken to provide a third example of this Europe–Asia divide, although the country is generally located among the new Asian republics for cultural and religious purposes. In strict definitional terms, other similar problems can also be identified. Cyprus, located closer to Syria, Lebanon and Asian Turkey is generally perceived to be a European country for historic and cultural reasons although the current division of the country provides much stronger Asian ties for the northern part of the island. Likewise, important tourist destinations such as the Greek islands of Rhodes and Samos are much closer, geographically, to Asian Turkey than they are to the Greek mainland and in other political, cultural and historic contexts could well form a natural part of Asia. The Canary Islands, again very important in tourism terms, are part of the continental shelf of north Africa, although politically part of Spain. Finally, the status of colonies, overseas territories and departments of European countries can also present some problems. Politically, remaining British colonies such as Anguilla and Bermuda are detached from the colonial power and thus do not have any direct involvement with Europe. The same is true of Dutch colonies in the Caribbean. However, French overseas departments in the Caribbean, Indian Ocean and Pacific are deemed to be fully integrated parts of France from a political perspective and, thus, could be deemed part of Europe in certain circumstances.

Definitional problems are not only the work of cartographers. Europe is frequently – and erroneously – used as an abbreviated term for the European Union and, thus, we read about the debate in Norway regarding that country's 'entry into Europe'. The legacy of the Cold War is that Europe is still widely seen as consisting of two parts, east and west, even though parts of Western Europe (Austria, Greece and parts of Italy) lie considerably to the east of areas of Eastern Europe (the former East Germany and the Czech Republic). Furthermore, a number of pan-European organizations include members from outside of the geographical boundaries of the continent. Membership of the European Broadcasting Union ensures that Israel participates in the annual Eurovision Song Contest and UEFA, the association football authority, does likewise in including Israeli clubs in their competitions.

Geography, therefore, presents one initial but not insurmountable challenge when addressing the tourism and hospitality industry in Europe. In practice, in this book, a relatively pragmatic approach is adopted whereby Europe is seen in terms of its political constituent countries and grey areas, such as Turkey and Russia, are treated in a flexible manner driven primarily by tourism and hospitality considerations. Thus the Turkish Aegean and Mediterranean coastlines have clear common ground with other sun destinations in Greece and Spain and compete for similar markets such that it would be illogical to exclude this region from discussion. The same could, of course, be said for Tunisia and Morocco, although these countries are not considered here. By contrast, eastern Turkey has much more in common with Asian neighbours such as Iraq and Syria and these areas are excluded from consideration here.

The second issue that arises in the context of this chapter is that of the meaning of the term 'tourism and hospitality industry'. In Chapter 1, we chose not to attempt a definition of tourism because this ground is well covered elsewhere. Here, the requirement is somewhat more practical because unless we are clear as to what we mean by the industry, it is difficult to consider its scope, size and organization in European terms. The conventional approach is to consider tourism and hospitality in terms of its component subsectors and thus to define the industry in terms of the facilities, businesses and other organizations with which the visitor comes into contact during her or his stay. This is the approach adopted by Baum (1989a) in defining the scope of the tourism industry in Ireland and it is one that we shall return to later in this section.

An alternative approach is to consider the industry in terms of the economic activity which occurs when a visitor interacts with the range of goods and services that are available for purchase, consumption or other usage. In this sense, the tourism and hospitality industry is customer-centred.

> The tourist industry is defined, not in terms of the production of particular types of goods and services, but in terms of the circumstances in which goods and services are consumed. Thus the sale of a particular good or service to a tourist is counted as a 'tourist expenditure' while the sale of the same good or service to a local resident is not. As a result of this difference in concept, the tourist industry overlaps the usual classification of industries defined according to the goods or services they produce.
>
> (Australian Treasury, in Leiper, 1979, p. 399)

Leiper (1979) builds upon this approach when he distinguishes between the incidental industries which serve tourists' wants and needs, and the tourist industry itself. In doing so Leiper, in common with many other writers, subsumes hospitality within tourism. Incidental industries comprise the shops, restaurants, public services and recreational facilities which tourists may utilize during a stay but whose users are normally the local community. Leiper recognizes that there may be considerable overlap between incidental and tourist services and that activities within the two groups may show considerable commonality in terms of the actual work undertaken and goods and services provided. Thus a tourist restaurant may offer a similar ambience and have the same menu as one which is targeted mainly at the local community and which, when patronized by passing tourist trade, by Leiper's definition, forms part of the incidental sector. Leiper sees the tourist industry as comprising: 'all those firms, organizations and facilities which are intended to serve the specific needs and wants of tourists' (Leiper, 1979, p. 400).

The important words in this definition are 'specific' and 'are intended to'. 'Specific' implies that the goods and services provided to the tourist are unique to the visitor and somehow different to those provided for the local community. The notion of intent implies that the facility or business was established with the intention to provide for tourists and not for the local community. The reality of the tourism and hospitality industry, in many parts of Europe, is that such clear distinctions are not always readily made. As we shall see in Chapter 3, in many parts of Europe, tourism evolved and developed over a considerable timespan. Attractions and facilities which are now major tourist 'draws' have long acted as resources for communities at a local or national level – major places of worship such as cathedrals are good examples. It is thus not always easy to designate such attractions within Leiper's two-type classification. To place St Paul's in London or Notre Dame in Paris within the category of 'incidental services' because they were not established specifically for tourist use is clearly absurd given their importance both as national centres of worship and as major tourist attractions. On a smaller scale, it is common in places such as Connemara in Ireland and the Scottish Highlands to find tourist-focused shops and other facilities which have evolved out of and alongside established local businesses – shops, pubs or garages – and where the original activity remains an important part of the operation, especially out of season. It is also difficult to place such concerns within either of Leiper's categories. At the same time, there clearly are businesses which have been established with the intention that they be for the specific use of tourists. The more recent the establishment of the location as a tourist destination, the more widespread are such businesses, as can clearly be seen in major Mediterranean beach resorts such as Benidorm where shops and restaurants intended for local use are located away from major tourist areas and where there is relatively little common usage of facilities other than the beach by visitors and the local community. However, even purpose-built attractions such as theme parks, which might reasonably have been assumed to meet the requirements for designation within the tourist industry, are frequently located on the basis of access from a substantial local as well as tourist market. EuroDisney's location in close proximity to a major population concentration within the Isle de France, primarily Paris, does not represent chance siting but recognition of the importance of substantial local as well as tourist markets to attractions of this kind.

Leiper's approach, in all probability, has greater applicability in the context of international tourism to the developing world where the social and economic distance between the local community and the visitor is such that the extent of 'overlap' between tourist and local consumption of goods and services is relatively small. The two groups operate through use of a discrete range of businesses which are dedicated to meeting specific tourist or local market needs. As economic prosperity within the local community increases, so there is a growth in the extent of common consumption of goods and services by, on the one hand, the international tourist and, on the other hand, the local community and the growing domestic market. This pattern can clearly be seen in a study of the growth of tourism and rising economic prosperity in countries such as Malaysia and Singapore. In Europe, the 'peripheral' regions of the south, notably Spain, Portugal, Greece, southern Italy and, more recently, Turkey, as well as parts of the western margins (Ireland, Scotland), have experienced this convergence in consumption rather more recently than other areas. Recent changes in Eastern Europe, however, mean that there is now evidence of considerable visitor – community 'gaps' in terms of consumption patterns in countries such as Romania and Russia, and Leiper's distinction does have greater applicability in these countries. However, in the rest of Europe, as we shall see in Chapter 3, the democratization of tourism in Europe and the era of mass participation have served to significantly reduce the gap between local and visitor consumption.

It is, therefore, probably more realistic to recognize that, for many businesses, the distinction between activity which is tourist or non-tourist generated is not easy to make and the fact of a mixed tourist and local market may not always be of that great consequence. There are, however, consequences for marketing policies and strategies which cannot be ignored while, in human resource terms, catering for an international as opposed to local clientele may have implications for the skills that are required. We will return to this theme in Chapter 7.

If Leiper's approach does not really work in the context of the European tourism and hospitality industry, we are drawn back to an understanding based on the component parts of the industry as defined by the use that is made of them by domestic and international tourists. Thus any business which provides goods and services to a visitor falls within the scope of the tourism and hospitality industry, irrespective of whether it also serves local community needs and without qualification on the basis of whether tourist-related business is the major or minor component of the business activity. Davidson (1994) provides useful clarification in support of this approach when he argues that tourism can be viewed as:

- A social phenomenon, not a production activity.
- The sum of the expenditures of all travellers or visitors for all purposes, not the receipt of a select group of similar establishments.
- An experience or a process, not a product – an extremely varied experience at that.                          (Davidson, 1994, p. 24)

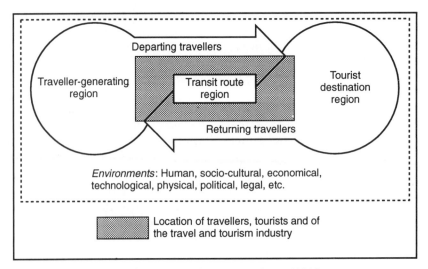

**Figure 2.1** Leiper's tourism system. (Source: Leiper, 1990.)

In a further analysis of the structure of the tourism and hospitality industry, Leiper (1990) considers the environment in terms of the process of flow through which the tourist progresses. He thus considers the tourism system to consist of the travel generating region, the transit route region and, finally, the tourist destination region. Leiper's model is shown in Figure 2.1.

Adopting a broad-based approach to an interpretation of what constitutes the tourism and hospitality industry has important consequences for our understanding of human resources issues in the tourism and hospitality industry. As we shall see in later chapters, approaches that are required with respect to, among other things:

- understanding of the tourism and hospitality labour markets (Chapter 4);
- developing a service culture based on human resource capabilities (Chapter 5);
- managing a multicultural market and workplace environment (Chapter 7);
- planning training and development for tourism and hospitality (Chapter 8); and
- provision of overall coordination for human resource management within the industry (Chapter 9);

are significantly affected by the breadth of interpretation that is applied to the tourism and hospitality industry. Because our definition here of the tourism and hospitality industry encompasses activities such as the public service (civil servants, police, immigration), banks and local garages as well as more conventional tourism and hospitality operations, approaches in all the above areas must recognize this diversity within the industry.

## SUBSECTORS OF THE TOURISM AND HOSPITALITY INDUSTRY

The tourism and hospitality industry consists of a number of major subsectors as well as a range of what might be called ancillary activities which provide support services for tourists. At its simplest, the components of the industry are identified as

- travel and transport;
- accommodation and catering; and
- leisure, recreation and business facilities (Davidson, 1989).

This classification simplifies the variety which is contained within each of the above but also neglects significant further components. A more comprehensive approach might include companies and organizations responsible for the following areas (recognizing overlap between areas which results in some duplication):

- travel and transport:
  - air transport
  - water transport (ferries, hovercraft, cruise liners, canal craft);
  - road transport (private, car hire, bus/coach, taxi, horse drawn);
  - rail transport;
  - air transport infrastructure services (airports, information, handling services, air traffic control);
  - rail transport infrastructure services (information, stations);
  - road transport infrastructure (information, motorway services, garages/petrol stations, rescue services, road toll services);
  - tour operators;
  - travel agents;
- accommodation:
  - hotels/motels;
  - self-catering accommodation (apartments, cottages, gites);
  - health farms;
  - camping sites/caravan parks;
  - holiday camps/inclusive all-weather parks (Centerparcs);
  - timeshare;
  - ferries/cruise liners;
- catering:
  - restaurants at all levels of service;
  - cafes;
  - bars/clubs (sports, country);
  - fast food;
  - outdoor and speciality catering (sports events, outdoor theatre, etc.);
  - transport catering (airports, airlines, trains, stations, coaches);

- entertainment:
  - clubs;
  - theatres/cinemas/concert halls;
  - outdoor theatre and music venues/festivals;
  - sports (non-participatory);
- sports and recreation:
  - participation sports (golf, water, equestrian, angling, etc.);
  - sports/fitness clubs and centres;
  - hotel sports and fitness facilities;
  - outward bound/activity centres;
  - organized recreation (ornithology, hiking, etc.);
  - national/regional parks;
  - beaches and other waterfront locations;
  - gambling (casinos, sports);
- history and heritage:
  - museums;
  - galleries;
  - historic buildings (cathedrals, castles, great houses);
  - historic sites (burial and worship sites, battlefields, land and maritime locations);
  - interpretation centres;
  - heritage and genealogical services;
- natural/scenic heritage attractions/sites:
  - coastlines, mountains, woodlands, etc.;
  - protected sites for flora and fauna;
- attractions (constructed);
  - theme parks;
  - animal parks/zoos;
  - interpretation centres;
- events:
  - sporting (Olympic Games, World Cup, grands prix);
  - cultural (European City of Culture);
  - festivals (Notting Hill Carnival, garden festivals, Cannes Film Festival, Montreux Jazz Festival);
  - shows (Chelsea Flower Show, Crufts Dog Show, county and local agricultural shows);
- retail:
  - tourist craft and souvenir shops;
  - duty-free shopping;
  - boutiques and speciality shops;
  - major department stores and similar shops;
  - food shopping;
  - airport/other transport shopping;
  - hotel shopping;
- business, conference/convention tourism and hospitality;
  - business centres (hotel, free-standing);
  - conference/convention centres (hotel, independent);
  - incentive organizers;

- tourism and hospitality information and facilitation:
  - travel agents;
  - tour guides;
  - tourist information centres/offices;
  - national, regional and local tourist boards;
  - motoring/travel organizations (AA, RAC);
  - media tourism and hospitality presentations (specialist magazines, newspapers, television, radio);
- tourism and hospitality support services:
  - bureaux de change (banks, hotels, airports, independent);
  - customs, immigration, tourist police;
  - government (national, regional) ministry responsible for tourism;
  - industry and professional associations (International Hotels Association – IHA; International Air Transport Association – IATA; International Civil Aviation Organization – ICAO; European Travel Commission – ETC; Tourism Society; Hotel Catering and Institutional Management Association – HCIMA);
  - voluntary associations (National Trust).

This listing, while not fully comprehensive in its contents, does, however, give a clear indication of the diversity of subsectors which, to a greater or lesser extent, constitute the tourism and hospitality industry in Europe. This complex amalgam of public, private and voluntary organizations and businesses provides the basis from which the full range of entrepreneurial, technical, operational and management employment options within tourism and hospitality can be identified. Consequently, it is important to retain this 'big picture' of the industry in mind at all times when addressing various human resource concerns. Much of what has been written about the industry from a human resource perspective in fact focuses primarily upon the hotel and catering subsectors or the provision of the three core services of food, drink and accommodation. This only represents the hospitality aspect of the industry. More limited discussion addresses transport, travel and leisure services but much of the complex range of additional activities is virtually neglected in relation to a consideration of organizational structure, ownership and staffing.

## THE TOURISM AND HOSPITALITY PRODUCT IN EUROPE

Beyond the identification of the various subsectors of the tourism and hospitality industry and the presence of most of them within the majority of countries, is it meaningful to consider tourism and hospitality in Europe as a unified and identifiable industry? Such unity would imply, at least, that there are significant common elements and features which are applicable to all or the majority of countries and regions in Europe. Such commonality could relate to:

- similar tourism and hospitality product profiles (natural, historic, cultural, created, activity-based);
- similar visitor markets;
- similarities in size of business, ownership or organizational structure;
- similarities in private/public sector involvement;
- similarities in economic impact and importance;
- similar social and political commitments to the tourism and hospitality industry; and
- similarities with respect to the service and technical skills utilization and productivity of the workforce in tourism and hospitality.

In order to assess whether it is meaningful to talk about unity within the European tourism and hospitality industry, it is necessary to evaluate the evidence with respect to each of the above criteria.

### Europe – a common tourism and hospitality product profile?

In geographical and climatic terms, Europe extends on one axis from the near Arctic in the north to the Mediterranean climate of the southern states. On the other axis, the range is from the maritime climate of the west influenced by the Gulf Stream to the steppes of eastern European Russia with its strongly continental weather. Thus, European weather is characterized by considerable diversity, lacking only the range of subtropical and tropical conditions from the full global weather spectrum.

While Europe comprises predominantly fertile and inhabitable lowlands, a mountainous spine from Spain in the west to the Carpathians and, arguably, the Caucasus in the east, with heights of up to 4807 metres in the Alps and 5633 metres in the Caucasus. A further mountainous northern spine runs the length of Norway. The great rivers of Europe flow in a predominantly north to south direction, draining into the large enclosed seas – the Mediterranean, Black and Caspian.

As a consequence of the physical geography of Europe, it is hardly surprising that tourist resources from a natural perspective are varied in response to the environment in which they exist. As we saw in Chapter 1, Burton (1994) divides Europe into three physical zones from a tourism perspective.

1. The Mediterranean basin – the focal point of the southward flow of summer tourists; in 1990 it attracted 148 million visitors;
2. The mountain chains that form the east–west spine of central and southern Europe. This region is the magnet that draws the dual seasonal flow of summer scenic tourism and winter sport tourism. It is also the region that divides the Mediterranean basin from
3. The industrialized lowlands of the northwest margins and of continental Europe. This region is the focus of business tourism and the area that generates day tourism to the local coast and countryside.                                   (Burton, 1994, p. 6)

This classification points to the diversity in the physical tourism product and it also represents a considerable simplification. In particular, the non-industrialized margins of north and northwest Europe are ignored and the natural tourist appeal of destinations such as northern and western England, Finland, northwest France, Iceland, Ireland, Norway, Scotland, Sweden and Wales is thus neglected. Northern Russia, potentially, also falls into this category. While by no means mass destinations, these areas represent important alternative tourism locations which are likely to grow in importance as other regions suffer from overcrowding, over-utilization of their natural resources and the reduced appeal of sun-focused vacations.

The consequences of physical and climatic diversity for the organization of the tourism and hospitality industry are considerable. The type of facilities and activities that are required for tourist use in the various regions of Europe are clearly varied, driven by the nature of the natural tourism product in the specific locality, whether it is mountainous, at the seaside or forest-based. This has inevitable impacts on the characteristics of the tourism and hospitality businesses that operate, notably on their size and ownership. Climate in particular also has structural implications, especially in relation to seasonality. With the possible exception of business and some limited forms of cultural, historic and retail shopping tourism, all European destinations are affected to a greater or lesser extent by seasonality factors. The season for a hotelier in Rhodes runs from March to the end of October and the business is generally closed during the winter months. The equivalent season in northern Norway may be May to August and in the west of Ireland a similar if not even shorter period. This means that much of the resource stock of European tourism is under-utilized, suffers from consequent under-investment and, despite strenuous efforts to extend the season with mixed success, is a business problem which much of Europe faces to a greater or lesser extent. All-weather resorts, such as Centerparcs, offer one limited response which is proving successful but on a modest scale relative to the overall size of the seasonality problem. As we shall see in subsequent chapters, seasonality also has an important impact on the management of human resources within the tourism and hospitality industry.

Europe's appeal as a tourist destination goes beyond its natural resources, however, and includes a wide range of traditional historic and cultural attractions as well as some of rather more modern appeal. Europe, as a whole, benefits from the effects of long habitation. Thus wherever visitors travel, there is tangible evidence of a long history, frequently of a turbulent nature, and this provides a major source of the appeal of Europe to its own inhabitants as well as to those from long-haul originating countries. The manifestation of history is certainly very different as a result of variation in the natural, cultural, religious and socio-political influences which affected regions and countries. Thus the architecture of cathedrals, castles and ordinary houses is very different in southern Spain from that found in Denmark or Greece, and this diversity, often evident within relatively short distances in Europe, is one of its main attractions.

However, the intensity of histories and cultures which have interacted over hundreds of years is such that, from a tourism management perspective, Europe's resources in this respect also exhibit many features in common. A major recurring theme is one of conservation, access and combining original purpose with the needs of visitors. This applies equally to the Alhambra in Granada, Spain, as it does to York Cathedral in England and the Acropolis in Athens, Greece. It is also a relevant issue on a much smaller scale to many towns and communities throughout Europe, faced with the challenge of preserving their history and living with and within it while at the same time providing and encouraging access to visitors from outside that community. This challenge is also one of controlling the impact of modernization and reconstruction upon tourist resources so that they are not destroyed or altered out of all recognition. At the same time, the reality is that visitors are, primarily, attracted to a small number of 'honeypot' locations, cities, buildings or heritage sites and that, for a country such as Britain, a substantial number of buildings and other historic and heritage locations may not have sufficient appeal to remain viable as a dedicated visitor attraction. Alternative commercial or other uses may be necessary in order to allow relatively low demand facilities to remain in reasonable repair.

Conservation of physical history and culture presents one set of challenges but very different considerations come into play when the issue of representational history and culture (music, dance, story-telling, theatre, crafts, fine art) is addressed. Here, Europe also exhibits considerable diversity, resulting from a variety of linguistic traditions but also different influences and heritage. At a certain level, as a result of history and the location of economic and political power in certain countries of Europe, there is a sharing of common culture. Thus the *Mona Lisa*, by an Italian, is one of the main attractions for visitors to the Louvre in Paris. Similarly, art galleries throughout Europe hold work by artists from many different countries as well as that which might be called national. This is seen to represent a common European heritage and culture. This practice is not without controversy at a political level as the debate over the Elgin Marbles, originally in Greece but now located in London, illustrates.

The notion of common culture is not so evident with respect to other aspects of culture and heritage where preservation, even as a tourist resource, is not always easy. There are strong commercial and consumer-led pressures throughout Europe which mean that tourists are more likely to patronize a disco than a culture show, purchase a Barbi or Disney doll rather than a locally crafted product and see a 'blockbuster' American film in preference to one made in the country they are visiting. This process of internationalization or globalization is by no means unique to Europe or, indeed, to the tourism and hospitality industry but has a particular impact, given the diversity in culture and history which is threatened. We will return to the theme of what George Ritzer (1993) calls the McDonaldization of society at a later point in this book. This process of cultural homogenization is a common theme throughout contemporary Europe and is one contributing factor in reducing the distinctive character and appeal of different countries and regions. It is also a trend that has considerable implications for the range and nature of human resource skills that will be required by the tourism and hospitality industry of the future.

The theme of globalization is an important consideration in reviewing Europe's tourism product profile. In terms of the tourism and hospitality resources which attract visitors to particular destinations, we have noted considerable natural and physical diversity within Europe but also more discernible common themes with respect to culture and heritage. This latter is particularly true when we consider relatively recent additions to the attractions profile in Europe, notably entertainment and theme parks of various types such as EuroDisney, Alton Towers and Blackpool Pleasure Beach, which generally have international rather than local focus in what they offer and in how they are organized. The range of facilities which support the development of tourism, namely accommodation, catering, transport and related industries, show considerable diversity in terms of size, ownership and structure in Europe. However, the underlying trend in tourism and hospitality, as in many other industry sectors, is towards increasing dominance by the major multinational companies, operating by direct ownership or through franchise or management contract arrangements. Supported by technology, strong marketing strategies (especially branding) and changing consumer expectations, this trend is already clearly discernible in the hotel, restaurant and retail subsectors and is becoming of greater significance in travel agencies, tour operators and airlines. A good example from the latter subsector is the range of equity and franchise arrangements which British Airways have made with British and European partners, such as TAT (France), Deutsche BA (Germany) and Brymon, City Flyer Express, Loganair, Maersk and Manx in the UK. Similar moves have seen a number of Western European airlines invest in strategic and equity alliances with partners in Eastern Europe. Globalization or, more strictly in this context, Europeanization has considerable implications for the management of people on a multinational basis, within partner companies with different cultures and history from the parent but all delivering what, to the customer, is presented as a common and consistent product and service standard. This theme will be further addressed in Chapters 5 and 7.

Thus the evidence for unity within the European tourism and hospitality industry, assessed from the point of view of product profile, is inconclusive but the trends, especially with respect to those aspects which are independent of natural or physical environmental factors, appear to suggest an underlying movement towards greater commonality and decreasing national or local individuality.

### Europe – common tourism and hospitality markets?

In terms of markets, the European tourism and hospitality industry receives visitors from three sources:

- domestic tourists (i.e. those from within the country in question);
- European tourists, from other countries within Europe; and
- intercontinental tourists, those arriving from outside of Europe.

These three segments are common to all European countries, although the emphasis on one or the other will vary country by country. The importance of domestic tourism to a small country such as Luxembourg is relatively less than it is in France or the United Kingdom.

In terms of international tourism, Europe is the pre-eminent region of the world, annually accounting for some 60% of all international arrivals, although this proportion, but not the absolute total, is in slow but steady decline. The main reasons for European dominance relate to characteristics of western countries but are likely to increasingly feature in the east as well. These reasons include:

- Proximity and size of European countries – Europe, in particular Western Europe, is a patchwork of relatively small countries, easily accessible to each other so that international travel may readily involve visiting two to three countries in a day – an unlikely occurrence elsewhere.
- High population densities close to many international borders, providing large, local markets for international travel.
- Good internal infrastructure, especially in Western Europe, making road, rail, sea and air travel relatively easy and efficient. This infrastructure is improving in some respects, for example with the opening of the Channel Tunnel, but also suffers from considerable congestion at peak times.
- Generally satisfactory facilities for tourists (accommodation, catering, etc.) in most parts of Europe, with the exception of parts of the east. The growing importance of multinational hotel, restaurant and travel companies means that uncertainty will increasingly be reduced in European travel to the benefit of some segments of the tourist market but with consequent losses with respect to the character and local authenticity of the tourism product.
- Reduction and, in part, elimination of many of the technical barriers to travel, within Western Europe, especially in the European Union. This is most clearly evident when travelling by road between, for example, Belgium and France or Norway and Sweden, where there are few physical impediments or delays to almost interruption-free movement across international boundaries. Travel in Eastern

Europe still remains rather more complicated (although considerably simpler than before 1989 – delays of up to twelve hours at road frontiers between Hungary and Romania are not uncommon but such problems are likely to reduce in the future as visa and related formalities are simplified or eliminated.

- Relatively affluent countries in Western Europe, generating high levels of international trade while also having the time and resources for considerable leisure travel.
- Lifestyle changes in Western Europe permitting more time for travel and enabling people to utilize short breaks for international travel.
- A concentration of population and relative affluence in northern countries of Europe, increasing the attraction of warmer southern countries as tourist destinations.
- Diversity in cultures and history concentrated within a small area, offering visitors wide variety within short travelling distances, either from their home or, if from further afield, within close proximity to each other. For many Europeans, international travel involves less distance or expense than inter-state journeys in the United States or Australia.
- Concentrated tourist attractions (natural, historic/heritage and constructed), all in relatively close proximity to each other.
- Perceived 'cradle of civilization' status which, whether justified or not, acts as a powerful magnet to visitors from outside of Europe, especially North America and the Far East.
- Strong family ties between affluent 'new world' countries such as those of North America and Australasia and all European countries, generating significant VFR traffic as well as cultural and genealogical tourism by those without existing family ties. This market, of long-standing importance to countries such as Ireland and Italy, is of increasing significance to the newly accessible countries of Eastern Europe.

The combination of these factors means that European countries take seven out of the top ten places in the world as international tourist destinations in terms of visitor arrivals (only the USA, Mexico and Canada feature from outside Europe) and eight out of the top ten based on international tourist receipts (with only the USA and Canada from further afield). According to World Tourism Organization (WTO) figures for 1991, the leading European countries in terms of international tourist arrivals are:

1. France;
2. Spain;
3. Italy;
4. Hungary;
5. Austria;
6. UK;
7. Germany;

8. Switzerland;
9. Portugal;
10. Czechoslovakia.

With the division of Czechoslovakia into two independent republics, Greece will now feature in the top ten of European destinations in terms of arrivals. The presence of Hungary and Czechoslovakia represent evidence for major changes in Europe post-1989, although when we consider expenditure data, neither of these countries feature among the top earners from international travel. These are according to WTO figures:

1. France;
2. Italy;
3. Spain;
4. Austria;
5. UK;
6. Germany;
7. Switzerland;
8. Netherlands.

What is equally significant in European terms is that seven out of the top ten tourist generating countries in terms of expenditure are also European (the exceptions are the USA, Japan and Canada), confirming the importance of intra-European travel to the dominant position that is held by the region. Top European generating countries are according to WTO figures:

1. Germany;
2. UK;
3. Italy;
4. France;
5. Netherlands;
6. Austria;
7. Sweden;
8. Switzerland;
9. Belgium;
10. Spain.

Data extracted from Pompl and Lavery (1993) suggest that non-European markets are of significant but varying importance to European countries. The United Kingdom, for example, has a traditionally high dependence upon non-European markets. In 1990, 42% of visitor expenditure was generated by Western European markets but 25% came from North America and 33% from the rest of the world (including Eastern Europe). Comparative figures for the Irish Republic show a rather smaller non-European proportion at 24% of which almost 80% is derived from North America. German expenditure figures by foreigners indicate that 32% is generated from outside of Europe, with the USA (8%) and Japan (4%) constituting the largest markets. The major dependence on European markets is particularly evident in Mediterranean countries. For Spain, less than 20% of visitors are from outside of Europe, a high proportion of these being from Latin America as Spain acts as a traditional gateway to Europe for visitors from that part of the world. For Portugal, the proportion of visitors from outside of Europe is 10.5% while the Greek figure is similar at 10%. Despite Italy's strong family links overseas, less than 8% of visitors are from outside of Europe. It is difficult to provide useful comparative data with respect to eastern European tourism as traditional, pre-1989 market patterns have changed dramatically for political, social, economic and logistical reasons. This latter factor means that data collection techniques are of limited value and accuracy. Proportionately, non-European markets are small but growing as tourism develops in key countries in the region.

Domestic tourism, the third market source, also varies in its importance to different European countries. It is also the most difficult element to quantify with accuracy because usually there are no obvious administrative sources of data collection (such as frontier points or hotel registration requirements) and also because domestic tourist activity merges into normal, non-tourist expenditure patterns to a much greater extent.

In the United Kingdom, the relative importance of domestic tourism has been in steady decline since the early 1970s, although the actual number of trips have remained stable. At the same time, however, overseas travel by Britons has increased greatly (Lavery, 1993). In the former West Germany, domestic vacations have remained stable at around 10 million since the early 1960s while foreign travel has increased dramatically (Hill, 1993). While similar underlying trends are evident in other Western European countries, domestic tourism is subject to considerable fluctuation. Aderhold *et al.* (1993), for example, note a slight increase in domestic vacationing by Norwegians in response to economic recession. The poorer countries of southern Europe, endowed with plentiful tourist resources in their own right, have the highest domestic tourism participation rate in Western Europe – approximately 90% of Portuguese who take holidays take them at home (Edwards and Sampaio, 1993). The countries of Eastern Europe have traditionally maintained a high level of dependence on domestic tourism, partly because of limited access to foreign currency and partly because of political controls. Much foreign travel was confined to neighbouring countries within the Eastern Bloc. While some of the political barriers to travel have been removed, the prime difficulties are now economic, with only a small proportion of the population able to afford the cost of travel abroad. Even the price of previously subsidized domestic tourism has, in relative terms, increased beyond the reach of much of the population of, for example, Romania where the price of a family holiday in an average Black Sea resort is roughly equivalent to an annual public sector professional salary.

As we shall see in Chapter 7, the character and composition of the tourism and hospitality market has important implications for human resource provision. Europe's tourism and hospitality markets show significant variation between north and south and between east and west. However, it is reasonable to argue that there are significant areas of commonality between much of the continent which permit legitimate discussion of Europe's tourism and hospitality markets in unitary terms. Product gaps are closing due to investment in the east and to the increasing importance of multinational, branded tourism and hospitality companies and this will further contribute to similarity. Ultimately, this may be to the detriment of Europe's market position, as it stands to loose the distinctiveness and variety that is so important at present. This may lead increasing numbers to make use of value travel opportunities beyond Europe to Asia, North America and Africa.

### European tourism and hospitality: common business structures and ownership?

As a generalization, it is fair to say that the European tourism and hospitality industry is characterized by small businesses, generally family – owned and managed. This characteristic is of profound importance to the management of human resources within the industry. There are clearly exceptions to this rule, primarily in the transportation subsector, but consideration of, for example, accommodation, restaurants, travel agents, retail and sports/recreation organizers point to a numerical dominance by free-standing, independent operators. At the same time, in all these sectors it is possible to identify exceptions to the rule and the growing presence of large multiples. This situation is, broadly, true throughout Western Europe, although the pattern of ownership and the impact of larger companies varies country by country. The situation in Eastern Europe is somewhat different because of the long-standing dominance of large, public-owned tourism and hospitality companies in many sectors. While an independent private sector is developing fast in most countries of the region, such structural change is inevitably slow and probably investment with the most impact at the moment is coming from multinational companies.

The small business structure of the Western European tourism and hospitality industry contrasts with that to be found in North America or Asia where larger multiples, in all subsectors, have a rather stronger, but by no means totally dominating, presence. As we shall see in Chapter 3, the European tourism and hospitality industry, in the east and the west, is a product of its history and this is largely one of slow, progressive growth over a one hundred year and often longer timespan. This history also reflects one of the prime characteristics of businesses in the service sector, that production and service cannot be centralized and stored for distribution to the customer. Thus, the tourism and hospitality industry in Europe has developed as a highly dispersed, fragmented 'industry of every parish' – each town with its own small hotels, restaurants, travel agencies, transport services, etc. Centralized ownership of some or all of these has only occurred through state control (in Eastern Europe) or as a relatively recent phenomenon with the growth of multiple ownership in the industry.

There are some exceptions to this picture in terms of business size and these primarily relate to large cities where significant redevelopment has occurred or to areas of relatively recent tourist development. Thus the hotel industry in London consists of significantly larger establishments than is the case elsewhere in the United Kingdom and ownership is considerably more group or multiple dominated than the national average. The same is true of other major commercial centres such as Paris and Milan. Cities which have witnessed high levels of relatively recent development also fit into this category. One legacy of the 1992 Olympic Games for Barcelona has been to significantly increase the number of hotel rooms available while also altering the average size and ownership structure of its hotel industry in the city. Parts of the Mediterranean coastline have also developed in a manner contrary to the general rule expounded earlier in that their hotel, apartment and other accommodation investment, dating from the 1960s and later, was designed with mass participation tourism in mind and is reflected in the high-rise building in resorts like Benidorm and Torremolinos. Similar, large-scale accommodation development can also be found in other parts of Spain, in the Portuguese Algarve, the Rousillon coast of France, along parts of the Italian Adriatic and in Corfu. Interestingly, a number of other Greek islands have avoided similar large-scale development. Some of these large-scale resorts are now perceived to represent the antithesis of sustainable tourism and hospitality development. While atypical of their country in terms of size, ownership and management of the large accommodation properties is not necessarily in the hands of multiples or large companies. However, the level of such involvement is rather higher than the national average in all the countries concerned.

Parts of the transportation subsector of the tourism and hospitality industry in Europe also represent exceptions to the general size and ownership rule. Railways in Europe are almost universally state monopolies, operating with high levels of public subsidy. The exceptions include small private railways in Britain and Switzerland which are mainly focused on the leisure visitor. Total privatization of Britain's rail network is planned although it is too early to predict the precise form that this will take, and there has been some expression of interest from companies involved in other areas of transport, notably coach operators and airlines. Interestingly, much of Europe's railway system, particularly that in Britain, was constructed with private, entrepreneurial capital during the nineteenth century and has gradually moved towards public ownership as the railway era gave way to that of the motor car and air travel. The introduction of new forms of high speed rail travel able to compete with other forms of transport is one reason for increasing private interest in investment in this area.

Air transport is also an example from the tourism and hospitality industry where large, frequently semi-monopolistic companies dominate the marketplace in Europe. There are historical similarities between airlines and the railways in that early activity in air transport was in the hands of small, private companies. The need for increasing safety regulation, the high level of capital investment required and the highly regulated airline market that emerged from the Second World War in Europe moved many of these companies into public ownership in the form of state monopolies. As national flag carriers, airlines also acquired a status and sanctity which has served to protect many of them from commercial reality up to the present day. State involvement in the airline industry remains high in most European countries, with the exception of Britain. A number of airlines are partially privatized, such as KLM, Lufthansa and SAS, but British Airways is the only European 'flag carrier' to operate entirely in the private sector, although its competitors claim that even BA receives favoured treatment in its access to prime takeoff and landing slots at London's Heathrow Airport.

Moves to deregulate the airline industry in Western Europe, while a rather slow and reluctant process, has stimulated the growth of an increasingly important independent sector. This consists of relatively small concerns operating to much tighter staffing and resource management criteria than is the case with the larger national airlines, and frequently utilizing smaller, more economical aircraft. The independents aim to compete both on major and on thin, regional routes. Good examples from a wide selection include British carriers British Midland and Air UK, Meridiana from Italy, Brit Air and TAT from France, Ryanair from Ireland, Braathens from Norway and Eurowings from Germany. However, the power of concentration and the control over reservations systems and associated technology that is held by the world's major airlines is such that independents are finding it increasingly difficult to compete in total isolation of the larger carriers. As a result, most small European airlines have marketing or closer ties with a selected major airline partner. Equity or closer ownership relationships include Air UK and KLM, Business Air and Lufthansa, and TAT, Deutsche BA and Loganair with British Airways. Arrangements outside of formal equity or ownership include City Flyer Express and British Airways as well as Virgin Atlantic's franchise operations on routes between London Gatwick and Athens and London City and Dublin.

Airline alliances are not confined to small–large relationships in the sense that has been outlined here. The survival of Sabena, the Belgian national airline, depended upon significant investment by Air France while merger discussions between Austrian, SAS and Swissair, while not brought to fruition at this point, point to the need for medium-sized carriers to cooperate in order to survive both in Europe and further afield. Discussions about a British Airways–KLM merger, which subsequently failed, were prompted by competitive fears in the global marketplace and both airlines have responded with alternative alliances in the wake of the breakdown in discussions. In addition to formal merger or equity stake arrangements, various looser options are being pursued by airlines in order to maximize presence in the marketplace while minimizing investment and cost. Various forms of code-sharing within Europe and beyond enable airlines to gain access to specific markets without necessarily ever flying one of their own aircraft or crew to the destinations in question.

> Code-sharing comes in several guises: an on-line change of plane with the same carrier . . .; when you fly from A to B with the same flight number, connecting from one airline to another; wet and dry leases [whereby one airline's flights are operated by aircraft and/or crew of another on a lease basis]; double designator codes – the same code but with one airline operating the service; when one airline books seats under its own code in another carrier; and franchise arrangements. (Collis, 1994, p. 37)

While the commercial value of arrangements of this nature may be evident, potentially there remain significant human problems attached to the inevitable loss of control that results from code-sharing arrangements. Collis (1994) refers to some of the problems that have faced British Airways in ensuring consistent standards of service from their partner airlines operating in BA livery and uniforms. The system works best where partner airlines share the same quality standards and culture as is the case with SAS, Swissair and Austrian in their Quality Alliance. However, as we shall see in Chapter 5, maintaining consistently high service from staff who work for a number of different employers can create problems for the company that, ultimately, must take responsibility for the overall product and service.

Predictions for the future structure of the airline industry suggest that alliances will be an increasing necessity for small as well as major carriers, and these examples are only a taste of the direction that airline restructuring is taking.

The new structure of the airline industry in Eastern Europe is still evolving at the present. National flag carriers remain important in countries such as Hungary (Malev) and Romania (TAROM) but are facing more direct and open competition from western carriers and from fledgling independents. Former East German airline Interflug was an early casualty of German unification. A number of Eastern European airlines, notably Balkan-Bulgarian Airlines and Malev, have entered into alliances with established western carriers and thus are likely to evolve as regional feeder airlines to their partner companies, Air France and Alitalia. The situation in the former Soviet Union is one of some confusion. Most of the newly independent republics now have their own airline, frequently utilizing former Aeroflot resources. There are also private sector airlines and examples include Ukraine International, Baltic International Airlines and Riga Airlines Express. Aeroflot, now confined to Russia, is currently facing major problems with regard to resourcing and safety. It is clear that the period of transition in Eastern Europe will result in considerable upheaval and change in the airline as well as other tourism and hospitality sectors before reasonable stability can emerge.

The move towards centralization and market control by a small number of large operators is most pronounced in the airline industry where the potential number of operators or business units can ever only be a fraction of those in the hotel, travel agency or restaurant subsectors. However, there is visible evidence of moves towards concentration in these areas, notably in travel agencies/tour operations as well as hotels. Tour operations in Britain, for example, are dominated by three major companies, Thomsons, Airtours and Owners Abroad, who control well over half the UK outbound fully inclusive (FIT) market. These companies, in turn, own an increasingly important segment of the retail travel agency business within which they are gaining market share from independent operators. Moving under the protective shelter of a large company is one response for the independent travel agent and the franchising arrangements of a company such as A.T. Mays provides the vehicle to undertake this without loss of business independence.

In most European countries, independent hotels still remain the dominant force, both in terms of the number of operating units and in relation to market share. Even in the United States, where the situation is perceived to be much more oliogopolistic, the ten largest hotel companies only control about 25% of the total hotel market. In Western Europe, equivalent figures are much smaller. Table 2.1 summarizes the place of chains within the hotel industries of a number of major Western European countries. Accurate figures are difficult to obtain and countries use different definitions of what constitutes a hotel so some caution is required in interpreting these data. Furthermore, the quality of what is included within the definition of a hotel varies significantly from country to country. In France, over 55% of hotel rooms fall within one-star and unclassified categories, the highest level in Western Europe.

Similar figures to those in Table 2.1 apply to other Western European countries, although in all cases the proportion of group-owned

**Table 2.1** Ownership of hotels in selected Western European countries

| Country | Total hotel stock (rooms) | % of establishments in chain ownership/ management | % of rooms in chain ownership/ management |
|---|---|---|---|
| France | 756 000 | 2 | 10 + |
| West Germany | 1 745 000 * | 1 | 10 |
| Italy | 975 000 | | < 10 |
| Spain | 477 503 | | 5 + |
| UK | 886 798 * | 6 | 27 |

*Sources*: Various.
* Bedspaces.

establishments is increasing at the expense of independent operations. The situation in Eastern Europe is somewhat different in that independent hotel operations did not really exist prior to 1989. The majority of establishments were operated within state monopolies, generally the national tourism company such as Inturist in the USSR and Orbis in Poland. Foreign investment, even prior to 1989, was almost exclusively by international groups. Therefore, the majority of hotels still remain either in state hands or are operated by multinational companies. Some small independent hotels are emerging, frequently with the support of expatriate capital. An example of this new form of ownership is the Hotel Helvetia in Bucharest, Romania, which was developed to a high international standard by Romanian émigrés living in Israel.

On the surface therefore the dominance of independent operators within the hotel sector in Europe (and especially the west) appears to be such that it will not be seriously threatened in the near future. Such a conclusion disguises market performance indicators and trends which are revealing increasing threats to the future of the small, independent hotel operator. If the impact of group operations is considered in relation to the quality and size of hotels in individual countries, it is clear that group operations are concentrated at the top end of the market and their hotels are, on average, considerably bigger than those of the independents. This has long been the prime divider between the group and independent hotel operation and, therefore, direct competition between the two was limited. However, the advent of group budget hotels, offering a low-cost, quality product but with reduced service accommodation, has posed a real threat to many independent establishments in countries where this form of hotel has the greatest concentration, notably France and the UK. The main hotel casualties of recession during the early 1990s in Britain have been operations in the one- and two-star categories, which have been least able to compete, price or product-wise, with hotels such as Travelodge, Travel Inn and Campanile. Further threats to the independent sector arise from the increasing use of computerized reservation systems tied to central booking telephone numbers, and the level of certainty that the market receives through branding in the lower and middle ranges of the hotel market.

Other subsectors within the European tourism and hospitality industry exhibit similar variation with respect to ownership, with a strong bias towards small, independent operations in most areas except those which are highly capital intensive, such as theme park attractions. The restaurant sector exhibits similar trends to that found in the budget hotel market. The subsector remains dominated by the small, independent operator but, at the fast-food and family end of the market, is witnessing the increasing involvement of multiple operations such as McDonald's, Pizza Hut, Movenpick, TGIF, Little Chef and Harvester. The losers in this scenario are small, local restaurant operations. The multiples frequently operate on the basis of franchise or similar licensing arrangements, thus eliminating or reducing the capital investment required by the parent company. Another interesting feature of the restaurant market is the high level of involvement by immigrant and ethnic minority groups, with restaurants reflecting specific culinary and cultural traditions. This has important human resource implications and is an issue that is further addressed in Chapter 7. Some other areas of the tourism and hospitality industry, as we shall see in the next section, have a high level of public ownership but much tourism provision in the leisure, sport and related subsectors is small-scale and private in ownership and operation.

Therefore, the verdict with respect to a unified European tourism and hotel industry from the point of view of its ownership and management must be indecisive. The strong presence of small, independent operators has been noted in some subsectors but contrary indicators are applicable in others, such as transportation. The overall movement is towards concentration into larger companies and a consequent standardization of product. This movement is at the expense of the independent operator. The Eastern European situation is somewhat anomalous in this regard, and it is difficult to predict the way in which the tourism and hospitality industry will develop in this part of the continent.

### European tourism and hospitality: a common role for the public and private sectors?

Both the public and the private sector are represented in the operation of the European tourism and hospitality industry. There are some functions which, in effect, operate as extensions or part of government services and yet are important components within a visitor's overall experience of a country or resort. These functions include immigration, customs and the police. Generally speaking, these areas do not recognize their role within the tourism and hospitality industry and they can operate in a manner contrary to the best interests of the sector. However, with a general reduction in formal frontier and customs controls within Europe, the role of these services has become rather less intrusive and threatening to the visitor; recognition of the training needs of personnel involved with these services has also contributed to this improvement. However, especially for visitors from outside of the European Union, arrival at Heathrow, London, or Charles de Gaulle, Paris, can be a daunting and protracted experience. Police services have responded to the needs of visitors in some locations by designating certain officers 'Tourist Police', thus identifying those with language and related skills who are best able to assist visitors.

Tourism planning, promotion and information also tend to be public sector responsibilities in most European countries. These functions may operate as a direct extension of the government ministry responsible for tourism or, alternatively, have a degree of independence as an autonomous agency such as Bord Failte Eireann, the Irish Tourist Board (Baum, 1994a). The breadth of the role of such agencies also varies considerably, from a concern that is primarily marketing and information-related (the British Tourist Authority and equivalent bodies in other northern European countries including Denmark, Germany, the Netherlands and Belgium) to roles that are much wider in ambit, including product development, regulation and training. This is rather more common in southern European states (Akehurst *et al.*, 1993). Poetschke (1995) identifies a number of different models for the management of tourism policy development, which vary according to the level of public and private sector involvement. Figure 2.2 represents these four alternative models, showing increasing private-sector industry involvement.

Within Figure 2.2:

> As you move from Type I to the right, the degree of industry involvement and control over planning for tourism development increases. A Type I governing structure, where the private sector provides input through a lobby group which it has formed, is the traditional form of government. Government sets and implements tourism policies and the private sector often finds itself in a position where it must lobby for change – usually a somewhat antagonistic process.
>
> A Type II relationship is usually characterized by the participation of the private sector in an Advisory Council. In this case, the government still sets and implements the policies but actively seeks advice from the private sector. This advice may or may not be listened to.
>
> In Types III and IV, the private sector actually gains some degree of control over the strategic decision-making process. Type III, a Commission, is typically more of a figurehead organization than

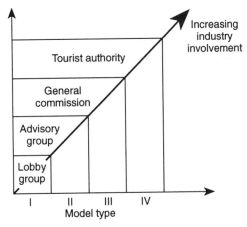

**Figure 2.2** Public–private sector partnership models for tourism policy managment. (Source: Poetschke, 1995.)

Type IV, a Tourist Authority. Both these groups are often charged with overseeing the strategic function for a country or region's tourism industry; however, the level of involvement by a commission is typically much less than that of a Tourist Authority.

(Poetschke, 1995)

The general trend in both Eastern and Western Europe is movement towards Type IV involvement and consequently at a practical level towards increasing the definition of the state's role in tourism and hospitality. The focus then becomes primarily marketing, releasing other responsibilities to other public and private agencies. Thus in Scotland the Scottish Tourist Board does not have any human resource development responsibilities, and requirements in this area are catered for by Scottish Enterprise and the private sector. Even in the primary marketing area, the general tendency is to reduce state investment where possible and to seek additional funds for this function from the private sector which, ultimately, will benefit from the initiative.

The logic for public sector support for tourism and hospitality marketing stems from the fragmented nature and small business size of much of the industry and also because, for most visitors, the experience includes purchasing components of their visit from a range of different operators, whether in the transportation, accommodation, entertainment/leisure or retail subsectors. Thus creating public awareness of the national, regional or local product profile requires coordination and, probably, sustained public investment. The rationale for government involvement in tourism at a level which might not apply in other industrial sectors is further articulated in terms of regional development. Akehurst *et al.* (1993) argue that for government intervention to be justified, tourism must be seen to have wider benefits than those purely of a regional nature. They identified a number of additional reasons for the level of support that does exist.

(a) tourism is a common good, the development of which benefits many firms collectively;
(b) in regions where tourism is not developed, it is an infant industry whose development to full commercial viability requires government support;
(c) the improvement of the tourism product, through measures such as the training of workers in the industry, carries external benefits in addition to the financial returns earned by the workers;
(d) there are secondary benefits from tourism development.

(Akehurst *et al.*, 1993, pp. 37–8)

The state in most European countries also runs a large number of tourism and hospitality-related operations, some of which may not see themselves as primarily concerned with this industry. Public, either national or municipal, museums and art galleries may be a case in point where the focus is frequently more on preservation of heritage than on facilitating visitor access and stimulating their interest. However, public tourism resources such as the Louvre in Paris and the British Museum and National Gallery in London are among those cities' most visited attractions. The problem from a human resource perspective is that unless the management and staff of public facilities such as these recognize that they are in the tourism and hospitality business, the level and quality of customer service may not match that offered within the private sector.

At a more commercial level, the public sector in Europe retains a considerable stake in the operation of tourism enterprises in many subsectors of the tourism and hospitality industry. This is not only true of Eastern Europe, where inevitably the move from public to private, while gathering some momentum, is relatively slow and painful. We have already noted public sector ownership of transportation, notably airlines, railway operations and bus and coach companies. Such ownership is declining but the transition is slow and state protectionist inclinations persist. The high costs of operating within transportation mean that state enterprise is likely to remain the dominant form of ownership in railways, but airlines and other forms of transport are more likely to move into the private sector.

State involvement does not stop at transportation. Hotel investment remains important in Eastern Europe but is also an indirect concern of the state through national airlines. Air France, at the time of writing, has been required to relinquish its stake in the Meridien hotel group while a similar prospect faces the Irish airline Aer Lingus, owners of Copthorne Hotels. Ireland, however, has other state-owned hotels in the Great Southern group which are now owned by the airports authority Aer Rianta but which were originally railway hotels which passed to the state with railway nationalization. The same was true in Britain where British Transport Hotels, as a subsidiary of British Railways, were in public ownership until the late 1970s. As recently as 1972, Borer was able to state that 'the list of British Transport Hotels . . . is today very long' (p. 182) and cited a wide range of establishments in all major cities (for example, the Charing Cross and the Great Western Royal in London) as well as in country locations (for example, Gleneagles in Scotland and the Manor House Hotel in Devon).

Other tourism and hospitality areas with significant public sector interest in Western Europe have included travel agencies (Thomas Cook was a publicly owned company for a number of years) and retail outlets, especially duty-free shops in a number of countries, including Ireland. However, overall, the trend is towards declining public ownership of tourism and hospitality enterprises as part of an overall privatization culture in many European countries. The overall effect of this process will be to create a more equitable commercial environment within tourism and hospitality on a pan-European basis. However, the impact is also likely to reduce the job security and status of employees within the tourism and hospitality businesses that remain protected by the state and this promises to have major industrial relations repercussions in a number of European countries.

Overall, the European tourism and hospitality industry is predominantly and increasingly private in its ownership. However, the public sector retains control in a number of key strategic areas and such control, while reducing, is unlikely to disappear in the immediate future.

### European tourism and hospitality: common economic impact?

The evidence with respect to this dimension has already been assessed in Chapter 1. What is evident is that the tourism and hospitality industry is of considerable importance to the economies of all Western European countries but to widely divergent extents, ranging from lows of 0.7% of Gross Domestic Product (GDP) in Germany (West) and 0.9% in Finland up to 7.4% in Austria, 5.4% in Portugal and 5.2% in Spain (Table 1.1). However, even in countries where the actual proportion of GDP appears to be relatively low, the nature of the industry is such that it is frequently of considerable regional or local importance. Tourism and hospitality tends to be strongest in those areas where other economic activity is weakest and the industry, therefore, makes a significant contribution to regional development. For example, in Germany tourism and hospitality is of considerable importance in the mountainous regions of the Black Forest and the Alps, where alternative economic activities and employment opportunities are not readily available. The same is true with respect to the Highlands of Scotland and the Pyrenees of France and Spain.

Tourism and hospitality were of considerable importance to the former regimes of Eastern Europe as a major source of hard currency. The same remains true today but the economic significance of the industry may be even greater in that alternative sources of wealth creation, primarily in the industrial sector, have declined greatly in the face of international competition and reduced disposable personal income in some countries. Tourism and hospitality presents what is seen as a relatively low investment alternative which also has the advantage of labour intensity in countries where job opportunities are limited and labour is relatively cheap. There are locations where tourism and hospitality are, undoubtedly, booming industries – the cities of Budapest and Prague are good examples – but in other areas, the level of investment required to bring product and service standards up to international levels should not be underestimated – the Romanian Black Sea coast is one example. Furthermore, domestic tourism and visitors from neighbouring Eastern European countries, the mainstay of the industry prior to 1989, have declined dramatically as citizens of these countries on the one hand are able to exercise their new-found rights to travel abroad, while on the other are also faced with the effects of escalating price inflation and declining living standards which puts even domestic vacationing out of reach.

The evidence, therefore, suggests some homogeneity with respect to the economic impact of tourism and hospitality in Western Europe, but also suggests a major divide between west and east and one that is likely to remain for the immediate future.

### Europe: a common social and political commitment to tourism and hospitality?

At a national level, commitment to the tourism and hospitality industry is varied between the countries of Europe. All countries acknowledge the economic and related benefits of the industry and back this recognition through varying levels of financial and related support for the development and marketing of the industry. This commitment is clearly shown by the speed with which tourism authorities react when periods with particularly adverse conditions ameliorate – tourism and hospitality is the industry to respond far quicker than others in its attempts to 'get back to normal'. This has clearly been seen in locations such as Croatia, emerging from war, and Northern Ireland, hoping for a permanent end to civil strife. However, the corollary of this responsiveness is that the tourism and hospitality industry is particularly vulnerable to the presentation of negative political or social images, which very readily can lead to tourists switching their loyalty to alternative destinations and countries. The total collapse of tourism to many parts of the former Yugoslavia is an extreme example but similar problems have been faced by the industry in Ireland and other areas of civil or social unrest.

In addition, there are increasing concerns, primarily at a local level, regarding the negative impact that excessive tourism development may have on the physical, social and cultural environment of a locality. Consideration is focusing on alternatives to high consumption tourism, which can bring with it congestion, pollution, crime, health and other related problems.

Measuring social and political commitment to tourism is problematic. We can consider direct public-purse investment in the development and marketing of the industry as one indicator. Akehurst *et al.* (1993) report the level of central government expenditure in absolute and per capita terms for the twelve member states of the European Union and this shows very significant differences among the countries concerned. Table 2.2 extracts key expenditure indicators from their study.

Of course, some caution is necessary in interpreting these figures because of different political structures within the countries concerned. Thus Germany's strongly federal system means an under-representation of total public expenditure as the individual Länder also are heavily involved in this area.

In a general sense, the economic reality of the late 1980s and early 1990s in most Western European countries was such that expenditure on tourism both by governments and at a more regional or local level

**Table 2.2** European Union states' central government expenditure on tourism, 1989–90 (£ sterling)

| Country | Central government tourism budget (million) | International tourism receipts, 1989 (million) | Per capita spend | Budget as % receipts |
|---|---|---|---|---|
| Belgium/ Luxembourg | 10.3 | 1838 | 1.00 | 0.56 |
| Denmark | 15.3 | 1387 | 3.00 | 1.10 |
| France | 43.7 | 9900 | 0.79 | 0.44 |
| Germany (FR) | 14.7 | 5195 | 0.24 | 0.28 |
| Greece | 74.5 | 1199 | 7.45 | 6.22 |
| Ireland | 23.4 | 642 | 6.69 | 3.64 |
| Italy | 63.8 | 7192 | 1.11 | 0.89 |
| Netherlands | 23.4 | 1812 | 1.59 | 1.29 |
| Portugal | 40.0 | 1552 | 3.88 | 2.58 |
| Spain | 65.9 | 9751 | 1.70 | 0.68 |
| UK | 58.3 | 6749 | 1.02 | 0.86 |

*Source*: From Akehurst *et al.* (1993), p. 49.

declined considerably in real terms. Governments argue that what they have attempted to encourage is increased focus and targeting of this public investment in order to maximize return. At the same time, there has been an increasing emphasis on developing a financial as well as policy-related partnership between the public and private sectors. As a result, increased involvement of private interests of the direction of tourism development and marketing is balanced by greater financial contributions from these sources. In Britain, this approach has been manifested in reduced budget allocations to the British Tourist Authority for its international marketing activity as well as to the English, Northern Ireland, Scottish and Welsh Boards for use at a regional and local level. In Ireland, Bord Failte has been given much greater direction in its marketing focus, with funding tied, in part, to meeting specific targets in selected markets.

An alternative analysis is to look at where the 'voice' of tourism and hospitality figures within political decision-making at a national or sub-national level. Few countries in Western Europe have a dedicated government minister with specific responsibility for tourism. Tourism tends to be amalgamated within a wider ministerial portfolio and, indeed, may not be readily identifiable as such. This is the case in Britain, where tourism is one responsibility of the Secretary of State for National Heritage. Baum (1994a), in an international survey that looks beyond Europe, found that in developed countries there was a considerable likelihood that tourism would not feature as a single identifiable ministry within governmental structures, unlike in the developing world where the industry is given rather greater prominence. The evidence of government action in the face of the competing interests of tourism and hospitality against those of other industrial and business sectors may also be an indicator of commitment. The tourism and hospitality industry in the United Kingdom might claim that restrictive restaurant and bar licensing, although much more flexible than a number of years ago, is harmful to the optimum development of the sector. Likewise, permission to route the M3 motorway through scenic Twyford Down in Hampshire might suggest that short-term economic interests and pressure from the road transport lobby carry more weight than the preservation of an important environmental and tourist resource.

A tourism and hospitality industry that develops in a manner that is socially responsive at the community level as well as in the context of the national political agenda is emerging as an increasingly important dimension in this equation, and here again the evidence is very mixed in Western Europe. Murphy (1985) brings together much of the essential thinking about this issue of community involvement and rights as part of tourism development. This thinking has been taken aboard in some locations, but the 'big picture' in Western Europe is one where government priorities frequently operate to overrule local wishes – the location of EuroDisney is, arguably, a case in point.

There is, therefore, some evidence to suggest that political commitment to the tourism and hospitality industry is not all that it might be in parts of Western Europe. In other parts, it is arguable that governments have been excessively responsive to the industry's short-term business interests and insufficiently concerned at the impact of excessive development on the overall environment and the long-term future of tourism to the region or destination. Parts of the Spanish Mediterranean coast, the Turkish Aegean and Mediterranean coastline and some ski resort developments in the French Alps exemplify this problem.

Most Eastern European countries have targeted tourism and hospitality as an industry that can make a significant contribution to economic restructuring and recovery. Thus tourism tends to be given a rather more prominent position in terms of government recognition than is the case in Western Europe. The main problems relate to the availability of resources to market effectively at an international level and the need to attract sufficient inward investment to ensure that the tourism and hospitality product meets international standards. Witt (1994) rather erroneously argues that 'hundreds of new hotels are needed throughout Eastern Europe in order to bring its tourism industry up to Western standards' (p. 223). In most countries of the region, hotel rooms are readily available, but the lack of recent investment is such that major refurbishment is required in order to bring these properties up to the required standards. Undoubtedly there are emerging business and tourist locations which do not have sufficient bedspace at present. However, to advocate widespread new development and the implicit abandonment of the old is to perpetuate non-sustainable development in an area where all aspects of the tourism and hospitality industry have developed over thirty to forty years with almost total disregard to these considerations.

Eastern Europe also faces a problem which is no longer of particular significance in more developed countries: that of social and economic distance between guest and host. This is a theme that we shall develop in more detail in Chapter 3. Visitors from Western Europe and beyond have, evidently, access to a level of economic resources that are totally beyond those accessible to the local community. Furthermore, the opportunity to travel and experience international tourism and hospitality standards is also denied those involved in the industry, previously for political reasons and now because of economic factors. As a result, community receptiveness to tourists may be tinged with resentment and frustration of a kind not so widespread in Western European countries.

However, there is one level in Western Europe where limited attempts have been made to create a unified tourism and hospitality industry in terms of common regulation and the removal of local or national barriers to development, and that is in the context of the European Union. The Commission of the Union has implemented measures in a variety of areas which have implications for the tourism and hospitality industry. These include measures:

- to reduce restrictive trade practices;
- to harmonize fiscal policies, especially taxation;
- to provide consumer information and protection;
- to facilitate labour mobility within the Union;
- to provide work-based protection to employees through the Social Chapter and other measures (see Chapter 6);
- to support environmental protection and standards, especially on beaches; and
- to facilitate investment and trade by citizens and companies from all member states within other countries of the Union.

These and a variety of other initiatives have considerable implications for tourism and hospitality businesses, as they do for other industries. In some areas of the economy, the diversity of measures are given cohesion through specific-sector policy frameworks. Long-standing examples include steel and agriculture. Policy with respect to tourism and hospitality has been rather slower to evolve. Robinson (1993) suggests that, in fact, tourism as an issue 'seems to have crept up on the policy-makers' (p. 12). As a result, what has evolved has been piecemeal and somewhat *ad hoc*. In the absence of any really comprehensive tourism policy within the Union 1990 was declared European Tourism Year, and the absence of any significant public impact testifies to the failure of the Commission to take any direct lead in the tourism field. *The Community Action Plan*, published in 1991 (CEC, 1991a), is the closest to a policy statement in the area to emanate from the Commission. The aim of the *Action Plan* is to include all aspects of tourism and to enhance the quality and competitiveness of facilities as well as improving awareness of tourism demand. The *Action Plan* is by no means comprehensive in the way that it addresses issues in the tourism and hospitality industry and the work programme that emanated from it has only been supported by very limited financial assistance.

It is difficult to identify any overall cohesion in the manner in which the tourism and hospitality industry is supported and developed on a Europe-wide basis. At a European Union level, there are limited measures which are designed to harmonize aspects of the industry's activities and to remove barriers to competitive trade. At a national level, support and commitment to the industry varies greatly from country to country.

### Europe: Common labour utilization, productivity, service and skills standards?

In many respects, this theme is one that is addressed in the subsequent chapters of this book. Given the somewhat indeterminate conclusions that have been reached with respect to other dimensions of the notion of a unified European tourism and hospitality industry, it is reasonable to anticipate diversity with respect to these human resource areas. Such, indeed, will be the broad conclusions reached later in this book.

## CHARACTERISTICS OF THE EUROPEAN TOURISM AND HOSPITALITY INDUSTRY AND THEIR HUMAN RESOURCE IMPLICATIONS

It might reasonably be argued that such an extensive diversion in order to discuss some of the main characteristics of the European tourism and hospitality industry is something of an indulgence in the context of a human resource book. However, it is argued here that without an understanding of the diversity that exists within the industry it is impossible to approach a consideration of human resource concerns with any degree of certainty. This diversity relates to the activities that take place within the industry, its main markets as well as attendant characteristics such as ownership and organization, economic impact, social and political commitment and the role of the public sector within the industry.

The planning and management of human resources is not a function that operates in isolation but is integral to all aspects of the operation of tourism and hospitality businesses. The same argument can be applied to human resource considerations at a macro level, whether dealing with the matter from a community, regional or national perspective. The essence of the concept of sustainable human resource management and development for tourism and hospitality, which we introduced in Chapter 1, is that it is inclusive in the way that it addresses the needs of the community in which such management and development takes place. Such inclusivity is only possible with a full understanding of the macro environment, in the case of this book the European to tourism and hospitality industry.

---

REVIEW AND DISCUSSION QUESTIONS

1. What problems does ambiguity in defining the boundaries of Europe create for an understanding of a European tourism and hospitality industry?
2. How useful is it to define the tourism and hospitality industry in terms of what the tourist does and where he or she spends money?
3. Imagine that you are responsible for the design and delivery of a new tourism and hospitality management development programme, with the remit to cater for all sectors and management jobs within the industry. What skills and knowledge might be included in such a programme to ensure that it caters for all the areas concerned?
4. Which is more important within European tourism and hospitality – its common features or those attributes which differentiate its sectors and different countries?

# The development of tourism and hospitality and the nature of employment in Europe

**3**

## THE DEVELOPMENT OF EUROPEAN TOURISM – FROM ELITE TO MASS PARTICIPATION

In order to understand the human resource environment within the contemporary European tourism and hospitality industry it is necessary first of all to review the origins of tourism and hospitality and its growth to its present status as a mass participation industry. This analysis must then be complemented by parallel consideration of the changing human resource environment which has evolved in support of the growing tourism and hospitality industry. This chapter will consider the development of tourism in Europe from being the minority privilege of the elite in the eighteenth century to because an industry of mass participation in Western Europe, with the potential to develop in a similar way in Eastern Europe. The driving forces behind this change, as we shall see, combine social, cultural, economic and technological factors. These same impulses have driven change with respect to employment in tourism and hospitality.

It would be naive to attempt to view the development of tourism in Europe as homogeneous. As we have seen in Chapter 2, the tourism and hospitality industry in Europe is highly diverse in its product as well as its structure and organization. For a variety of cultural, social, economic, political and technological reasons, European tourism and hospitality has evolved in a patchwork form, some locations reaching maturity some considerable time before others were recognized as destinations of any significance. It would be beyond our scope here to attempt anything that goes beyond a selective and thematic appraisal of the development of tourism in Europe and how this has impacted on employment within the sector. In doing this, the focus will, inevitably, be on those countries most clearly associated with the move towards mass tourism, primarily Britain but also France, Germany and other countries in the northwest of Europe.

Europe, or to be more precise, Western Europe, is the cradle of modern tourism as we know it or, as Pompl and Lavery (1993) put it: 'It was in Europe, particularly in Great Britain, that the tourist industry was invented, refined and developed' (p. xi).

The tourism and hospitality industry can be traced back to the growth of urbanization and conquest in ancient Egypt, Greece and Rome. In her consideration of the origin of hotels in Britain, Borer (1972) notes that: 'The first inns in this country, where travellers could eat, drink and sleep after a day's journey, were built before the English ever arrived here, for they were introduced by the Romans' (p. 9). These establishments, as elsewhere in the empire, were designed to support the efforts of war and colonial administration and were thus focused at specific rather than general travel markets, to place the activity in a contemporary context.

However, in the context of this discussion, the true antecedents of modern mass tourism can be identified in the 'Grand Tour' which flourished during the period from the sixteenth to the nineteenth centuries. Originally a selective, primarily aristocratic prerogative, the classical tour, mainly originating in Britain, included France, Italy, Switzerland, Germany and the Low Countries, and is well described as 'a tour of certain cities in Western Europe undertaken primarily, but not exclusively, for education and pleasure' (Towner, 1985, p. 301).

The original conception of the Grand Tour and related journeying to fashionable resorts and spas of the eighteenth century was very much as an extension to the normal pattern of aristocratic living and this is reflected in the employment structure that existed in support of travel at this time. Essentially, the rich and well-bred travelled with all or part of their normal retinue of servants. In the case of domestic travel to Bath, Deauville or Weymouth this could well consist of much of the household. Accompaniment on the Grand Tour was, generally, on a rather more modest scale but would probably include a tutor plus one or more personal servants. Accommodation was found in the great houses of families from the same class and background and only on rare occasions would commercial establishments be frequented during travel. Thus, the employment impact of travel at this time was limited and the development of identifiable tourism-related jobs cannot be really attributed to this period.

While the Grand Tour had its heyday in the eighteenth century, one significant feature of its evolution is the length of time committed to the experience, which fell from an average of 40 months in the mid-sixteenth century to just four months in the 1830s at the dawn of railway travel (Towner, 1985, p. 316). This propensity to shorten the experience over time is a characteristic of the development of tourism generally and continues to be an important feature in market trends today. It reflects changes in lifestyle, social, economic and working conditions, the impact of improved transport and other technologies, but, probably most significantly, the popularization of the experience from selective to relatively mass participation. Buzzard (1993) rightly argues that industrialization in Europe provided the main focus for this change, in that modern tourism arose 'as a broadly accessible form of leisure travel no longer based in the overt class and gender prerogatives of the Grand Tour' (p. 18).

This link between industrialization and the development of mass tourism accounts, in part, for the importance of Britain in the development of tourism as an industry. According to Feiffer (1985), even in the era preceding the impact of the railways, by 1820 about 150 000 British travellers a year were visiting Europe, representing a considerable growth from the time that has been described as the cultural 'golden age' of the Grand Tour (Poon, 1993, p. 30).

Initially, the pattern of this change was one which represents replication in that the growing affluence of the new, urbanized middle classes developed tourism in a way that included much that had featured in the elitist travel experiences which preceded their own ventures. Thus domestic travel, for example, gravitated towards the seaside locations made famous by royal and aristocratic patronage, such as Brighton, Weymouth and Deauville in France. At the same time, some specific resorts such as Blackpool developed to meet the needs of the newly 'enfranchised' tourist classes. Similarly, the new post-Industrial Revolution model of European travel from Britain followed the same main arteries as the Grand Tour, but on a scale which would have been impossible without the technology of the railways and the organizational and entrepreneurial skills of travel industry innovators such as Thomas Cook. Young (1973) in discussing Cook points to the latter's unique contribution when he says that 'his originality lay in his methods, his almost infinite capacity for taking trouble, his acute sense of the needs of his clients, his power of invention and his bold imagination' (p. 21).

Cook pointed the way towards the industrialization of tourism, its presentation as a consumer commodity available to all who could afford the time and cost. The packaging of the tourist's experience, which was a key feature of this process, implicitly gave recognition to the complexity of assembling the diverse components of tourism which was beyond the expertise of most potential travellers, especially among the newly affluent middle and skilled working classes. These groups of new travellers were primarily from the growing urban centres, benefiting from changes to the technology of travel but also from factors such as access to financial resources available to only a small group prior to the Industrial Revolution and from the advent of paid holidays and the impact of increasingly universal education in many European countries.

Changes in the pattern and structure of the tourism industry (and in particular its commercial packaging) had inevitable consequences for the nature of work in the industry. In many ways, this represents a clear parallel to the much more widely recognized changes which occurred within other industry sectors, notably manufacturing, mining and, latterly, agriculture. Supporting the travel of the aristocratic rich, whether while in transit or at a temporary destination, was in reality an extension of the home routine for the travellers and their retinue, little different from the movement between, for example, London, Bath and the country house to reflect the social seasons in Georgian England. Thus, those employed were the normal serving staff of the travellers or of their hosts and the nature of work as well as the relationship between the travellers and those that served them derived from existing 'upstairs–downstairs' conventions in the great aristocratic homes of most European countries.

The advent of travel by the middle classes or the bourgeoisie initiated significant change in this respect because, firstly, these new travellers were not able to avail themselves of the hospitality of their social peers in the resorts and cities that they visited and thus were required to make use of commercial accommodation as well as public transportation, initially the stage coach and subsequently the railway and steam packet. Secondly, they did not have the retinue of serving staff to allow the transfer of whole households to new locations. Local assistance during travel and while at the destination was required to support the tourist experience. Finally, the new travellers did not have the leisure time traditionally available to the aristocratic rich. For commercially driven business families, leisure provided a limited and controlled change from the normal working routine for maybe one or two weeks; thus the impracticality of moving the full household was further underscored.

The circumstances of employment in support of the fledgling commercial tourism industry may have changed as a result of widening participation but consumer expectations were much slower to develop. Thus the master/mistress and servant culture remained central to the provision of travel, hotel and associated services to the tourism industry of the nineteenth century and indeed beyond, reflecting not only its origins in the master–servant working connection but also the clearly defined relationships between social groupings at that time. Tourism was by no means a democratic activity but was largely confined to a relatively small (if growing) minority of the population in most European countries, and the nature of work in commercial enterprises in support of the industry reflected this elitism. The subsequent development of employment in tourism has continued to 'track' the main features of the industry's development and can be linked to the model of imitation which has characterized its change from elite to highly populist activity.

The process of replication from the exclusive in holidaymaking to mass participation in like activities and similar locations is one that has been repeated throughout the development of tourism as a popular and increasingly universal activity. In many ways, a loose analogy to Archimedes and displacement can be used.

The initial stage is one where the first contact between the fashion trendsetters, the rich or the adventurous (whom we may call Group A visitors), with a specific tourism destination or wider locale is made.

This early phase relationship survives for a limited period of time, whereupon increasing numbers (Group B visitors), perhaps more hedonistic in focus and more restricted in their access to monetary resources, follow. Larger-scale and cheaper travel and accommodation provision is developed and the cost of the destination decreases or, put another way, its affordability becomes more widespread. The total value of the new tourist influx may not be significantly greater than that of the original visitors and, certainly, the environmental and social cost will be much greater. The popularization of the destination leads to its abandonment by the pioneering visitors who established its status for tourism and they move elsewhere, frequently further afield or to relatively undeveloped tourist locations.

This process is repeated at both ends of the spectrum. Continued development of the original destination and the downward pressure on cost attracts visitors in larger numbers and from groups previously unable to avail themselves of the resort for cost and access reasons (Group C). This influx, in turn, will result in the migration of Group B to new destinations, possibly those to which Group A moved earlier. This group, in turn then, moves on to destinations new and the process continues in effect in a continuous spiral, ever wider as the ripples in a pool after a stone has been thrown into it. The drive for change comes from a combination of economic, fashion, lifestyle and technological factors which work together to provide tourism opportunities to an increasingly large proportion of the population. This process is essentially that which Steinecke (1993) calls one of 'imitation-segregation'. Steinecke illustrates this process in tabular form and his ideas are presented and extended in Table 3.1

This model looks at the displacement concept with respect to a finite and defined population, within primarily the Western European context. Thus it is possible to map the development of tourism in, say, Britain or Germany by applying the successive stages. There are arguments which suggest that this notion of replication or displacement is over-simplistic in that it does not cater for models of tourism and hospitality development which omit one or more of its stages. Blackpool, for example, developed as a resort to cater for the leisure needs of the industrial working classes in the northwest of England and did not go through a prior period of catering for aristocratic or middle class markets.

Steinecke's model is one that draws on the notion of economic change and development within market-driven or relatively open economies and does not cater for the development of tourism within the former planned economies of Eastern Europe. In the former Soviet Union and its associated states in Eastern Europe, the development of low-cost social tourism, organized through agencies such as trade unions and community organizations, enabled participation on a mass scale without the barriers imposed by access to major economic resources. Clear similarities with socio-political tourism organized for, in particular, young people in National Socialist Germany during the

1930s can be seen. Primarily but decreasingly domestic in focus, this form of tourism was, according to Hall:

> ... viewed as essential to the well-being of citizens and to their economically productive capacities. The availability of leisure and tourism was an important component of the cycle of production and reproduction. Being strictly subordinated to political and ideological considerations, however, domestic tourism had a largely organized, group character. (Hall, 1991, p. 84)

Hall continues by quoting Halász (1960) who outlined Hungarian provision for this form of tourism in the late 1950s which included:

> ... a widespread network of holiday resorts. On the recommendation of the trade unions, the workers can enjoy holidays at reduced prices, or, as a special reward, even free. There are special holiday resorts for mothers with small children. Through the nurseries, schools and youth organizations many thousands of children and

**Table 3.1** Periods of development of tourism

| PERIOD | Landed classes | CLASS Bourgeoisie | Lower class | CAUSES OF CHANGE |
|---|---|---|---|---|
| 17th/18th c. | Grand Tour | | | |
| 18th c. | Spa | Grand Tour/ educational journey | | *Growing industrial middle class* |
| 18th c./early 19th c. | Seaside resort | Spa | | |
| Mid 19th c. | Mediterranean *in winter*/Rhine tour | Seaside *resort (domestic)* | Excursion *train* | *Advent of railway travel; paid holidays* |
| Late 19th c. | Alpinism/ Mediterranean in summer | Rhine tour/ Mediterranean in winter | Seaside resort (*domestic*) | |
| Early 20th c. | World Tour | Alpinism/ Mediterranean in summer | Seaside resort/spa (*domestic*) *Holiday camps* | Early impact of the motor car on leisure travel |
| Mid 20th c. | *Multiple vacations (domestic and international)* | *Long-haul destinations* | *Mediterranean in summer; social tourism* | *Jet airline transportation; reductions in travel formalities/ restrictions* |
| Late 20th c. | *Multiple, activity-linked vacations, long- and short-haul* | | *Long-haul sun destinations* | *Jumbo jet travel* |
| 21st c. | *Increasingly blurred distinctions between the three groups within developed countries?* | | | |

*Source*: Steinecke (1993). *Italics* indicate this author's additions.

young people spend their vacation in the summer holiday camps either entirely free or for a very small sum.

(Halász, in Hall, 1991, p. 85)

Social tourism is, of course, not an exclusively Eastern European phenomenon and continues to operate in countries such as Belgium and France as well as, to some extent, under the auspices of charitable organizations in Britain and the United States where parts of the summer camp movement provide a good example of social tourism in operation. Richards (1992) traces the origins of social tourism in Western Europe back to the 1930s and the passing of laws on paid holidays. He proposes three models of social tourism as identifiable in the 1980s. One is that already discussed in the context of Eastern Europe, where all forms of tourism were social in their focus. The northern European model emphasizes individual consumption, with social tourism by the state limited to the most underprivileged groups. The third model, akin to the first, is that which prevailed in southern Europe, which was more collective in focus and emphasized state provision of low-cost accommodation for low-income groups, with distribution controlled by social services and trade unions (Richards, 1992 p. R1).

Even social tourism in Eastern Europe was not, however, entirely immune from the imitation-segregation process as access to more attractive holiday locations, especially the opportunity for foreign travel within the Soviet bloc and beyond, became prized and contested privileges, available to a growing political and economic elite.

In addition, the model implies that there is no infilling at the levels which Steinecke's 'lower class' have just vacated. In a sense, this is true as the evidence of declined seaside resorts such as Seaton Carew in northeast England and Bangor and Bray in Ireland testify. However, at an international level, the model may well take on a transnational dimension, with resorts or destinations which have been vacated by the 'lower class' categories of Germany or the Netherlands meeting the needs and aspirations of newly enfranchised travellers from Eastern Europe instead. Some Spanish locations are currently experiencing this transition.

The model also has relevance when we consider the growing importance of domestic and outbound tourism within emerging developing countries of, for example, Asia. India with its increasingly important middle classes and rapidly industrializing countries such as Korea, Malaysia, Taiwan and Thailand all provide cases of the Steinecke model at work, albeit with somewhat different locational examples but with the key difference of timescale. These countries may well move through a very rapid displacement process so that widespread tourism participation is achieved within twenty to thirty years, compared to the two centuries of development in Europe.

This extension of Steinecke's model effectively maps the development of tourism from an elitist occupation of a small minority of the population to one with truly mass participation within most developed Western societies. As with all models, it must be treated with some caution in that there are dangers of simplification and a tendency to ignore the complex interrelationship of many factors in creating change within tourism. However, it is indisputable that the development of tourism to its mass participation status within most developed economies represents one of the most wide-reaching social phenomena of the second half of the twentieth century. Looking to the future, the author's addition suggests that the clear distinctions which have existed in terms of 'class' participation in tourism in Europe over the past two centuries may well blur as technology makes travel cheaper and more accessible, in terms of time, to larger sections of the population. Differentiation, in terms of tourist participation, may well become increasingly interest as opposed to fashion determined.

Steinecke's model focuses, of course, entirely on the behaviour and perspective of the growing number of tourists and appears to assume a passive response from host communities. Models of sustainability as discussed in Chapter 1, as well as widening demands for community involvement within tourism planning and development (Murphy, 1985), question the simple assumptions of tourism as solely consumer-demand led in its growth, especially when a contemporary and future gloss is imposed. A lack of passivity by the local community is by no means new. For example, local friction between tourists, especially as the number and profile of visitors changed, and residents has been a common if under-reported theme in the development of European tourism. Berry (1992), considering the 1890s, notes disquiet at the 'takeover' of San Remo by the British during the winter, especially the development of facilities which included 'a Presbyterian Church and two Church of England Churches, an English Druggist, an English Nurses Institute and four English doctors' in competition with local providers. Thus tourism development is not entirely externally driven by factors within originating countries and locations. The local environment and the responsiveness of the host community to the tourist invasion can, in its own right, influence the nature and volume of visitor arrivals.

The model, as extended after Steinecke, represents the movement of tourism from a minority, elite activity to one where, in developed countries at least, tourist activity in its broadest definition is accessible to the vast majority of the population. Tourism can be viewed as a normal consumer activity, competing with other commodities for a share of the discretionary income of most households, but nonetheless part of everyday consumption. Burton (1994) quotes figures regarding the proportion of the population of Western European countries who travel abroad and, without defining the timeframe within which the figures operate, points to international travel rates of 69% for Germany, 67% for Belgium, 65% for the Netherlands, 50% for Sweden, 35% for the UK, 8% for Spain and 7% for Greece. Clear inferences about links to, on the one hand, geographical factors and, on the other, the economic strength of the country can be made. Alternative sources look at the overall vacation participation rates, including domestic tourism, in different countries and this leads to figures of around 80% in Scandinavian countries and a range of between 50% and 75% in other northwestern European countries but lower figures for southern Europe.

Comparable figures for Eastern Europe are not readily available but it is reasonable to presume that they will be considerably lower and, given the decline in state-sponsored social tourism in the region as well as an absolute decline in economic prosperity in some countries, are likely to represent falls from pre-1989 participation rates.

This change from elite to mass consumption, which can be traced over a two hundred year period – with considerable acceleration since 1945, – may be attributed to a diversity of social, economic, political and technological/communications factors. It is easy to pinpoint key factors such as legislation to ensure paid vacations for employees; the railways, the motor car and the advent of fast and cheap air travel; and the relaxation of travel restrictions by most countries. However, the reality represents a complex amalgam of determinants, reflecting change in the wider social and economic environment of most countries. It is impossible, therefore, to attribute one of the most significant changes of the twentieth century to any single factor or, indeed, to any specifically definable group of factors. Despite the antecedents to mass tourism which have been pinpointed in this chapter, the scale and scope of participation in travel today is an entirely new phenomenon, which has no real parallel before the mid-nineteenth century or even later.

## EUROPEAN TOURISM AND HOSPITALITY – THE DEVELOPMENT OF EMPLOYMENT

Inevitably, therefore, the scale of employment in support of contemporary tourism and hospitality reflects these changes so that the industry can now claim to be the world's largest sector employer. The development from work which was essentially an extension of the normal serving function in the home to that which has organizational characteristics akin to other industry sectors, especially within services, has been dramatic and has been driven both by the scale of change and by its social and economic features. Wood (1992a), in a discussion about the hotel and catering sector which constitutes a major part of tourism and hospitality, states:

> It is generally accepted that the historical origins of the hotel and catering workforce lie in the class of domestic servants who maintained the homes of the ruling classes in the latter half of the nineteenth century and the first half of the twentieth. (p. 17)

Saunders (1981) argues that the growth of the hotel industry in the early twentieth century came at the same time as domestic service faced its first phase of serious decline and that many serving employees made the transition to hotel work as a result of a combination of 'push' (increasing domestic technology necessitating fewer serving staff) and 'pull' factors (more attractive and secure conditions). Thus, the change was a reflection, in part, of the effects of industrialization and urban living on the home. It is argued here that the origins of this change actually lie earlier, in the mid-nineteenth century, and reflect the effects of increasing industrially generated affluence and the consequent growing level of participation in tourism by the urban middle and subsequently working classes. However, there is little argument about the process involved which saw an initial transfer of employment from one sector to another, although the growth since that point reduces the significance of these origins.

Because of its early industrialization, the process discussed here took place rather sooner and in more pronounced fashion in Britain than in other European countries but similarities can be seen in the process of industrialization within the hotel and catering sector in France and Germany. However, in countries or regions which faced expansion of tourism and hospitality without a significant industrial or urban history, the move into employment in related sectors was, inevitably, somewhat different. The growth in tourism and hospitality-related jobs in the countries of the Mediterranean or the rural areas of western Ireland and Scandinavia has much in common with similar more recent transitions in the developing tourism economies of, for example, the Caribbean, Malaysia and Thailand, where the shift is directly from agricultural subsistence or employment to tourism and hospitality sector work. A seasonal combination of work in the two sectors was and remains a significant feature of work in these countries.

Little is documented about the origins of employment in the myriad of other sectors which comprise the tourism industry beyond the dominant hotel and catering subsector. However, it is reasonable to speculate about a number of areas which have their antecedents in the social fabric and culture of many countries. Good examples lie in the fields of entertainment and traditional crafts where occupations which are now focused, in a dominating way, towards meeting tourist needs and extracting the tourist dollar have their origins in traditions carried out in communities and the home for centuries. It is argued that many of these activities could and would not survive without the support and impetus of tourist interest; it is also arguable that the authenticity of much traditional culture and art has been compromised by its 'packaging' for tourist consumption. Long and Wall (1995) argue that this effect is in evidence in Bali. The 'industrialization' of traditional craft production processes and marketing, frequently advocated within tourism planning in the developing world, inevitably has a major impact on the nature of work in the sector and moves production and ownership from the level of the cottage to that of the factory. A similar process can be identified with respect to traditional dance and music in most European countries. It is arguable that some of the highly stylized forms of employment offered in theme parks and similar environments have a direct linkage to traditional entertainment forms and thus can be seen as a modern manifestation of the commercialization of tradition. In the context of EuroDisney, which represents American and therefore 'alien' culture, this is clearly a highly contentious issue and one which purist supporters of French culture would strongly seek to refute.

Other areas of tourism employment also owe their origin to activities which had been part of the local landscape long before the emergence of tourism. Examples include the work of the ski instructor in the Alps and that of offering fishing and pleasure trips along all of Europe's Atlantic seaboard. Here again, a merging of employment with other sectors is evident, providing more than one source of work and income to the local population on a seasonal basis. The relatively recent prominence given to agri-tourism also depends on this model, where people whose traditional occupation and income, derived from the land, is supplemented by work which uses those same agricultural resources to meet tourism and hospitality needs, but often working to complementary peak seasons. Agri-tourism, while by no means a new concept, is now to be found in much of Western Europe and is being promoted within a package of tourism development measures in a number of Eastern European countries. Diversification of this kind has been strongly supported by both national governments and the European Union in an attempt to reduce reliance on subsidies within the agricultural sector and to maintain rural employment.

As we have seen in Chapter 2, tourism and hospitality's development has also provided opportunities to extend existing economic activity, and therefore employment, from services designed primarily for the local community to meeting the needs of visitors. A wide range of business areas can fall into this category, including banks, clubs, garages, pubs, restaurants, shops and taxicabs, all of which may have commenced trading with a primarily local market focus and have changed and frequently grown through the patronage of tourists. Many retain dual markets but the growth of the tourism and hospitality industry has not only distinctly affected the character of the establishments but also the level, sustainability and nature of employment available in them. While the businesses in question may well survive in the absence of tourist clientele, it is unlikely that they would be able to employ the same level of staff as they do within a mixed market. Of course, the success of existing businesses in attracting tourist trade frequently results in the establishment of dedicated establishments, catering almost exclusively for visitors and thus creating new employment opportunities within the existing skills base.

This phenomenon of the merging of local consumption with tourist consumption, of businesses serving what are, on the face of it, two very distinct markets, is characteristic of locations which have evolved into tourist centres rather than those which have been purpose built. Thus a study of businesses and employment in towns such as Clifden in Connemara, Ireland, Callander in Scotland, and Rhodes town in Greece will illustrate how employment in tourism, including self-employment, has developed on the lines of the above model through a combination of local business market diversification and expansion as well as new, dedicated investment. By contrast, 'created' tourist resorts such as Brighton and Bournemouth in England, as well as the more recently built Magaluf in Majorca or Golden Sands in Bulgaria, developed with businesses and employment primarily focused on meeting tourist needs. Mature resorts, such as those identified in England, have seen a merging of their markets in a reversal of the process described above, with existing tourist businesses such as shops increasingly serving the local as well as the visiting customer.

Tourism and hospitality work has not only evolved in such clear form out of traditional, existing employment activities. In common with most industries, new categories and types of employment have been created to cater for technological-, market- and service-led change during the transition to mass tourism. Airline crew represent an interesting but hybrid example of this process. Airline pilots and related support staff have, obviously, a recent history and it can be argued that their antecedents lie in hobby and military flying. This is reflected in the number of military pilots in particular drawn into civil aviation during the post-war period, but the military still remains a source of recruitment for many airlines today. By and large, however, the work is recent in its creation. By contrast, cabin staff in aircraft as well as those involved in ground handling, while relatively new positions in themselves, undertake work which has much in common with other areas of tourism employment, notably in hotels. Indeed, recruitment by airlines of staff with hotel backgrounds is quite common. Tourism and hospitality today also generates highly technical employment which has little by way of origin in other employment areas, although contemporary parallels exist in other sectors. This is true of areas such as financial management and information handling in tourism businesses as well as the technical and technological aspects involved in theme park management.

## NEW WORK PATTERNS IN TOURISM AND HOSPITALITY

A historical perspective on the growth of tourism and hospitality in Europe also points to the development of new work patterns in response to the structure of the industry which evolved, focusing on seasonal, part-time and short-term work. The growth of these employment structures can be linked directly to the changing demands of the industry as it evolved to mass participation status as well as to other factors in the economic, political and social environment.

Seasonality has already been mentioned in the context of work which is combined with other activities, such as agriculture, fishing or, in Ireland, local authority capital projects. Seasonality is not exclusive to tourism and was not new to much land-based activity. The insecure and transitory nature of the seasonal work of sheep shearers and harvest-time employees, for example, pre-dates the industrialization of agriculture but was given particular impetus by new divisions of labour on the land from the nineteenth century onwards.

However, mass tourism in those parts of Europe where it is over-whelmingly concentrated into a relatively short period of the year created demand for labour on a scale and in skills areas previously unknown. Seasonal tourism, which can be of little more than three months' duration in some peripheral regions of Europe, developed so that labour was drawn from a number of sources. Local employees were attracted through accommodation with their existing main source of work (as has already been indicated), and this pattern is common in many Greek islands as well as on the western fringes of northern Europe. Alternatively, tourism drew on the local, non-working popula-tion, such as women in the home, the long-term unemployed as well as school and college students during their vacations. Tourism-related employment has offered the first experience of paid work to a large section of the population in areas that have a high dependency on visitors. Finally, the development of tourism created new patterns of employment migration, with people moving temporarily to work opportunities in holiday resorts in the south of France, the English coastal resorts as well as Spain and Greece. This is a phenomenon which remains in evidence in its traditional form but is also exempli-fied, at a somewhat more contemporary level, by the movement of tour company representatives, entertainers and timeshare salespeople from northern Europe to the Mediterranean during the summer months. Thus a process of seasonal movement in response to tourism work opportunities has developed a strongly international flavour, facilitated by cheap and available transportation as well as the easing of travel and working restrictions. Baum (1993b) discusses the traditional patterns of work-related migration within European tourism which has a long-standing history from the 'periphery' regions of Europe to the 'centre', the main urban centres. It is particularly prevalent among Irish, Italian and Spanish employees during the off-season and Baum notes that this can result in permanent loss of skills to the 'periphery' as workers settle to full-time and non-seasonal employment in the larger European cities. These movements are considered in greater depth in Chapter 7. In a general sense, the impact of seasonality, with the inevitable workforce instability that it creates, can be very sig-nificant in terms of operational standards within the industry, the pres-sure to provide adequate and rapid training, staff motivation and loyalty, and also in the insecurity that is induced among employees.

Seasonality is not widely addressed in the literature but another di-mension of the new working environment within tourism, that of part-time work, is much more widely researched and considered. It is also discussed in greater detail in Chapter 6. Wood (1992a), while neglecting the impact of seasonality on employment within hotels and catering, gives in-depth recognition to part-time work and reports a number of studies which address the effects of this growing work form on both hospitality businesses and also on their employees, especially women. The nature of demand in the tourism industry is such that part-time options have long been recognized as an important strategy to meet labour requirements at peak times. Thus in the hotel industry there is a well-established tradition of utilizing a regular pool of casual or part-time staff within banqueting, stewarding and housekeeping departments, and this practice may have derived from traditions inherited from entertaining in the great houses of the eighteenth and nineteenth centuries. Other tourism and hospitality industry sectors have daily demand patterns which only warrant part-time work. Bed and breakfast establishments and youth hostels, for example, may only offer work for limited periods of the morning while infrequent flight and shipping schedules to islands in Scotland and Greece do not require full-time staffing in support at the local stations.

These forms of part-time work have evolved as a natural response to the requirements of the business cycle within tourism. Part-timers operated alongside a substantial core of full-time, long-service employees in hotels and other businesses with relative harmony although facing the personal pressures of insecurity and poor remuneration which is characteristic of this form of work. The basic employment model, however, remained that derived from the industrial and agricultural sectors, of full-time employment with the expectation of continuing work with a single employer although, until the post-war period, without employment protection and security. The implicit expectation was that should business levels require, full-time working opportunities would emerge instead of the part-time work on offer.

However, post-1960s economic restructuring in many Western European countries has seen the growing importance of service sector employment, with a far greater structural reliance on a part-time, flexible and predominantly female workforce. This restructuring reflects in part a major underlying change within the economies of most Western European countries, following similar patterns in the United States, but it is change that has been actively facilitated by the policies of governments on both sides of the Atlantic. This issue and its social impact will be considered in rather greater depth in Chapter 6. The change has, at its heart, a recognition by governments and employers that flexible work practices allow companies to fine-tune their labour needs both to changes in the business cycle (on a daily, weekly or longer timespan basis) and in response to more fundamental restructuring, such as alterations in market profile, shifts in guest expectations and the introduction of technological alternatives to labour. Government intervention in the United Kingdom as well as in other European countries has been designed to facilitate flexibility in the workforce by removing employment protection from part-time workers and eliminating wage controls. At the same time, the position of trade unions in the affected sectors has been greatly weakened. In part, the European Union's Social Chapter is designed to counter the worst excesses of this change but its impact is difficult to assess at this point.

The outcome, however, is clearly in evidence with an increasingly high proportion of new employment opportunities in Britain, for example, being offered on a part-time basis within the service sector. Within this, tourism and, especially, hotel and catering have been responsible for a significant element in employment growth. A study by Robinson and Wallace (1983) in Britain noted that the growth of employment in hotel and catering between 1971 and 1981 was over twice that in the service sector in general, and that this increase, for women, was almost exclusively part time. Part-time jobs also accounted for 69% of new male posts. The authors point out that this growth in part-time employment has taken place at the expense of full-time employment, especially among women. The recent introduction of flexible working contracts by the British hotel group, Forte, based on a core twenty-hour guaranteed week, is an example of employment restructuring which uses part-time work on a large scale as a norm rather than the traditional contingency role which it played.

The nature of much tourism work is that it is readily accessible to those with relatively little specific training. At the same time, conditions and rewards are such that employees frequently are drawn to alternative, allied sectors such as contract or institutional catering where these attributes have traditionally been more attractive. Thus, labour turnover in some sectors of the tourism industry is high, although this situation is by no means new and was noted by George Orwell (1933) on the basis of his experiences in pre-war Paris. As a result, levels of worker mobility are high, both at the unskilled and the managerial level. Wood (1992) discusses a number of studies into aspects of labour turnover, primarily at the unskilled level. At the professional level in the hotel industry, Baum (1988) found that managers in Irish hotels moved to new posts, on average, within 15 months of taking up appointments. In part, high labour turnover is a factor of seasonality but also derives from what Riley (1991) describes as the characteristically weak internal labour market of much of the tourism industry. Riley compares the features of strong internal labour markets which are characteristic of professions such as medicine with the contrasting features of tourism and, in particular, hotel and catering. Further discussion of Riley's work will be found in Chapter 4.

However, as is the case with part-time work, there is some evidence that the introduction and maintenance of an ethos of temporary employment can be attractive to some service industry sectors. The fast-food industry has, arguably, pioneered this approach, building its staffing on the short-term expectations of primarily students and young people not wishing to enter into long-term or career-focused commitments. The approach allows for the introduction of highly repetitive and deskilled work routines which employees can follow without the danger of longer-term motivation problems. Other benefits to the company are flexibility and low wage costs (Ritzer, 1993). The temporary, revolving workforce, however, represents a model which can be attractive to tourism businesses with a large number of low skilled positions, and which can systematize and standardize a substantial number of working routines as well as having a relatively transitory customer base.

Tourism and hospitality in Europe, therefore, has become a mass participation industry with increasing trends towards the creation of a workforce which mirrors its consumer market in its breadth. The growth of seasonal, part-time and temporary working opportunities in most sectors of the industry means that, for many young people and women returning to work, positions in tourism-related companies represent an early exposure or reintroduction to the world of employment. At the same time, these same employees are, frequently, relatively seasoned tourists in their own right and have participated in both domestic and international travel to a considerable extent. Thus, for the first time, we have tourism employees who are versed and experienced in the needs that their customers have, and the gap between the two groups no longer has the importance that it did even in the immediate post-war years.

The changes in patterns of work within tourism would not have been possible had the overall guest–worker relationship remained the same as it was during the early days of tourism development. Tourism and hospitality within most of Western Europe has developed to a point where, with respect to a substantial proportion of both visitors and those working in the industry to meet their needs, there is no longer a significant difference in their attitudinal, social and economic backgrounds. This is most apparent when we consider the relationship between visitors and those working to meet their needs in resorts such as Blackpool and Benidorm but is an increasing feature of tourism within developed economies worldwide. However, the gap is still very evident, primarily for economic reasons, within developing countries as well as in parts of Eastern Europe. Yet the master–servant relationship which lay at the root of the early history of tourism employment has much less potency within modern tourism, although vestiges of it still do exist, and to a certain degree are perpetuated by the trappings of businesses within the sector, for example on cruise liners and in hotels and restaurants. However, democratization is also becoming much more common in this area. The Ritz Carlton's motto that 'We are Ladies and Gentlemen serving Ladies and Gentlemen' is an extreme case in point. Another example is represented by the recent announcement that Lauda Air, the Austrian company, have redesigned their cabin staff uniforms to match the normal attire of their business customers – which includes jeans – to 'create an environment that is casual but polite, and leads to a more personal contact with customers' (Churchill, 1994).

In many respects, these examples should bring us to a position that is in complete contrast to the one where we started, when traveller and server were totally detached in social, economic and cultural terms. What is more, both parties fully accepted this social distance, tacitly buying into the Malthusian notion that divisions in society were part of the natural order of things and that each person had their place and role. The democratization of tourism and hospitality, supported by legislation, has created an environment where – in theory at least – server and guest are equal. Critical to this process has been the exposure of tourism and hospitality workers to travel and international guest status in their own right, something unthinkable at its current level and scale even forty years ago.

---

REVIEW AND DISCUSSION QUESTIONS

1. Consider aspects of the history of the tourism and hospitality industry in a town or region with which you are familiar. What are likely to have been the main reasons for its development? What were the main features? Does any evidence remain of the original form of the industry in your locality?

2. With reference to a town or region with which you are familiar, can you find any evidence in the local history of tourism and hospitality to support or reject Steinecke's replication or displacement model?

3. Consider the vacation and travel opportunities that you and your family (immediate, grandparents) have enjoyed over the past forty to fifty years. Does any identifiable pattern emerge in the type of holidays that were taken, the locations that were visited and their distance from home? Can you account for changes to your family vacation patterns over that timeframe?

4. Utilizing your own work experience or other contacts, interview a senior and mature tourism and hospitality employee or someone, now retired, who used to work in the industry. Try to establish the main changes that have occurred in that person's experience in the nature of work that was undertaken and that which is prevalent in that occupation today. Consider the reasons for such changes and their implications.

5. What are the implications of decreasing 'social distance' between guests and employees for the management of a tourism and hospitality business?

6. Does serving guests in the tourism and hospitality industry need to be servile?

# 4 The tourism and hospitality labour markets

WHAT ARE LABOUR MARKETS?

Chapter 2 has demonstrated that the tourism and hospitality industries in Europe are characterized by diversity both on the basis of intranational (within countries) and international (between countries) criteria. Diversity is compounded by imprecision in defining the actual boundaries of the tourism and hospitality sector and variation between countries in how they actually attempt this exercise. The 'porous' parameters of the industry which, at its margins, merges into a variety of other economic sectors is a characteristic to which we are driven to return repeatedly. It is a source of frustration to those who prefer to work within the precise and comforting boundaries provided by absolute definitions, whether derived from official or other sources. It can also be a source of challenge when it is recognized that the heterogeneous range of activities which constitute tourism and hospitality are bound together by their contribution to a common goal, that of meeting the comfort, logistical and leisure needs of the traveller away from home.

As we have seen in Chapters 2 and 3, the characteristics of the tourism and hospitality industry in Europe have a major impact on the nature of work in the sector. Thus the range of subsectors, the size of businesses, their ownership, the markets they serve and the impact of seasonality illustrate the factors which contribute to determining, for example, the range of tasks which are undertaken, the numbers employed and the skills required. However, while these associations are undoubtedly very important, they cannot be seen as the exclusive determinants of the tourism and hospitality labour market.

In its broadest sense, the labour market comprises the total working environment at local, regional, national or transnational level. Thus we can talk about the labour market of a small town, such as the location of the 1994 Winter Olympics, Lillehammer in Norway; of a metropolitan city, for example the 1992 Summer Olympics venue, Barcelona in Spain; of a distinct region of a country, such as Calabria in Italy; of an entire nation state; or, finally, of the whole European Union or, indeed, the total continent of Europe. A labour market consists of all industry sectors, their personnel requirements and skills needs, as well as those currently outside the actual workforce, whether unemployed, temporarily unable to work because of illness or injury, or undergoing specific vocational training or more general preparation for the workforce within the schools system. Economists and others who view labour markets from a macro or theoretical perspective tend to describe the environment as one akin to a well-oiled machine, driven by supply and demand within a free market. However, as Riley (1991) rightly points out:

> Behind the assumption of a perfect market is a perfect flow of information between buyers and sellers of labour. In a perfect world the buyers would know how many have the skills they desire, how many would like to learn them and where these people are. Conversely, people would know how many vacancies there are, in what organizations and at what rate of pay. (p. 7)

Perfect labour markets, however, do not exist in the real free market world and, despite major investment in labour planning, the total management of the labour market was not a conspicuous success in the planned economies of Eastern Europe either. This is because labour markets at macro or micro level represent a complexity of interactions which do not lend themselves to management and balancing in the manner demanded by the theoretical model.

> At any one time, people will be seeking employment or trying to change their jobs. Simultaneously, employers will be seeking new employees. Wage rates will be set, recruitment policies implemented, people will need training, people will have to move. This is the daily life of labour markets. Thousands of independent decisions made by employers and employees make up the trends in mobility, the surpluses of or shortages of supply, the excesses or lack of demand. In other words, whatever the state of supply and demand in a labour market, it is brought about by the independent and unconnected decisions of thousands of people.
>
> (Riley, 1991, p. 7)

In addition to this, the character of this wider labour market is determined by a wide range of macro environmental factors, some of which pertain specifically to the geographical unit in question (town, county, region, country, etc.) while others are shared with other units. Some of these factors include:

- the culture and history of the locality or unit;
- the economic system within which it exists (free market, planned economy, etc.);
- the range of existing wealth creating industry sectors (agriculture, heavy industry, light industry, services, including tourism, etc.);

- changes to the industrial structure of the unit (the decline of coal mining and steel production and the rise of light assembly work in South Wales is one example while another is that of Liverpool where the decline in traditional port employment has been paralleled by growth in the leisure and tourism sector (McDonald, 1994));
- the profile of businesses in terms of size and ownership – multinational companies tend to have a very different relationship to a local and even national labour market than that characteristic of a small, family-owned business;
- local, national and, indeed, global economic performance, factors which will influence demand for good and services produced, the price that will be paid for them and the level and character of employment that will be generated as a result;
- the demographic structure of the unit and trends within it (the falling birthrate and increasing longevity of older people in much of Western Europe, for example);
- the range of skills available within the existing workforce and among school leavers and college graduates and how these relate to industry demand;
- competition between companies and industry sectors for available skills within the workforce and among school leavers and college graduates;
- the structure, organization and focus of educational and vocational training provision within the unit;
- the extent of inward and outward labour mobility to and from the unit in question and the barriers and incentives that exist to such mobility (for example, rights of free labour movement within the European Union or at a national level);
- policies enacted at a local, regional, national and transnational level by governments, councils, legislative and representative assemblies with respect to matters which may include:
  - fiscal/economic policy;
  - education and training;
  - employment creation and related incentives;
  - employment protection measures;
  - workplace conditions and practice, such as those covered in the European Union's Social Chapter;
  - health and safety at work provisions;
  - support for export;
  - attraction of inward investment;
  - immigration/employment of expatriate labour.

A labour market, therefore, is a dynamic concept responding to a diversity of factors some of which can be controlled at a local, regional or national level but also including others which are entirely beyond such management and which cannot be treated as static and unchanging. This reality has major consequences for the manner in which, at a micro level, managers plan and initiate all aspects of their human resource policies within a company. At the macro level, likewise, planning with respect to areas such as vocational education provision and the introduction of special measures to alleviate youth unemployment, for example, must be responsive and flexible in recognition of constant change within the labour market. Recognizing the dynamic nature of the labour market environment and the consequences that this has for planning human resource needs at a macro level is a central theme within Chapter 9 of this book.

## WHAT IS THE VALUE OF UNDERSTANDING LABOUR MARKETS?

What is the practical value and purpose of an understanding of the labour market to those involved, as employers and employees, within it? From the employer's perspective, the labour market external to the company provides the source for the recruitment of new staff as well as the pool which personnel made redundant or released for other reasons join. The wider labour market also provides the major benchmark against which it is possible to gauge a range of major human resource policies and practices, some of which are discretionary and some of which are externally imposed. Thus a company's policies with respect to the full range of human resource functions are influenced by the characteristics of the labour market in which it operates. Depending on the nature of the company's business, its skills requirements and a range of other factors such as labour mobility, the labour market reference point for any particular business may be local, national or even international. For example, the recruitment of semi-skilled factory floor or cleaning personnel will necessitate action within different labour market parameters than will be the case with respect to staff with specialist scientific research skills. Labour market considerations determined by the range of influences which we have addressed above will impact upon a company's policies and practices with respect to a large number of areas. These may include:

- recruitment of personnel in the open market, from schools/colleges and through head hunting from other employers;
- staff training and development;
- promotion and enhancement policies;
- severance/redundancy policies;
- employment of part-time, casual and seasonal staff;
- contracting or franchising out of functions to supplier companies (catering, cleaning, office services, etc.);
- rates of remuneration, including overtime, bonus payments, profit-sharing, etc.;
- conditions of service such as hours of work, flexible time-keeping, paid holiday entitlements, maternity and similar benefits;

- trade union representation;
- social and other benefits; and
- health and safety provision.

Riley (1991) does not fully accept the above argument that a company's internal environment is essentially a response to external factors of the kind listed above. He argues that, within companies, independent rules may be established to determine how some or all of the above operate in practice. Riley distinguishes between the external labour market at whatever geographical level we wish to consider it, which is basically governed by the range of macroeconomic, social and political factors that we have considered earlier, and the internal labour market within the company (or arguably the industry sector) itself. He argues that:

> The concept of the internal labour market is based on the idea that sets of rules and conventions form within organizations which act as allocative mechanisms governing the movement of people and the pricing of jobs. Such rules are about promotion criteria, training opportunities, pay differentials and the evaluation of jobs, but most importantly, they are about which jobs are 'open' to the external labour market. It is the concept of openness which represents the interface between what goes on inside the organization and the external labour market. (Riley, 1991, p. 12)

We will address the consequences of this distinction between internal and external labour markets in greater depth later in this chapter.

Likewise, from an employee perspective, an understanding of the main features of the labour market provides the basis for decisions with respect, for example, to educational and training choices, both at the initial stage and as retraining, selection of employment and employer, negotiating strength with potential and current employers, career promotion and enhancement, mobility between employers as well as geographical mobility within a region, country or internationally, participation in special schemes during periods of unemployment, and participation in trade union and related activities, as well as a range of attendant considerations.

As regards both the company and the individual, the relationship with the labour market in which they exist, whatever parameters are used to define its geographical boundaries, is highly individual. It is possible to review the characteristics and structure of the labour market in question against the range of determining factors that we have already considered and many of these will impose similar constraints on all employers as well as all employees. However, it is also important to recognize differing circumstances, constraints and needs within both groups (companies and workers) and these will impact upon the way in which members of both groups relate to the labour market.

# GLOBAL LABOUR MARKETS

In keeping with trends in all aspects of business, labour markets, even at a relatively local level, are increasingly dependent on the international and even global context in which they exist. Historically, labour markets could exist in relative isolation from events and developments in the next town, in the neighbouring country or on the other side of the world. Industrialization started the process which has destroyed the virtual self-sufficiency of communities and created the complex range of dependencies which characterize modern business. Migration of labour to the new industrial locations occurred on a scale which previous mobility had not permitted. At the same time, opportunities in new labour markets, especially in North America, attracted migrants to leave their primarily rural homes in Europe and travel overseas on a scale previously unknown. Economic migration, as opposed to the political mobility of those avoiding persecution in their own land, has taken place on a previously unknown scale and scope during the past one hundred and fifty years. Examples include European and especially Irish migration to the United States and Australia since the 1840s, a movement that continues today; immigration from former colonial possessions into France and Britain from the 1950s onwards; movement out of countries such as Vietnam and Hong Kong to Australia, Canada, Europe and the USA since the 1970s, reflecting a combination of political and economic circumstances; and movement west within Europe since the collapse of the Soviet Union and its dependent governments in Eastern Europe. Some of the consequences to the tourism and hospitality industry of migration are considered in more detail in Chapter 7.

Globalization of markets and business structures as well as the political will to remove the barriers to trade and labour mobility has had the effect, on the one hand, of creating truly international labour markets, especially in certain vocational subsectors, while at the same time blurring the geographical boundaries of others which have traditionally been fairly local in their focus. As a result, some specialist skills are the cause of truly international recruitment searches at an individual or collective level. Shortages of specific computing skills, for example, have led major American companies to actively recruit in south and east Asia. Alternatively, within the increasingly global economy, companies are willing to relocate their operations to countries and localities where availability of skills is greater and the cost of such skills is lower than is the case in the labour market within which they have previously been operating. The relocation of clothing manufacturing plants from the United States to neighbouring Latin American countries is an example of this process as are movements in south and east Asia to relocate highly labour-intensive industries out of expensive locations such as Hong Kong, Singapore and Taiwan into China. This process of globalization of the world's labour force is a relatively controversial subject and its impact depends on whether it is seen from the perspective of the beneficiary or the loser. Johnston (1991) argues that:

> The globalization of labor is good for the world. It allows human capital to be deployed where it can be used most productively. Countries that recognize it as a positive trend and facilitate the flow of people will benefit most. (p. 124)

On this basis, the European Union model of free movement of labour can be seen as a positive step within globalization. Overall, it is likely that, in terms of skills which are in short supply throughout the world, the net beneficiaries of mobility will be the most advanced industrial countries while, for the poorer countries, globalization of labour means the relocation of low wage, high polluting industries from the developed to the less developed world. A similar analysis can be applied in considering the potential impact of the GATT free trade arrangements. Johnston's analysis concludes in an upbeat manner, which ignores nationalist, racist and, consequently, protectionist trends in Europe and other parts of the world:

> The globalization of labor is inevitable. The economic benefits from applying human resources most productively are too great to be resisted. At least some countries will lower the barriers to immigration and at least some workers will be drawn by the opportunity to apply their training and improve their lives. But more likely, many countries will make immigration easier, and many workers will travel the globe . . .
> The world will be changed as a result. As labor gradually becomes international, some national differences will fade. Needs and concerns will become more universal, and personnel policies and practices will standardize . . .
> Two forces will drive workplace standardization: companies responding to global labor markets and governments negotiating trade agreements. For a global corporation, the notion of a single set of workplace standards will eventually become as irresistble as the idea of a single language for conducting business.
> (Johnston, 1991, p. 126)

Labour globalization and relocation is not a widely exercised option within the tourism and hospitality industry because the tourist attraction, which visitors come to see, generally cannot be moved to alternative locations, although this process may occur in specific technical support areas such as aircraft maintenance. In other respects the recruitment of cheaper labour from elsewhere to meet low skills requirements in the tourism and hospitality industry is commonplace. As we will consider in more detail in Chapter 7, migration within Europe is from peripheral countries such as Ireland, Italy, Portugal and Spain in order to work in the hotels of London and other north European cities. This is a long-standing tradition and the consequences of this process are discussed by Baum (1993b), who refers to:

> . . . the pull of the 'core' regions, offering the attractions of different lifestyles, higher rewards, year-round employment and associated benefits. This issue is one that is, perhaps, critical within the whole economic development of the 'New Europe' and has implications for regions not currently within the European Community. The main flow of tourists (international and domestic) within Europe, is essentially from 'core' to 'periphery', although some 'honeypot' locations are identifiable in the 'core' areas (London, Paris). By contrast, the traditional flow of labour is from the 'periphery' to the 'core' (for example Irish emigration to London and the movement of Italian and Spanish labour to France and Germany, a process directly in reverse of the main tourist flows). Greater facility for labour mobility is likely to increase this flow of workers. Migration within Europe and to Europe has greatly increased in recent years, for a diversity of reasons (economic, political and cultural) and this process has already increased through a 'rippling' process, incorporating areas further and further from the economic core of Europe, such as Turkey, North Africa and the countries of Central and Eastern Europe. As a consequence, the 'peripheral' countries face the prospect of losing their trained and skilled tourism labour to those countries in the 'core'. This, in turn, is likely to adversely affect standards of product and service in the regions losing their skilled labour. There is every reason to believe that this process will continue, providing cheaper labour for the tourism industries of the 'core' countries and drawing skills away from the periphery.
>
> (pp. 81–2)

Likewise, countries such as the Philippines and Sri Lanka have acted as traditional sources of labour for hotel industries in Europe, the Far East and the Gulf states.

Transnational economic integration also provides the basis for major changes to assumptions about traditional labour markets. In particular, the free movement of labour within the European Union, alongside the free movement of investment capital, means that on the one hand companies can locate activities in countries or localities where the skills and labour cost environment are most favourable to their needs. British policy, which seeks to reduce both the cost and bureaucracy of employment by, among other things, declining to sign the Social Chapter, has been designed to attract investment from its European competitors, a policy which appears to have had some success. On the other hand, labour has the theoretical opportunity to seek out employment openings wherever they exist within the Union and Baum (1993b) above details how this process operates in the tourism and hospitality industry. Former UK government minister Norman

Tebbitt's much quoted advice to job seekers from areas of high un-employment to 'get on their bikes' and avail themselves of job opportunities elsewhere in Britain now has an increasingly European dimension. However, linguistic and cultural barriers mean that intra-European Union labour mobility remains relatively small in scale although it is increasing in significance.

## TOURISM AND HOSPITALITY LABOUR MARKETS

Within the context of wider labour market considerations, it is possible to give particular attention to the characteristics of labour markets within specific subsectors of the economy. Such sub-labour markets, while in no way operating in isolation of the wider economic, social and political context which drives the broader external labour market environment, have features and behavioural patterns which set them apart to greater or lesser degrees from that wider context. Thus it is possible to identify a tourism and hospitality labour market at all the geographical levels that we have already considered – local, regional, national and transnational.

In Chapter 2, we identified some of the major features of the tourism and hospitality industry in Europe. One of these was that commonality is not always easy to identify at a transnational level and that the industry is characterized by inevitable diversity for geographical, historical, cultural, political, social as well as business and market reasons. However, there are a number of broad features which can be identified as representative of tourism and hospitality in Europe and these, when set alongside the range of generic determinants discussed earlier, provide the main influences on the labour market within the sector. These features include:

- an industry dominated by small businesses with a high level of family or self-employment in a number of its subsectors (hotels, restaurants, retail activities) on the one hand, and by large, traditionally state-owned enterprises (e.g. transport) in others on the other hand;
- an industry which experiences high levels of fluctuation in demand for its services in terms of annual seasonality as well as variation within the timeframe of the typical week and day. This has major consequences for the supply of labour, especially in the context of the small business operation;
- an industry constrained by its service-sector characteristics (which we shall consider in greater detail in Chapter 5) but which include the inseparability of production and consumption; the intangibility of the product; its perishability, meaning that it cannot be stored or warehoused; and the local nature of its demand, which means that it cannot be offered centrally to the market;
- an industry where, in some European countries, traditions in terms of the style and ceremony of service remain very important unlike in

North America, a feature which has important consequences for the nature of work and its flexibility;

- a labour-intensive industry in most of its sectors which, despite the impact of technology, is unlikely to alter substantially in the foreseeable future;
- an industry which, as a consequence of its labour intensity, is dominated in many subsectors by unskilled and semi-skilled jobs. Riley (1991) develops a model from earlier work of the Hotel and Catering Industry Training Board (1984) in the UK, which looked at the manpower structure of hotels, restaurants and institutional catering. This model is reproduced as Figure 4.1 and illustrates clearly the dominant position of what he calls operative staff within these sectors;
- an industry which, because of its skills profile, is readily accessible to workers with a minimum of formal training and where training focuses on widely transferable skills, especially in the customer contact zone. This 'openness' works to the advantage of the industry, especially in locations where a high seasonality factor is in operation, in that it is relatively easy to draft additional labour into the industry as demand increases and to shed employees at times of reduced demand. However, the negative corollary means that trained tourism and hospitality employees are readily 'poached' by other industry sectors because of their generic and readily transferable skills;
- an industry within which some sectors are dominated by traditions of low pay and perceived poor conditions, as we shall see in Chapter 6.

Riley (1991) analyses this labour market environment in terms of the hotel and catering sectors, with specific reference to the concept of internal labour markets. Riley differentiates between the structural

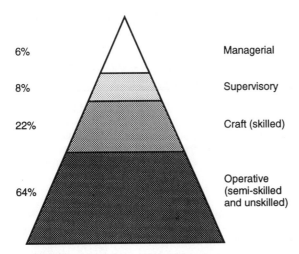

**Figure 4.1** A skills model for the hotel and restaurant sectors. (Source: Riley, 1991, after HCITB, 1984).

features of strong and weak internal labour markets and this differentiation goes some way in explaining the characteristics of employment within many subsectors of the tourism and hospitality industry. Table 4.1 identifies the features of the two internal labour market types.

It is Riley's contention that the labour market within the hotel and catering industry meets most of the criteria for 'weak' status. This analysis is based, primarily, upon observation of the industry in the United Kingdom and the fit is quite good in this respect. Certainly,

**Table 4.1** Features of strong and weak internal labour markets

| Strong | Weak |
| --- | --- |
| • Specified hiring standards | • Unspecified hiring standards |

*(representing the extent to which specific jobs demand a particular qualifications and experience profile for entry)*

| | |
| --- | --- |
| • Single port of entry | • Multiple ports of entry |

*(representing the extent to which recruitment for particular posts are restricted to one source in terms of qualifications and experience or whether a diversity of backgrounds can qualify as applicants for the post)*

| | |
| --- | --- |
| • High skill specificity | • Low skill specificity |

*(representing the extent to which the job demands specific technical or knowledge-based skills)*

| | |
| --- | --- |
| • Continuous on-job training | • No on-job training |

*(representing the extent to which specific and ongoing training is necessary in order to progress within the job or, alternatively, where initial training provides the totality of expected training for the job).*

| | |
| --- | --- |
| • Fixed criteria for promotion and transfer | • No fixed criteria for promotion and transfer |

*(representing the extent to which further training and experience are specified for promotion and transfer)*

| | |
| --- | --- |
| • Strong workplace customs | • Weak workplace customs |

*(reflecting the strength of trade unions and professional associations in influencing the organization of work and the workplace)*

| | |
| --- | --- |
| • Pay differentials remain fixed over time | • Pay differentials vary over time |

*(reflecting the strength of trade union and professional control over pay and conditions, especially in terms of protecting the status and reward differentials between higher skills posts and those at a lower level)*

*An additional dimension to those proposed by Riley is:*

| | |
| --- | --- |
| • *Fixed roles/responsibilities* | • *Flexible roles/responsibilities* |

*(reflecting the extent to which rigid job demarcations exist in the workplace or to which flexibility in work roles/multi-skilling applies)*

From Riley (1991), p. 12. *Italics* indicate this author's additions.

when comparisons are made against these criteria between, for example, access to management within the hotel industry and professional careers in medicine, the contrast between strong and weak internal labour markets can be seen in relatively clear relief. However, as is the case with any framework, what we see is a simplified representation of the real situation and Riley's argument does not portray an absolute description of the situation within the hotel industry on a Europe-wide basis. In Switzerland and a number of other European countries, hotel employment has a far stronger tradition of perceived 'professionalism' than is the case in Britain and, as a result, some vocations within the industry, including management, food preparation and food service, are likely to exhibit rather stronger internal labour market characteristics. Many hotels in Eastern Europe have also developed traditions of considerable strength within their internal labour markets but within a rather different context. One major hotel in Bucharest, Romania, for example, recruited virtually no new staff from its opening in 1986 until 1994. Limited internal promotion was strictly on the basis of seniority and all workplace customs were rigidly specified. Such practices, allied to a rooms to staff ratio of 1 : 2, are under major threat from moves towards a free market and the entry of foreign competition into the hotel business.

Riley's model was not designed to transfer fully into the wider tourism and hospitality sector. The diversity of the industry, encompassing as it does subsectors as wide-ranging as sports coaching, museums and other attractions, heritage sites and transportation as well as hotels and restaurants, includes many working environments or internal labour markets which exhibit predominantly strong characteristics. Such employment opportunities include museum curators, airline pilots and tourism consultants, where the open employment environment characteristic of lower skills areas is not typical. However, even these relatively protected areas are weakening to some extent. During Ronald Reagan's presidency, the American government's willingness to replace the highly specialized skills of established air traffic controllers through recruitment and training of alternatives when threatened by the consequences of strike action represents a good example of a weakening labour market. Likewise, the Irish airline Ryanair employed less expensive Eastern European pilots during the mid-1980s when the cost of labour prohibited the use of local alternatives.

We must also remember that Riley's model is designed to cater for labour markets within the private, free-market domain of the economy. There remain, in Europe, substantial parts of the tourism and hospitality industry which are public-sector owned and operated. These include government departments and agencies involved in marketing and information services (national, regional and local tourist offices) as well as transportation (railways, airlines and bus services), hotels and other services. The public sector frequently operates to different labour market rules than those which apply within a free market and, as a result, there are tendencies which push the internal labour market in this sector towards that described by Riley as strong. The ongoing debate about public subsidy for state-owned airlines and the attendant restructuring of the workforce in countries such as France, Greece and Ireland illustrates the situation with respect to public ownership and the labour market. Much of the tourism and hospitality industry in Eastern Europe is in a transition phase from public to private and, likewise, is not really suitable for the application of the Riley model.

The tourism and hospitality industry as a whole in Europe is an amalgam of subsectors which represent both weak and strong labour markets. Overall labour market management by governments in most countries of Western and, increasingly, Eastern Europe is undergoing a general process of weakening, so as to facilitate greater flexibility within the workforce at lower cost to both the state (through training and benefits) and the employer through wage costs and additional benefits. A range of legislation in the United Kingdom since 1979 has been designed to meet these ends, eroding the position of trade unions within the workplace, deregulating a wide variety of workplace practices, supporting the deskilling of tasks within both the public and private sectors and removing minimum wages protection in a number of industries through the abolition of the Wages Councils. However, National Minimum Wages (NMW) operate within most countries of the European Union and undoubtedly act to strengthen the labour market within industries affected. According to Wood (1992b), only Ireland and the United Kingdom do not operate legally enforceable NMW. In other countries, the situation is as follows:

- France, Luxembourg, the Netherlands, Portugal and Spain all have a statutory minimum wage;
- national collective agreements create legally enforceable general minima in Belgium and Greece; and
- Denmark, Germany and Italy set minimum rates through legally binding industry-level agreements (Wood, 1992b, p. 303).

As we shall see in Chapter 6, the European Union's Social Chapter is also, on the face of it, a move in the direction of strengthening the labour market, which is in part why the United Kingdom has refused to sign it. However, much of the impetus for change is driven by the private sector and it is unlikely that the Social Chapter can counteract the effects of such developments. Examples above from America and Ireland illustrate the process of labour market weakening at work in the tourism sector.

The issue of flexibility in the workforce is one that is central to the weak–strong labour market debate and has been added to Riley's model within Table 4.1. Flexibility has two important dimensions when we consider the tourism and hospitality labour market. Employers seek flexibility in terms of the numbers that are employed within a business in order to cope with cyclical variation in demand, whether based on annual seasonality, peaks and troughs within the week or day or in order to cater for the high demand created by special events, whether a wedding in a hotel or transport to the Olympics or other 'one-off' sporting events. The traditional response to the need for this form of flexibility has been reliance on part-time, casual, short-contract and seasonal staff. All subsectors of the tourism and hospitality industry have employed this approach to flexibility which is manifest in the work undertaken by, for example, representatives employed by tour operators and located in resorts for the duration of the season, seasonal hotel and airline staff, breakfast kitchen and service staff in small hotels, banqueting staff in hotels and convention centres, and self-employed tour guides. Such staffing arrangements are attractive to employers in that labour is only costing them when it is required. However, control over matters such as operational and service standards may be jeopardized by the lack of permanence within the workforce. Problems can also arise at times of peak labour demand because other employers may offer better or more extended employment to those in the pool from which a company normally draws in order to exercise its need for flexibility. One response by Forte Hotels in the United Kingdom has been to offer guaranteed minimum hours to staff working in areas where the impact of variable demand is most felt. Under this arrangement, staff are contracted to work or be paid for a minimum of twenty hours per week but may be required to work considerably longer as required. It is argued that the flexible contracts involved will make the concept of overtime virtually redundant (Bartlett, 1993). The personnel involved are permanent and fully trained members of staff and cannot opt to work elsewhere as is the case with other arrangements.

The second aspect of flexibility relates to the tasks that are undertaken by employees within the workplace. Traditionally, workplace demarcation was relatively fixed in many sectors of the tourism and hospitality industry. The classical parti system in hotel kitchens, for example, identified the specific tasks which lay within the responsibility of each member of the kitchen brigade and little interchange of functions took place. The notion that kitchen staff could work outside of that specific domain, for example through participation in service functions, would have been beyond comprehension to many who worked within that system. Vestiges of the classical parti system still exist in countries such as France, although working practices combined with the advent of technology and the deskilling of some tasks through the use of alternative, convenience products has eroded its significance. Similar, clear, role definitions have been features of work within airlines, railway systems and other sectors of the tourism and hospitality industry.

Such inflexible working practices have made it difficult for businesses to respond to variable demand and, especially within small businesses, to compete effectively while at the same time maintaining cost competitiveness in the marketplace. The manufacturing sector has pioneered a response to the need for flexibility in this sense by developing a core of permanent full-time employees who are trained in a variety of skills in order that they may move from function to function as required. The weakening of the internal labour market within tourism and hospitality can be seen in the extent to which similar approaches have been adopted within the sector. Small hotels have long practised flexibility through the employment of personnel who can work in a number of departments and who, typically, may face a working day which involves service at breakfast, housekeeping functions during the morning, and bar or restaurant service at lunchtime to complete the day. Specialist training courses have been designed in order to meet industry's demands for the range of skills required to undertake such work (Baum, 1987). Similar flexibility is evident in new working practices, especially of smaller airlines where cabin staff may well be involved in a variety of other functions, including check-in, baggage handling and related tasks. This has the effect of reducing the requirement for ground station staff at small airports where the airline offers limited services. Examples include British Airways Express Scottish island services as well as those operated by Ryanair between Ireland and the United Kingdom. However, there are also countertrends within the tourism and hospitality industry, which militate against such functional flexibility. Guerrier and Lockwood (1989a) discuss the effects of strengthening the departmental structure in hotels by giving greater local authority and autonomy to department heads and their staff. One effect of this process is to make cross-departmental flexibility more difficult to achieve because departments become rather more unit focused and also develop strong local cultures of their own.

Guerrier and Lockwood (1989b) also offer an interesting model of flexibility within the hotel industry which, if implemented, will further reinforce our interpretation of the internal labour market within this sector as predominantly weak. The model builds upon the two dimensions of flexibility which have already been considered above. Guerrier and Lockwood draw on work by Atkinson (1985) for the Institute of Manpower Studies in the United Kingdom.

> They [the Institute of Manpower Studies] define four different types of flexibility: functional flexibility, concerned with the versatility of employees and their ability to handle different tasks and move between jobs; numerical flexibility, concerned the ability to adjust the number of workers or the number of hours worked in response to changes in demand; pay flexibility, concerned with financial reward systems that encourage functional flexibility and reward scarce skills or individual performance; and 'distancing' strategies which involve contracting out operations to shift the burden of risk and uncertainty elsewhere.
>
> (Guerrier and Lockwood, 1989b, p. 9)

Atkinson then continues by describing an ideal model of the fully flexible firm. This consists of a numerically fixed core group of employees carrying out the key activities of the firm demanding very specific skills who are difficult to replace and hold full-time, permanent career positions within the company, with job security implicit in their position. In return for such flexibility, the core group are expected to operate in a fully flexible manner in functional terms. Within this ideal model, the core of the company is surrounded by three peripheral groups which insulate the core from the effects of changes in demand and take the brunt of the need for, in particular, numerical flexibility. The first of these groups are employees on permanent contracts but with little prospect of enhancement and limited job security. They undertake tasks which are generic in their skills demand. Functional flexibility is not demanded of this group but labour turnover is high and thus numerical flexibility can readily be achieved and may be encouraged through the deliberate recruitment of personnel who are unlikely to stay for long. The second peripheral group consists of short contract, part-time and job-share staff, offering both functional and numerical flexibility to the company. The final component within the model consists of external or 'distanced' groups who are not employed by the company, including subcontractors, agency staff, self-employed workers and those providing outsourced products.

Guerrier and Lockwood applied this 'ideal' model to the hotel industry in the United Kingdom through a study which included both extensive interviews and an in-depth investigation of practice in two hotel units. The outcome of their study is summarized in Figure 4.2.

Guerrier and Lockwood's conclusions suggest that, within the corporate hotel structure, the Atkinson model does work, but with some modification to take account of the head office and unit-based structure of such companies. Within a single unit hotel company, it is more likely that the 'ideal' model would apply. Guerrier and Lockwood divide the core staff of a multi-unit hotel company into three components. Firstly, there are 'company core staff' consisting of the cadre of senior and middle management within the hotel such as the general manager, deputy or resident manager, assistant managers and graduate trainees but usually excluding department heads. They are so defined because they operate within the company's career structure and potentially have access to career opportunities elsewhere within the group. Normal progression includes periods with responsibility for a number of functional areas in the hotel. Traditionally, but less so today, this route has required a period in food and beverage as a prerequisite for general management. Thus this group of staff are expected to exhibit maximum functional flexibility and are a highly skilled, versatile and committed group which the company cannot afford to lose in any great number. Career tracking schemes which companies such as Hilton International have instituted focus on this group of core staff and contribute to the planning of both their geographical and status progression within the organization.

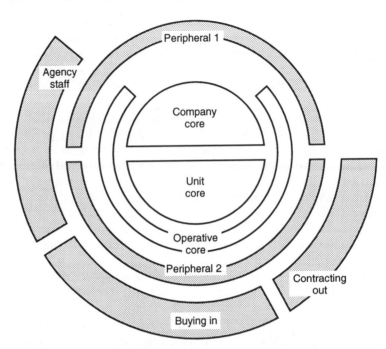

**Figure 4.2** Core and peripheral staff in hotel operations. (Source: Guerrier and Lockwood, 1989b, p. 11.)

The second group of core staff are unit based, with access to career opportunities within a single unit but less so within the whole corporate structure. The unit core consists of heads of department, supervisors and some operative staff. By contrast with the Atkinson model, this group lack functional flexibility and work in their specialist areas of food preparation, housekeeping, food and beverage service, etc. Flexibility comes in terms of their ability to 'trade down' to operative tasks as and when required. According to Guerrier and Lockwood, this group constitute the most stable within a hotel by contrast with more transitory senior managers and peripheral staff. Mobility within the company is limited and enhancement tends to be achieved by movement to alternative but local opportunities.

The third core group is that of skilled operatives, notably in the kitchen, in-front office, housekeeping, and food and beverage service. These personnel are performing key functions in the hotel in a relatively functionally inflexible way, but are in high demand within the labour market and have the opportunity for considerable mobility if they wish. Thus building a stable core within a hotel at this level can be difficult. Mobility can be accommodated within a larger company while loyalty can be sought through incentive and promotion schemes at unit or company level. The Swiss hotel industry makes interesting use of this core group in that the positions in many hotels remain stable with defined operative functions attached to each. However, links to hotel schools provide a guaranteed source of *stagiers*, mainly from abroad, who rotate through the positions on a six-monthly cycle, providing core stability but with different personnel filling the actual posts.

In terms of the periphery, Guerrier and Lockwood's work conforms rather more closely to that of Atkinson's 'ideal' model. Their first group consist of full-time, permanent employees with limited security and career opportunities. They have many characteristics in common with the operative core and undertake similar functions in the hotel. The main difference relates to labour turnover as this group is frequently drawn from groups in the labour market with little long-term interest or commitment to the company or, indeed, to the industry. The group may consist of skilled 'cosmopolitans' seeking to exercise their skills as a means of supporting an urge to travel – the Australian and New Zealand influence on hotels in London exemplifies this, students, transient foreign workers and others with no interest in the security available to core staff. This group are of particular importance to hotels in cities such as London but also in resort towns such as Brighton and Bournemouth in England or Cannes in France, as well as other regions of Europe with a strongly seasonal summer or winter tourist trade. They may have greater skills than those normally available within the local labour force but, because this group is essentially transient, problems may arise with regard to attaining and maintaining service to the expected quality.

The second peripheral group consists mainly of part-time and casual staff, living locally to the hotel. The part-timers may have a long-term commitment to the hotel but such loyalty is less frequent among casuals, who will, typically, be on the 'pool' of a number of hotels at the same time.

The final component that Guerrier and Lockwood identify on the periphery is that of distancing strategies. Such approaches may involve contracting out various functions within hotels, frequently laundry requirements, maintenance and cleaning contracts, as well as the provision of pastries to the kitchen. The range may extend considerably beyond these areas and include the employment of agency or subcontracted staff for lobby shops, the leisure centre and car park operations. Similar strategies not identified by the authors are also used in housekeeping and security. Guerrier and Lockwood do not identify core hotel activities as likely to be 'distanced' in this way. However, a recent study by Hallam (1994) points to a growing practice in London hotels of restaurant franchising, either to an individual or group operation. This practice is well established in North America, where some major hotel/restaurant chain alliances can be found. The advantages to the hotel of using external sources of labour are flexibility in response to cyclical demand and a reduction in the permanent payroll.

Guerrier and Lockwood's model provides a useful vehicle for the analysis of the labour environment in major hotels and has applicability beyond the United Kingdom. However, some caution is required in its application as aspects of the work are already dated, especially in view of major management restructuring by companies such as Accor and Forte, which aim to reduce the numbers of middle managers and vest greater autonomy and responsibility on department heads and supervisors. This process is likely to draw this latter group into the company core, in that these posts will increasingly be occupied by staff without the specific technical skills background normally associated with head of department status who can expect to move to positions of greater responsibility at unit and corporate levels. At the same time, greater autonomy is being allocated to individual hotel units, with a corresponding downsizing of the corporate structure. Novotel, part of the Accor group, for example, has introduced measures to flatten the management hierarchy both within units and at a regional level. The idea is that each hotel runs as an autonomous unit, fed with help and advice from a central office. Each general manager reports directly to the regional managing director, thus eliminating the role of regional managers. At the same time, the management line within each unit has been shortened to a considerable extent (*Caterer and Hotelkeeper*, 1993). In addition to these changes at management level, as has already been suggested, peripherality has also been reinforced by an extensive increase in the use of distancing strategies since the Guerrier and Lockwood study was carried out.

Guerrier and Lockwood's study was of the hotel industry only in one European country. Wood (1992a) implies the need for caution in that the level and extent of workplace flexibility is very varied between different companies and also between businesses of different size and ownership. There is little by way of empirical information by which to extrapolate this model into either a wider tourism context or to other European countries. Certainly, the hotel and restaurant industries of some European countries retain traditions and a culture which may militate against functional flexibility as well as against some of the distancing strategies discussed above. In other tourism subsectors, there is some evidence that Guerrier and Lockwood's model may have applicability, although with some modification. The downsizing of some major European airlines and the staffing models adopted by smaller, independent airline operations have both focused on the creation of a minimum core staff grouping supported by various peripheral groupings. The emphasis is on both numerical and functional flexibility, especially among ground and cabin staff. Distancing strategies are also commonplace through the use of handling agents at airports other than major hubs as well as in areas such as engineering, cleaning and catering services. The increasing importance of central reservations, for both airlines and hotels, also represents a form of distancing, although the staff may well be part of the company's payroll. They can be located entirely independently of the company's main operating base, allowing for a reduction in labour and office costs, as is the case with British Airways who have located this function near Newcastle, or Forte whose Travelodge central reservations is located near

Birmingham. With the reduced costs of international telecommunications and the growth of multinational computerized reservations systems (CRS), there is no reason why such functions should not locate even further afield, where costs are even further reduced, thus allowing tourism to model aspects of its work on the manufacturing sector. Attractions also commonly contract out functions such as catering. However, companies such as EuroDisney, where corporate identity and a homogeneous image are of critical importance, have not gone down this route to any significant degree, although other forms of flexibility are utilized.

In essence, the process of increasing all forms of flexibility within the tourism and hospitality workforce is one that can only reinforce and increase the weak nature of its labour market. Flexible working practices go entirely contrary to the major features of a strong labour market. The same can be said for the process of deskilling which is a feature of work in most industrial sectors and has certainly had some impact in tourism and hospitality.

As Wood (1992a) notes, the issue of deskilling and degradation of work is one of the most important themes in recent industrial sociological debate and represents a complex amalgam of theoretical discussion and empirical analysis of the nature of work within a diversity of industry sectors. Wood cites Braverman (1974) as the originator of much of the discussion about deskilling from a Marxist perspective. Braverman approaches the issue on the basis that, within a capitalist economy, the objective of the owners and managers of capital is to maximize control over the labour force as a means of ensuring increased profits. The argument which Braverman pursues is that scientific management – or Taylorism – has been key to this process of increased control because it divorces the conception from the execution of work, defining a clear distinction between the roles of management and labour, thus degrading and deskilling the role and contribution of the latter. Braverman's argument has much in common with that of Ritzer, although the latter does not place his analysis within the theoretical construction of Marxism. According to Ritzer, control of and in the workplace is one of the central aspects of the process which leads to deskilling in a variety of service areas. At the centre of this process is the substitution of human by non-human technology.

> The basic idea, historically, is to gradually and progressively gain control over people through the development and deployment of a wide variety of increasingly effective technologies. Once people are controlled, it is possible to begin reducing their actions to a series of machine-like actions. And once people are behaving like human machines, then it is possible to replace them with mechanical machines, most recently and notably, mechanical robots. With the replacement of humans by machines, we have reached the ultimate stage in control over people – people can cause us no more

uncertainty and unpredictability because they are no longer involved, at least directly, in the process. (Ritzer, 1993, pp. 100–1)

Ritzer applies this analysis to a number of case sources in the service sector, notably but not exclusively within fast food.

Much of the food prepared at McDonald's arrives at the restaurant preformed, precut, presliced, and preprepared, often by nonhuman technologies. This serves to drastically limit what employees need to do – there is usually no need for them to form the burgers, cut the potatoes, slice the rolls, or prepare the apple pie. All they need to do is, where necessary, cook, or often merely heat, the food and pass it on to the customer. The more that's done by nonhuman technology before the food arrives at the fast-food restaurant, the less the workers need to do and the less room they have to exercise their own judgements and skill. (Ritzer, 1993, p. 105)

Wood (1992a) discusses theoretical constraints within the deskilling debate but also presents considerable evidence which is fully consistent with Ritzer and supports the contention that, despite the low skills starting point, further reduction in the skills requirements in some sub-sectors of the tourism and hospitality industry is a widespread and ongoing process. Other examples can be found in the airline business where the everyday application of skills has been considerably reduced in the piloting of commercial aircraft. Automatic systems can effectively take over virtually all pilot functions. However, the presence of the skills in the flight deck crew remains essential in order to cater for the eventuality of an emergency or system failure. Robotic control of other means of transport such as trains and monorails (for example, the Docklands Light Railway in London) is also becoming commonplace and has thus substituted as well as reduced the skills requirements in certain areas. In many respects, substitution, deskilling and flexibility go hand in hand because the simplification of one task or a range of tasks may well place it within the skills reach of employees who also have other responsibilities and who previously would not have been able to undertake the tasks in question – pilots assuming engineering and navigational roles in aircraft is an example of the combination of deskilling and flexibility.

There is an inherent contradiction in this discussion of deskilling within the tourism and hospitality labour force. This will become manifestly evident in Chapter 5 where a central theme is the use of empowerment strategies to upgrade the responsibilities and demands of jobs at the front-line within the tourism and hospitality industry and thus to improve a company's competitive position in terms of service delivery. Empowerment is certainly incompatible with the control dimensions of McDonaldization, and what we are seeing is an increasing divide within the tourism and hospitality industry and the creation of distinct service cultures and strategies to cater for very different markets and market philosophies. Kanter (1983) highlights the contradictory directions which appear to be evolving with respect to control on the one hand and empowerment on the other. She highlights the 'old' type of organization where activities are segmented into discrete compartments and isolated from their context but, interestingly, on the basis of a non-systems approach – a definite contrast to McDonaldization. Segmentalism, according to Kanter, 'inhibits innovation at every step of the solution-search process' as follows:

> The motivation to solve problems declines in segmented systems. Segmentalism discourages people from seeing problems – or if they do see them, from revealing this discovery to anyone else ... If people's activities are confined to the letter of their job, if they are required to stay within the fences organizations erect between tasks, then it is much less likely that people will ever think beyond what they are given to do or dream about things they might do if only the right problem came along.     (Kanter, 1983, pp. 29–30)

Although starting from a different set of premises, Kanter with segmentalism, therefore, has much in common with Ritzer and McDonaldization in her analysis of the negative impacts of standardization and the application of formula responses within the working environment. Both segmentalism and McDonaldization are incompatible with empowerment – a conundrum or managerial paradox that we will address in greater detail in Chapter 5.

## CONCLUSION – A RETURN TO THE MACRO ENVIRONMENT

In concluding this chapter about tourism and hospitality labour markets, it is useful to return to the macro environment within which they operate. Riley, as we have seen, links many of the key issues which face sectors of the industry – some of which we will return to in Chapter 7 – to the weak nature of the internal labour market that operates within these sectors. The attributes of the weak labour market provide both benefits and difficulties, whether you view the industry from an employer or employee perspective. Pizam (1982) addresses these attributes in the context of unskilled and semi-skilled labour in the tourism industry from two wider environmental perspectives, which he designates societal characteristics and industry characteristics. Figure 4.3 summarizes these influences in relation to some of the main issues facing the industry at the level to which Pizam is referring.

The characteristics of society which Pizam identifies as important determinants provide an important agenda of labour market influencers in a general sense, not necessarily specific to tourism and hospitality. They certainly reflect the optimism of the early 1980s in some respects but have only qualified validity over a decade later. What consideration of Pizam's analysis does emphasize is the changing nature of factors which influence the labour market within tourism and hospitality. Thus any consideration of this environment cannot afford to be static but must respond to a dynamic and ever-changing combination of both macro and micro environmental factors.

Certainly the growing importance of services within all Western European economies remains an important attribute and the restructuring of the new Europe, both in the west and the east, is likely to see increasing dependence both on high technology such as information and financial services and on labour intensive areas of the sector, notably tourism and hospitality. Traditional industries in the manufacturing, agricultural and extractive sectors have declined in Europe and further concentration of these into relatively small geographical areas – or, indeed, to other parts of the world – will further reduce their significance.

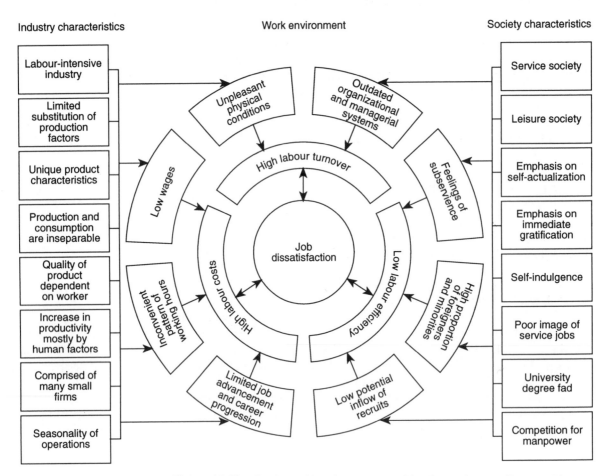

**Figure 4.3** Tourism's work environment and its determinants. (Source: Pizam, 1982.)

Pizam identifies greater leisure time as his second social impactor. In many respects, his analysis is accurate although projections that this process would continue and result in a general reduction in working time have not really been fulfilled. In the United Kingdom, for example, the last fifteen years have actually seen an increase in average time worked by those in employment; however, the numbers out of work have also increased dramatically, suggesting a reallocation of work time rather than its actual reduction among those with the resources to enjoy greater leisure time. What remains true is that, whatever the availability of theoretical leisure time, people are increasingly investing a higher proportion of such time on activities within tourism and hospitality. Demographic factors in Europe, notably an increasingly healthy and active older population, will further reinforce this trend.

Pizam identifies greater emphasis on self-actualization as an important social trend and implies the need of the tourism and hospitality industries to cater for such employee needs. The sustainable human resource paradigm addressed in Chapter 1 implies support for an employment model which offers greater scope and responsibility to employees. In the next chapter, we address the concept of empowerment among front-line staff, and this also is consistent with offering a motivational environment which is in tune with the pinnacle of Maslow's hierarchy. However, there are counter-trends in tourism and hospitality and within the service sector in general, notably the impact of labour-saving technology, standardized service delivery and deskilling (a theme that we have already touched upon in this chapter), encapsulated in the work environment portrayed so effectively by George Ritzer in his book, *The McDonaldization of Society* (1993). In his thesis, Ritzer analyses the impact of the processes of efficiency, calculability, predictability and control on the working environment within a wide range of service employments and his conclusions do not paint an optimistic scenario for the achievement of self-actualization within much tourism and hospitality work.

Pizam defines the demand for immediate gratification as an emphasis on immediate material benefit which impacts to the detriment of a working environment such as that in the tourism and hospitality industry. In particular, the dead-end nature of many semi-skilled and unskilled positions in the industry, together with a lack of evident pathways for progression in terms of monetary reward and responsibility, combine to alienate many young people from work in the sector. Again, recognition of the notion of sustainability in the human resource domain may lead employers to create working environments where progression paths are more clearly defined and the prospect of enhanced rewards enunciated. However, an understanding of Riley's concept of the weak internal labour market suggests that the very characteristics which create a low-paid, low-skills environment also provide considerable opportunity for rapid, meritocratic promotion within the industry.

Self-indulgence as a social phenomenon has many links to the demand for immediate gratification. Pizam uses the social trend by way of contrast with the conditions faced by the lowest skilled and poorest paid members of the tourism and hospitality workforce. In many respects, this is not a new social attribute. In Chapter 3, we have addressed in some detail the notion of social distance between tourists and those who serve them and, on the whole, it is a distance that has decreased within developed economies as tourism has moved to become more democratic and mass participatory in character. Many tourism and hospitality employees, even among the lower skilled and poorer paid, have the expectation of a degree of role reversal as they are also able to indulge in various forms of vacation and leisure activities. Such expectations do not exist among employees in the developing world or in much of Eastern Europe, where the gap between international visitors and those that provide for them has, if anything, greatly increased following the economic instability born of recent political changes.

The image problem of some service jobs, especially those in the low skills category, represents a problem that hospitality and tourism share with like sectors. Pizam approaches this issue at a macro level from the point of view of equating servitude and service, thus linking work in the service sector to a perceived status of inferiority, especially in parts of the developing world with a colonial legacy. The new and fast-evolving tourism and hospitality environment in parts of Eastern Europe also faces this problem. Again, in the context of the preceding discussion about self-indulgence, moves towards the democratization of many societies and of the customer–worker relationship can contribute to reducing this image problem.

Pizam also notes that growing participation rates in higher education, or what he describes as the 'university degree fad', creates an educated workforce who are reluctant to seek employment in the unskilled and semi-skilled employment areas of tourism and hospitality. Pizam could have argued further that, taking their lead from practice in North America where upwards of 60% of all graduates have worked for McDonald's at some point in their high-school or college careers, in many European countries these graduates are basing their reluctance on exposure to the industry through part-time and seasonal work. Such work may be in the fast-food sector, but also in bars, restaurants, hotels, as timeshare salespersons or tour operator representatives in Mediterranean or Alpine resort locations. Furthermore, exposure to work at the semi-skilled or unskilled level influences attitudes to careers in management or specialist areas within the industry.

Pizam's final environmental influence returns us to our earlier discussion of macro labour market determinants because he notes that, in many countries, the tourism and hospitality industry is facing an increasingly competitive market environment for quality labour. As he rightly notes, 'those industries and firms that have the ability to reward employees with high wages and pleasant working environments constantly win this competition and attract the best employees' (Pizam, 1982, p. 7). As we have argued at some length earlier, the tourism and hospitality industry has such diverse subsectors that parts of it will be net beneficiaries of such competition but, by and large, the mass of semi-skilled and unskilled positions on offer are not attractive by Pizam's criteria.

The industry-specific side of Pizam's model deals with a range of issues which form themes in subsequent chapters of this book. Labour intensity, limitations on substitution, the nature of the tourism and hospitality product, the inseparability of production and consumption, and, implicitly, the issue of professionalism are all addressed in Chapter 5 and its focus on the service quality–human resource management link. The issue of working conditions is at the centre of Chapter 6 while training concerns are central to Chapter 8.

---

## REVIEW AND DISCUSSION QUESTIONS

1. In relation to a tourism destination with which you are familiar, identify some of the major factors which influence the structure and characteristics of the local labour market.
2. To what extent are Riley's strong and weak internal labour market features applicable to different subsectors of the tourism and hospitality industry?
3. Does the extent to which the tourism and hospitality industry exhibits weak internal labour market characteristics vary between different countries of Europe?
4. How useful and realistic is it to consider a global labour market for the tourism and hospitality industry?
5. Apply Guerrier and Lockwood's core and periphery model to a subsector of tourism and hospitality industry other than hotels. How useful is it in understanding the structure of human resources in that sector?
6. Identify examples of technology substitution, deskilling and flexibility in the tourism and hospitality workplace. What do they contribute to an understanding of Riley's labour market model?
7. Pizam identified the societal and industry characteristics which impacted upon the tourism and hospitality labour environment as long ago as 1982. How relevent are they to today's tourism and hospitality industry in Europe?

# 5 Tourism and hospitality: the service imperative

## SERVICE QUALITY AND THE TOURISM AND HOSPITALITY ENVIRONMENT

In this chapter, we shall consider the importance of service quality as a business strategy within the tourism and hospitality industry in Europe and demonstrate the central role that human resource management plays in attaining this quality. Recognition of this link has been implicit in much of the discussion to this point, commencing with the analysis of the human resource dimension within sustainability. As Watson (1988) notes, the concept of quality in the tourism and hospitality industry has changed dramatically over the past quarter of a century.

> Not long ago, quality was nearly synonymous with luxury and personalised service, but this is no longer the case. We now know that quality can exist at all levels of price and service.
>
> (Watson, 1988, p. 20)

This is an important change which has clear links to our earlier analysis of the historical context of work within the tourism and hospitality industry. The era of mass participation in travel and tourism and the consumption of hospitality products and the democratization at the centre of change within the guest–server relationship have created a level of expectation concerning the overall experience provided by the industry that transcends the luxury–budget divide. Service quality, it is now recognized, is not some absolute standard, imutable and fixed for all time and part of the defining differentiation between what customers can expect from, on the one hand, the Savoy in London and, on the other, the Prom View in Blackpool. Rather, it is a concept which rides piggyback upon the expectations that the customer brings to the particular business, whether it is five star or unclassified. Thus, the customer has clear expectations of service and its quality hallmarks, whether he or she is travelling first class or economy, eating in the Cafe Royal or a fish and chip shop, or attending a gala performance at Covent Garden or the pier head bingo evening. While this notion of relative quality in service has been increasingly recognized by successful companies in tourism and hospitality, it is by no means universally applied. There are award-winning airlines from both Europe and the Far East where the standard of service for economy passengers is poor. The accolades, however, come from their first and business-class products. By contrast, British Airways, in their series of customer-focused initiatives since the late 1980s, have laid great stress on meeting the needs of all their customers and creating appropriate levels of service quality wherever on the aircraft their passengers are located (Goodstein and Burke, 1991; Robson, 1993).

Service quality is frequently presented as primarily a marketing-orientated concept, designed to assist companies to win and keep customers. Lewis and Chambers (1989) adopt this approach in their discussion of the concept of relationship marketing, by which they mean the ability of companies to build up genuine loyalty in their customer base which protects the level of repeat business that is so important to all tourism and hospitality operations. The quality of service, and especially the personalized, flexible and individualized response which frequently makes all the difference to the customer and determines whether he or she will return, are essential marketing tools within this model. Lewis and Chambers (1989) discuss relationship marketing in the following terms:

> Relationship marketing is defined as marketing to protect the customer base. It sees the customer as an asset. Its function is to attract, maintain, and enhance customer relationships.     (p. 63)

Lewis and Chambers go on to quote Theodore Levitt (1981) of the Harvard Business School, who describes the essential nature of the relationship to be found in the service encounter in somewhat more prosaic terms.

> The relationship between a seller and a buyer seldom ends when the sale is made. The sale merely consummates the courtship. Then the marriage begins. How good the marriage is depends on how well the marriage is managed by the seller. That determines whether there will be continued or expanded business or troubles and divorce, and whether costs or profits increase.
>
> . . . It is not just that once you get a customer you want to keep him. It is more a matter of what the buyer wants. He wants a vendor who will keep his promises, who'll keep supplying and stand behind what he promised. The age of the blind date or the one-night stand is gone. Marriage is both more convenient and more necessary . . . In these conditions success in marketing, like success in marriage, is transformed into the inescapability of a relationship.     (Levitt, in Lewis and Chambers, 1989, pp. 65–6)

Christopher, Payne and Ballantyne (1991) see relationship marketing as a process which extends beyond caring for the customer base.

> Relationship marketing implies a consideration of not just better relationships with customer markets but also the development and enhancement of relationships with supplier, employee, referral, 'influencer' and internal markets.
>
> (Christopher, Payne and Ballantyne, 1991, p. 30)

This concept has implications for the manner in which a tourism and hospitality company relates to its overall business environment because maintaining stability and good relations with all critical groups in that environment (for a hotel, these may include suppliers of food and other products, travel agents who influence customer choice, the existing and potential labour market as well as those who influence it such as employment agencies, and the staff of the hotel as an internal market) becomes a matter for active concern and not just passive acquiescence. Of course, if all parties are themselves tuned into relationship marketing, the matrix of relationships becomes highly mutually supportive and enhances the business performance of all concerned.

## CHARACTERISTICS OF SERVICE

Cooper *et al.* (1993), in considering the place of service within tourism, locate it squarely within marketing. Service enters their discussion through a consideration of the characteristics of tourism which set the industry and its products apart from other industries and products. They identify three characteristics which separate tourism as a service from manufactured goods and present these distinctions in what is called a 'goods and services continuum' (Cooper *et al.*, 1993, p. 231), as shown in Figure 5.1.

This continuum applied within the tourism context in turn owes much to the work of Albrecht and Zemke (1985), although focusing on just three of the concepts which the American authors employ. Mahesh (1988, p. 10) takes Albrecht and Zemke's classification of the differences and develops them further. He highlights the difference between between services and products as follows. The first seven points are derived from Albrecht and Zemke, the final two being his own additions.

- Sale, production and consumption of a service take place almost simultaneously, while there is usually a long lead time between production and sale of a product, in other words the concept of inseparability as used in the continuum. Also known as heterogeneity, inseparability means that it is difficult to distinguish between the

**Figure 5.1** Goods and services continuum. (Source: Cooper *et al.*, 1993, p. 231.)

production of the tourism service and its consumption, especially when the customer is personally part of that production process. This has important implications for the management of quality in the tourism and hospitality industries, in that the level of checks and inspection characteristic of the manufacturing sector cannot be applied.

- A service cannot be centrally provided, inspected, stockpiled or warehoused – it is usually delivered where the customer is by people who are beyond the immediate influence of the management. This feature includes the notion of perishability, by which a hotel room, an empty car on a theme park ride or an aircraft seat unsold at time of departure represents a loss which cannot be recouped. Systems are required to ensure optimum use of the facilities and these usually focus on pricing and marketing strategies. However, there is also a strong human resource dimension to the process; for example, in some hotels front-office staff may take responsibility for agreeing tariffs with late check-in guests and so must have the skills and authority to do so.

- A service cannot be demonstrated, nor can a sample be sent for customer approval in advance of purchase. This notion of intangibility also has strong marketing implications and attempts are made to overcome the problems that it causes at a marketing level through literature, video and computer technology, as well as some element of sampling – for example, a free weekend in a timeshare complex. However, such substitution does not overcome the inherent problems caused by the individual nature of the tourism and hotel experience and its dependence on the human element for its delivery.

- Following on from the above, a customer receiving the tourism or hospitality service generally owns nothing tangible once the service has been delivered – its value is frequently internal to the customer.

- The tourism or hospitality experience is frequently one that cannot be shared, passed around or given away to someone else once it has been delivered. The experience is, in some respects, unique, even among a group who are ostensibly sharing the same itinerary or facilities. This is a result of their differing expectations, previous experience, motivation in taking part in the experience and a variety of other concerns which may be affecting them at that time. This phenomenological argument need not be taken to extremes and from a marketing point of view it would be difficult to do so, but from the human resource management perspective, recognizing and responding to this individuality among customers is a very important skill. 'Have a nice day' may be an apt and sincerely meant farewell, appropriate to a group embarking on a day's sightseeing, but would cause offence to customers setting off for a funeral!

- Delivery of a tourism or hospitality service usually requires some degree of human contact – the receiver and the deliverer frequently come together in a relatively personal way. Although technological substitution for some aspects of service delivery has become important in some sectors of the industry (for example, automatic check-in and check-out in hotels and ticket-vending machines in airports), there is a definite limit to how far this process can go and consumer demand, if anything, is for increased personal service rather than its reduction.

- Quality control over a tourism and hospitality service requires the monitoring of processes and the attitudes of all staff. This, inevitably, presents certain problems in the industry, largely because of the heterogeneous nature of the delivery of these services.
- Unlike a bad product, bad service cannot be replaced – at best, it is possible to be sensitive to customer dissatisfaction and recover the situation with such good service that the customer may both forgive and forget the bad service received earlier.
- It is both difficult and undesirable to attempt to standardize service – the more spontaneous and custom-built a service, the greater its value in the customer's eyes. This is probably the most contentious dimension within the classification in that there are many examples from the tourism and hospitality industry where companies have attempted to standardize service delivery, for example in fast food, budget hotels and theme parks. This is an issue discussed at some length by Ritzer (1993) and will be developed in more detail later in this chapter.

## HUMAN RESOURCE IMPLICATIONS OF A SERVICE QUALITY FOCUS

Mahesh derives five major implications from these differences which impact upon the management of businesses in the tourism and hospitality industries, all of which are directly related to human resource concerns. In this chapter, we will use Mahesh's five implications in order to provide a structure to the discussion of the role of human resources in achieving quality service within the tourism and hospitality industries. The five are summarized by Mahesh as follows.

First, the customer's perception of service quality is more directly linked to the morale, motivation, knowledge, skills, and authority of front-line staff who are in direct contact with customers, than in the case of a product selling organization. Secondly, rather than being responsible for their staff, management should become responsive to staff. This is easier said than done for most line managers tend to view their jobs as control centred rather than freedom centred. The supervisors and managers of front-line staff should have the managerial skills to motivate their staff to be effective. Thirdly, traditional tools of quantification of output and work measurement have to be replaced by the subjective tool of customer satisfaction. Fourthly, as a service cannot be stockpiled and customers are in direct touch with staff, the power of the union to pressurize management increases manifold. Fifthly, bureaucratic organization structures and mega-organizations that suffer from what Toffler (1985) calls 'gigantiasis' a disease whose major symptoms are the hardening of decisional arteries and their ultimate breakdown, are ill-suited to excellence in service. The structure has to be adaptive, decentralized, and downsized to respond speedily to changing customer needs.                               (Mahesh, 1988 pp. 10–11)

Let us examine Mahesh's analysis in a little more detail, taking the five implications that he identifies point by point.

### Front-line staff

Mahesh first of all focuses on the critical role of front-line staff in the service encounter and their 'packaging' in terms of such diverse attributes as morale, motivation, knowledge, skills and authority. This analysis is fairly widely accepted within many service organizations but, perhaps, owes its most effective conceptualization to Jan Carlzon, past president of Scandinavian Airline Systems (SAS). Carlzon introduced the concept of the 'moment of truth' into the service vocabulary (Carlzon, 1987). Carlzon described a 'moment of truth' as every point of contact between the customer and front-line staff of the company, thus applying it to every contact, however seemingly trivial, that a customer has with a staff member of the company in question. In SAS terms, Carlzon estimated that perhaps 50 000 'moments of truth' occurred each operating day and equivalent figures can be calculated for all tourism and hospitality organizations. 'Moments of truth', although frequently small in scale (hotel check-in, drinks service in an aircraft, the purchase of duty frees in an airport, assistance with a theme park ride), are make-or-break occasions, when the company has the opportunity to disappoint the customer by failing to meet his or her expectations, to get it right by matching those expectations, or to excel by exceeding those expectations. From an organizational and management perspective, while it is heartening to exceed expectations, the key objective must be to consistently meet customer expectations and to minimize occasions when customers are disappointed.

The tourism and hospitality industry presents particular challenges in managing 'moments of truth' because of the fragmentation of the experience for many customers. Within a hotel, for example, guests come into contact with a wide range of staff attached to different organizational units within the establishment (front office, housekeeping, restaurant, business centre, etc.) even during a relatively brief stay. Plotting the 'moments of truth' for a typical guest stay in a hotel can be highly illuminating in this respect.

Even more complex is the range of 'moments of truth' encountered by the customer of a typical package holiday company. From the purchaser's perspective, he or she is buying from one company and yet the reality is that a wide range of intermediaries are likely to contribute to the total experience. These may include businesses over which the tour operator has some level of control and can monitor service standards but will also include exposure to organizations or individuals where no such control exists, although the 'moments of truth' will be judged by the customer with the umbrella company in mind. These intermediaries may include:

- the retail travel agent;
- insurance companies;
- ground transport to the airport;
- airport handling agents;
- airport services (shops, food and beverage outlets);
- the airline;
- immigration and customs services;
- local ground transportation;
- the hotel or apartment;
- tour services at the destination;
- companies and individuals selling a diversity of goods and services (retail, food and beverage, entertainment, financial establishments, timeshare vendors); and
- service providers on return (e.g. photo processing).

Many of these companies and organizations are, of course, beyond the control of the tour operator and most customers would not directly attribute problems with them to the company through which they booked. However, good or bad experiences or 'moments of truth' with the local police, beach vendors and taxi companies will colour the visitor's perceptions of the total experience in a way that does not really apply with respect to the purchase of other goods and services. Tour operators, of course, are legally responsible under consumer protection legislation in many European countries for the satisfactory delivery of many of the components within the package tour experience, but such liability cannot include the full range of bodies listed above. One response from the tourism and hospitality industry is to reduce the risk of inconsistent or unmanaged 'moments of truth' within the holiday experience by maintaining as close regulation and control over as many of the intermediaries as is possible. This may be achieved by vertical integration of as many of the providers within the tourism system as possible. Using Leiper's (1990) model which we discussed in Chapter 2 (Figure 2.1), such integration includes components within the travel generating region, the transit route region and the tourist destination region.

Such integration may result in tour operators acquiring their own retail travel agents and airline as well as hotels and ground tour operators at the destination. There are other benefits besides greater control and consistency in the delivery of service but the potential to manage and control as many 'moments of truth' within the guest experience as possible is one of the main attractions of vertical integration. This process may involve outright ownership of the various components or, alternatively, the establishment of a network of partners, all of which operate to agreed standards and systems and may even adopt the sponsoring company's branding.

Similar strategies which have a similar effect include isolating the guest from many of the uncontrolled variables, or 'moments of truth', at the holiday destination. The Club Méditerranée, Centerparcs, Butlins-type holiday camp and other all-inclusive resort concepts all fit into this model. The guest will typically only come into contact with employees selected and trained by the sponsoring company in relation to all the activities that the guest may wish to undertake, and so the guest will be insulated from the uncertainty of contact with the diverse range of local providers which typically, contributes to the makeup of the vacation experience.

This level of control and standardization of service is not feasible with respect to many tourism destinations, nor, indeed, is it desirable for many visitors themselves. The local encounter is a central attraction within the vacation experience, whether it is in an Irish bar in Connemara, a nightclub in Paris or as part of a farm holiday in Hungary. In a very real sense, then, the range of 'moments of truth' which the tourist will encounter can involve the total population of the tourist destination locality and not just those specifically employed to meet guest needs. The welcome and assistance that the visitor receives from the community as a whole becomes an important factor in ensuring an extended or return visit to the locality or in helping to decide that 'once is enough'. In many communities, there is a certain ambivalence to visitors, who can create congestion on roads and in facilities, behave in ways that are not compatible with local practice or exhibit levels of conspicuous affluence unattainable within the host location. A major challenge for the tourism industry in both the public and private sector is to support the education of the local community about tourism and tourists, so as to ensure a welcome or at least to avoid outright hostility. At the same time, tour operators have the responsibility to ensure that their visitors are sensitive to local customs and culture and behave accordingly. Tourism awareness programmes at community and national levels have become quite widespread in locations as far apart as Hong Kong and Hawaii as well as in some European destinations. Likewise, responsible tour operators do provide information and briefings for visitors on the locations they are visiting as well as behaviour that is and is not acceptable. These strategies will all contribute to ensuring that the uncontrolled variables within the 'moments of truth' cycle are positive in their outcomes and do not negatively affect the overall perception that the visitor derives from his or her visit.

Creating a true service culture at company or national level implies that the term 'front-line' must be used in its widest possible sense. For a community or nation to continue to attract visitors, especially those returning after the initial visit, ensuring positive 'moments of truth' at each commercial service and less formal encounter becomes imperative. The whole population are part of the relationship marketing effort. In societies where traditions in work as well as in a wider social context have made people suspicious of the stranger and indifferent or hostile in their attitude to service, creating this environment is a major challenge. The countries of Eastern Europe face this challenge as probably their main human resource issue. As Airey (1994) points out, 'In Central and Eastern Europe it is only recently that the satisfaction of the customer has become a key issue' (p. 8).

In practical terms, companies developing tourism enterprises in Eastern Europe have responded to the problem of a lack of a service culture by circumventing the issue. The recently opened Sofitel in Bucharest, Romania, employed no front-line staff with hotel experience, preferring to rely on enthusiastic but untrained young people to meet their needs. Likewise in Russia, within the same hotel group, Chaieb (1994) reports that 'the hotel [Novotel] prefers to train via its own means, by hiring unprepared candidates who, at least, have no bad habits' (p. 4).

Vikhanski and Puffer (1993) report the same approach with respect to McDonald's in Moscow, where front-line staff were selected on the basis of having no prior work experience:

> The idea was that it would be easier to instil McDonald's work habits and standards in people who knew no other way to work than to disabuse people of unacceptable work habits they had acquired in previous jobs. (p. 104)

Other reported strategies include resort hotels in the Crimea recruiting front-line staff from former care employees, nurses, social workers and the like because these are deemed to be the only group to whom the notion of customer care has any realistic meaning.

### Responsive management

We have considered the importance of every 'moment of truth' to the total guest experience and as a central feature within the achievement of quality service. The management of the 'moments of truth' cycle is a critical process and, according to Albrecht and Zemke (1985), requires a fundamental mind shift from traditional control-based supervision and management: 'When the moments of truth go unmanaged, the quality of service regresses to mediocrity' (p. 31).

The traditional approach to managing relationships within a company can be seen to operate on a hierarchical basis, as in Figure 5.2. What is important in this model is that the decision-making process flows from the base of the pyramid to its apex, the senior management level. The customer contact zone is figuratively and, frequently, literally adrift at the bottom. A caricature of this model at work, which has more than a touch of realtity in it, is the situation where staff in a busy hotel restaurant swarm to serve the general manager when he arrives for lunch and, in doing so, neglect the needs of paying guests. Staff at each level in this model are primarily concerned to satisfy their

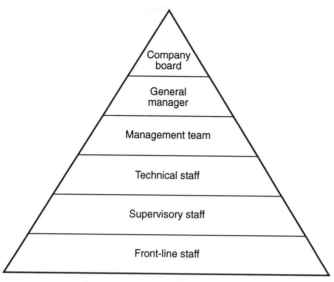

**Figure 5.2** Traditional management hierarchy.

immediate superiors within the hierarchy, even if this means neglecting the real customers of the business. Figure 5.3, by contrast, shows what Ken Blanchard calls the inverted service triangle, a philosophical inversion of traditional management hierarchies (Mahesh, 1994).

This simple reversal of the triangle has major ramifications for the operation of service within tourism and hospitality businesses. The energy flow remains upwards but is the complete reverse of that which

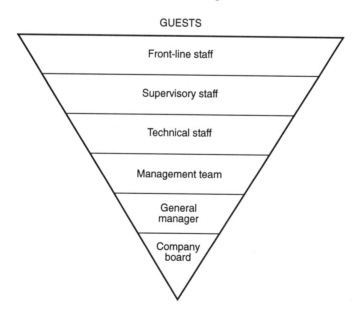

**Figure 5.3** The inverted service triangle.

operates within the traditional model. In this approach, the customer contact zone becomes the most important component within the management of the organization. Everything else is subservient to that aspect of the service process. Jan Carlzon saw the relationship between front-line staff, those responsible for handling the many thousands of 'moments of truth' on a daily basis, and the technical, supervisory and management functions as one of service, with the back-of-house team existing primarily to facilitate the critical work of those at the front line. Carlzon put it like this: 'If you're not serving the guest, your job is to serve those who are.' Disney's application of this principle is to consider all employees as cast members, with those at the front-line sharp edge as 'on stage' and those working behind the scenes as 'off stage'.

The inverted triangle demands an approach to management that is not control based but is designed to facilitate the work of operational staff. Management are there to assist their front-line colleagues provide a better service to guests, who Carlzon sees as a company's prime assets. By providing this superior service, of course, a tourism or hospitality company is enhancing its competitive position and increasing the likelihood that repeat business will be generated.

Cook Johnson (1991) clearly demonstrates the link between perceived superior service within the hotel sector in North America and management style. In her study, establishments were rated by guests and employees on the basis of their service and three groups were formed on the basis of this rating analysis.

- Service leaders – the group of hotels where, on average, 92% of employees and customers rated these organizations as consistently very good in their service – the top quartile.
- Service average – the group of hotels where 79% of employees and customers rated service as consistently very good – the middle two quartiles.
- Service problems – the group of hotels where only 62% of employees and customers rated service as consistently good – the bottom quartile.

Cook Johnson then used this classification to look at the ways in which superior service is delivered by front-line staff and management. She notes that the 'service leader' group of companies have attributes which clearly point to the importance of the relationship between those delivering the service and those providing support to enable them to do so. Service leader companies:

- are highly focused and consistent in everything they do and say in relation to employees;
- have managers who communicate with employees;
- facilitate rather than regulate their employees' response to customers;
- solicit employee feedback about how they can do things better;

- stress the importance of teamwork at each level of the organization; and
- plan carefully the organization's recruitment and training needs.

Cook Johnson concludes her analysis by summarizing the characteristics of service leaders in the following terms. Service leader companies are those which are recognized for:

- their unfailing commitment to service principles;
- their investment in people to ensure staffing competence;
- a management philosophy which stresses communication, a proactive orientation and employee feedback; and
- a dedication to teamwork. (Cook Johnson, 1991)

The link between service quality and the management environment within companies is one that is also considered by Mansfield (1990). She identifies four key principles in the development of customer care within tourism companies (pp. A-68–A-69):

1. Customer care starts at the top, meaning that commitment to the principle of customer care must emanate from senior management levels within an organization. Successful management 'is not only about the right management style but also an attitude, ethos or culture of the organization which overrides the management techniques used, such that in the absence of other instructions these values will dictate how an employee will behave.'
2. 'Customer care involves everyone within the organization.' It is not just about front-line staff. In keeping with Carlzon's argument, Mansfield contends that the contrary view 'only serves to reinforce the electricians' or administrators' opinion that the standard of service they give in support of front-line staff is not important. How can cleaners do the right job unless they fully appreciate the customers' needs and the importance of their role? High standards of customer care cannot be achieved by ignoring seasonal, part-time or voluntary staff who represent the face of the business to many customers.'
3. 'Care for your staff and they will care for your customers.' Too often organizations look first to the customer, whereas the emphasis should be placed on the staff. 'Improving the experience of the staff encourages a better service and a better experience for customers. More customers are obtained thereby improving the climate in which management and staff work. Investment and greater professionalism follow success and the cycle of achievement is reinforced.'
4. 'It's a continuous process', meaning that 'customer care is not a quick fix project but a long-term plan.'

Mansfield's analysis places considerable emphasis on what Lewis and Chambers (1989) call the internal marketing process. Internal marketing can be defined as:

> ... applying the philosophies and practices of marketing to people who serve the external customers so that (1) the best people can be employed and retained and (2) they will do the best possible work.          (Berry, 1980, in Lewis and Chambers, 1989, pp. 51–2)

A compelling conclusion from what both Cook Johnson and Mansfield argue is that service quality is much more likely to be delivered within a supervising and managing culture that conforms with the sustainable model introduced in Chapter 1 than within the traditional tourism and hospitality personnel paradigm. Foster (1991) highlights this distinction clearly in relation to British Airways. She discusses the change within BA from a traditional management environment to one where managers recognize the power and importance of internal marketing and its benefits to customer service standards.

> In the early 1980s, before the changes began, BA was a very hierarchical organization. Decisions could only be made at the top, and were often the result of protracted committee meetings. Managers and employees at more junior levels felt powerless to achieve change. Employees believed that they were cogs in the big BA machine and often felt their concerns were unheard or unanswered.
>
> BA management has since become much more participative, caring and involved. We believe that a company's management style must be consistent with the way in which it expects its staff to treat its customers: if we want our crew to be always attentive and ready to help with the passengers, then they have the right to expect that their managers will always be attentive and ready to help when they require assistance.          (Foster, 1991, p. 223)

The concept of internal marketing and the application of a supportive management culture which enables the delivery of quality service leads to the notion of **empowerment** of front-line staff, which is a concept that has gained considerable currency within service-focused companies in recent years. It is also a concept which, as Figure 5.4 demonstrates, is used to market what companies see as the competitive advantage of service excellence.

Empowerment means enabling and encouraging front-line staff to make decisions that will help to solve customers' problems or meet their needs without reference to an interminable management hierachy. The ability to deal professionally and competently with immediate queries, problems and complaints is an attribute that is rated very highly among customers of tourism and hospitality organizations and makes a major contribution to effective relationship marketing. One common recognition of this is the no-quibble goods return policy that is adopted by many retailers. Customers purchase with greater confidence but front-line staff are also in a position where they can

"*It was more than considerate of the Marriott night porter to trace my lost wallet – it meant he had to re-trace my entire journey through Vienna.* All I could remember was that I'd been travelling on a Southern District streetcar. Miraculously, from this tiny piece of information, the night porter from the Marriott hotel managed to trace the route I'd travelled, the particular streetcar I was on, and my wallet. I was astounded that he went out of his way so much to help me. But as I now know, everyone at Marriott works this way. Personally assuming responsibility for the needs of every guest. It's called Empowerment. And thankfully, they never seem to find anything too much trouble."

Vienna, January 27th 1993.

ALWAYS IN THE RIGHT PLACE AT THE RIGHT TIME. **Marriott** HOTELS · RESORTS · SUITES

**Figure 5.4** Marriott Vienna advertisement: empowerment. (Courtesy of Marriott Hotels and Resorts, London.)

contribute to overcoming customer problems and complaints by immediate refund or replacement. This is not total empowerment but rather a recognition, by management, that the customer care zone requires clear operating guidelines to which staff can work.

Similar absolute policies are more difficult to apply when the purchase is less tangible than that from a shop, for example a restaurant meal, theme park ride or transportation arrangement. It is not possible to replace an unsatisfactory hotel experience, although the establishment can attempt to recover its position through a full or partial refund or the offer of a future complimentary stay. Thus, front-line staff need to be able to assess and evaluate each particular situation with confidence and authority and have to be empowered to provide a solution in so far as one is available. Guidelines are clearly important so as to enable front-line staff to respond in a consistent manner, and in some cases relatively standard provision may be acceptable – for example, a complimentary meal for delayed airline passengers and compensation, within specified scales, for those off-loaded due to over-booking. However, generally speaking, effective empowerment is 'ring-fenced' in so far as financial decisions are concerned so that staff have the authority to act up to a specified level without reference to supervisory or management authority. The American Ritz Carlton company permit all employees to change anything, on behalf of guests, up to a value of $2000. Rather greater freedom may be available if no direct financial consequences are involved. Novotel, part of the French Accor group, use the word subsidiarity to describe their approach to empowerment. Serge Ravailhe, formerly managing director of Novotel UK, when interviewed in 1993 described the concept in the following terms:

> Subsidiarity is another way of saying that employees should be encouraged to take responsibility for decisions. Whatever decisions employees make, at least they have made them. If they can't make a decision on a problem then they pass it to the next person above them and they try to make it. Its like carrying the ball instead of passing it all the time. (Anon., 1993)

Ravailhe accepted that, from time to time, subsidiarity would lead to employees making the wrong decision, but argued that it was important that they had made the decision for themselves and learned from mistakes. Of course, such a system requires the total absence of a punitive environment when mistakes are made or employees will avoid making decisions of any consequence.

Customers undoubtedly greatly value the effects of empowerment. Albrecht and Zemke (1985) relate the case of a British Airways survey into what customers considered to be important in their flying experiences and this supports the approach which Novotel have adopted. Four factors stood out as of paramount importance:

1. Care and concern;
2. Spontaneity;
3. Problem-solving;
4. Recovery.

Albrecht and Zemke quote the response of Donald Porter of BA to these findings.

> 'Care and concern are fairly clear, I think,' says Porter. 'We weren't surprised to find this a key factor, although I think we'd have to confess that we couldn't claim a very high level of performance on it.
>
> 'Spontaneity made us stop and scratch our heads a bit. Customers were saying "We want to know that your frontline people are authorised to think." When a problem comes up that doesn't fit in the procedure book, can the service person use some discretion – find a way to jockey the system on the customer's behalf? Or does he or she simply shrug shoulders and brush the customer off?
>
> 'Problem-solving was pretty clear, we felt. Customers thought our people should be skilled at working out the intricacies of problematical travel schedules, handling complicated logistics, and in general getting them on their way.
>
> 'The fourth factor sort of threw us. It had never really occurred to us in any concrete way. "Recovery" was the term we coined to describe a very frequently repeated concern: if something goes wrong, as it often does, will anybody make a special effort to set it right? Will someone go out of his or her way to make amends to

the customer? Does anyone make an effort to offset the negative effects of a screwup? Does anyone even know how to deliver a simple apology?

'We were struck by a rather chilling thought: if two of these four primary evaluation factors were things we had never consciously considered, what were the chances that our people in the service areas were paying attention to them? For the first time, we were really beginning to understand and come to terms with the real motivational factors that are embedded in our customer's nervous system.' (Albrecht and Zemke, 1985, p. 34)

Empowerment, as the Cook Johnson study clearly suggests, also implies trust and confidence by management in the front-line work-force. For example, many traditional service organizations, where empowerment is not a concept that is fully adopted, restrict access to annual capital budgets and operating plans to management ranks only and on a 'need to know' basis. By contrast, the Disney Corporation provides operational personnel with full access to these tools, entrusting them to translate the strategic plan from the board room to the point of action within the theme parks (Johnson, 1991, p. 42).

Empowerment of front-line staff is not solely a matter customer handling. If we accept Christopher, Payne and Ballantyne's (1991) definition of relationship marketing to include, in addition to customer markets, those relating to suppliers, employees, referrals, 'influencers' and the internal environment, it is logical to think of empowerment extending to the management of and interaction with these groups as well. Thus front-line staff require the training and support in order to take responsibility and make decisions with respect to a wide range of external groups, all of whom, ultimately, contribute to the success or otherwise of the business.

Real empowerment of staff, however, is not something that takes place as a result of a head office circular and attached guidelines. Empowerment is a direct factor of, on the one hand, effective human resource development policies which give staff the skills and confidence to act autonomously and, on the other, a supervisory and management culture that is based on trust and partnership and not control and censure. Thus front-line staff will only be able to act outside prescribed boundaries if they are equipped with the information and skills to do so but, more importantly, if they know that their managers will support whatever action they decide upon and will not penalize or undermine such decisions.

Empowerment is, therefore, the result of a combination of corporate and senior management commitment with appropriate training and support at all levels. Sparrowe (1994), in an empirical study of the factors which contribute to the fostering of empowerment, identified two such factors.

> First, the relationship employees have with their immediate superiors appears to be a significant element in the development of empowerment. To the extent that supervisors are unable to develop positive exchange relationships with employees because of job demands, frequent shift rotation, or burnout, those employees are less likely to enjoy meaning, choice, impact, and competence in their work activities. Policies and procedures that enable supervisors and employees to establish effective relationships over time would function to support empowerment efforts.
>
> Second, the importance of culture in efforts to foster empowerment ... Constructive norms and shared behavioral expectations appear to facilitate employees' experience of meaningfulness, impact, choice, and competence at work. (Sparrowe, 1994, p. 69)

The effects of a genuine empowerment of front-line staff can also have a significant effect upon reducing the social distance between customers and those providing the tourism and hospitality services. When management demonstrates, in a public way, that all their staff have automony and the full trust of the company, they are stating their own evaluation of these staff, both as employees and as people. Guests, in the presence of this attitude, are much more likely to respond to those serving them on the basis of equality. Mahesh (1994), in his seminal book on the corporation and the individual within it, argues cogently for a trust in the better side of human nature, and this attitude is at the root of effective empowerment. The issue of social distance or the service/servitude conundrum is one that we have already reflected in our discussions in Chapters 2 and 4. Real empowerment of the kind espoused by the Ritz Carlton organization in the United States, where guests and staff are seen as social equals temporarily undertaking different roles, can make a real contribution to overcoming problems in this area, providing that macro social and economic conditions permit. Thus the effects will be far greater within the developed economies of Western Europe than within their Eastern European counterparts.

The case for empowerment is by no means conclusive. In Chapter 4, we have already considered the work of George Ritzer (1993) and the concept of McDonaldization as well as the earlier concept of segmentalism which Kanter (1983) proposed. These processes seek to reduce the human input to service delivery to an absolute and well controlled minimum as well as denying the employees a perspective on the total production or service delivery system. Control of the workforce is a central tenet within successful fast-food businesses and others in the tourism and hospitality sector. Control is incompatible with empowerment in its true sense because empowerment means relinquishing control while at the same time ensuring that front-line staff have the skills and confidence to represent the company to customers and help to meet their needs in the best possible way.

### Measuring success by customer satisfaction levels

Jan Carlzon's argument, in refocusing the business approach of SAS during the 1980s, was that that traditional asset audits of airlines and other capital-intensive tourism and hospitality businesses were fundamentally flawed. An airline's worth was traditionally based on the value of its fixed assets, primarily aircraft. Carlzon, however, argued that a true estimate of the company's worth comes from an enumeration of its satisfied customers because they alone will ensure the business's survival and profitability.

Mahesh (1988) takes this argument a step further by considering the role of traditional productivity measures within the service sector, an analysis that has particular applicability within the tourism and hospitality sectors. Any measures to enhance employee output and increase efficiency must be weighed against consequences for the level of customer satisfaction, thus moving the discussion away from objective productivity criteria into a rather more subjective arena. Certainly, productivity criteria can be utilized in order to set work targets in certain areas of the industry – house assistants can be given a specific number of bedrooms to service within a set time and airlines can set a seats-to-cabin-staff ratio for their aircraft. However, such targets have to be weighted against variable and sometimes unpredictable yield and therefore may create considerable pressure when the hotel or aircraft is operating to full capacity. In such situations, customer satisfaction may suffer as a result, with guests having to wait for a room at check-in or experiencing delays with cabin service. The balance between productivity improvements on the one hand and ensuring customer satisfaction on the other is therefore a delicate one and any attempts to alter it must be supported through the introduction of enhanced technology and/or additional training. However, there is a point of some contentiousness here in that Albrecht and Zemke (1985) argue that the fewer people who are involved with the delivery of a service, the better it is likely to be for the customer.

There is no doubt, however, that major changes in employee output as measured by numbers employed have taken place within the European tourism and hospitality industry. Major airlines, for example, have downsized considerably in staffing terms while at the same time retaining their route and flight density. Perhaps the leading example of this process was British Airways which, as part of its transition from public to private ownership from 1982 onwards, reduced its worldwide workforce from 59 000 to 37 000. At the same time, according to Goodstein and Burke (1991):

> It is interesting to note that within a year after this staff reduction, virtually all BA performance indices had improved – more on-time departures and arrivals, fewer out-of-service aircraft, less time 'on hold' for telephone reservations, fewer lost bags, and so on. The consensus view at all levels within BA was that downsizing had

reduced hierarchical levels, thus giving more autonomy to operating people and allowing work to get done more easily.

(pp. 11–12)

What is interesting is that Goodstein and Burke do not include passenger satisfaction among their performance indicators, an omission that Carlzon, in the same line of business, would criticize. However, all BA's success as an international airline as measured by user surveys, demand and profitability stems from the post-transition period. One of the most publicized areas of change within BA took place in the division which operates services within the Scottish Highlands and Islands. By moving staffing and management to a far more flexible work practice environment based on multi-skilling and a reduction in the number of staff located at local stations, a loss-making social service to isolated communities was turned round to profitability.

Of course, such changes cannot be solely attributed to organizational and personnel restructuring. Enhanced technology, within the reservations and other support systems also plays its part. European airlines have sought to change in a broadly similar way to BA, although in some cases without the benefits of private ownership. The European hotel industry has also enhanced productivity and reduced its rooms-to-staff ratio significantly in response to demography and labour shortages in some countries, as well as through reorganization, the use of technology and changes in the hotel product concept, especially in the budget sector. One of the most traumatic aspects of change in Eastern Europe has been the need to restructure the workplace so as to be competitive in Western European terms. Romanian hotels, for example, faced with government requirements to seek foreign partners in the private sector, face 50% staff reductions as well as the need to greatly improve rather than reduce the range and quality of services available to the customer.

At the end of the day, this debate comes down to recognizing the importance of customer satisfaction as the overriding imperative within a successful tourism and hospitality company. Without such satisfaction, business success and profitability cannot be achieved. This demands a fundamental reorientation on the part of many companies in the sector. Quinn (1990), in talking about his retail business, identified the culture that he seeks to achieve:

> A company where all the key decisions are based on an overriding wish to serve the customer better. A company where everyone in it sees serving the customer as their only business.

### Vulnerability to union pressure

Mahesh (1988) argues that the charateristics of service industries, especially the inability to stockpile, means that the sector is particularly vulnerable to union pressure. The logic of this argument is clear. During major industrial action in the coal or automobile industry, for example, companies are able to draw on reserve stock and thus, in the short term, lessen the impact of the action. Likewise, industrial action within the distribution system, such as the railways, means that manufacturing companies can maintain production for a period of time and stockpile their wares for later distribution and sale. Neither of these options are available to businesses in the tourism and hospitality sector. Business lost for whatever reason cannot be re-couped and therefore industrial action in an airline, hotel or food service company means totally lost revenue to the company. Likewise, industrial action within the tourism distribution system, such as airlines or ferries, has major immediate and longer-term consequences for pro-viders at the destination, notably hotels, retailers and ground transport companies, who are unable to secure alternative business at short notice.

This argument has a compelling force of logic to it but is undermined by the very patchy level of union representation within the industry in Europe. We shall discuss reasons for this in greater detail in Chapter 6. Some sectors are highly unionized, notably airlines and hotel workers in some urban areas. A strike by Dublin barworkers in 1994 was able to close 70% of public houses in the city to coincide with the soccer World Cup. However, in rural areas such action would have been totally ineffective. Furthermore, if we accept Riley's (1991) analysis of labour markets within the major subsectors of the tourism and hospi-tality industry, it is unlikely that unionization of the industry in Western Europe will have the force and impact that Mahesh suggests. Riley's model of the weak internal labour market, as we have already seen in Chapter 4, includes the attributes of weak workplace customs, unspecified hiring standards, multiple ports of entry and low skills specificity, and these all act to counter the potential impact of unioniza-tion. The small business structure of much of the industry also counters the potential for union impact. So does specific employer exploitation of these attributes, through which use of seasonal, part-time, youth and female labour in some subsectors of the industry has acted to counter any potential for strengthening within the internal labour market. There are exceptions to this situation. In part because of the strength of the apprenticeship training system in Germany's hospitality sector, some stronger internal labour market characteristics are in evidence and the role of trade unions as active partners in the education and training process has much greater weight.

Thus we have a situation in the tourism and hospitality industries of Western Europe where the potential for union power is considerable but where the reality is somewhat removed from meeting this poten-tial. The situation in Eastern Europe is one where, under the old com-mand economies, theoretical union membership levels were high but the exercise of industrial power was minimal. The period of transition, with generally high levels of unemployment in all sectors, will probably see a weakening of the position of organized labour so that similarities with the rest of Europe will increase.

## THE BUSINESS STRUCTURE OF THE INDUSTRY

Mahesh (1988), finally, argues for the downsizing of companies as a major implication of service sector characteristics, primarily because of simultaneous production and consumption and also because of the need to be responsive to individual customer needs. The notion of empowerment, which we have already considered, points strongly to an emphasis on local decision-making, allowing front-line staff to provide service that is geared to meeting the specific and immediate needs of guests rather than offering a standard, centralized response to such concerns. The logic of empowerment, furthermore, extends beyond the immediate front-line to unit and area management within large companies, allowing them the autonomy and authority to develop their businesses in response to local needs.

The reality of the tourism and hospitality industry in Europe is that the need for the sector to be 'adaptive, decentralized and downsized' (Mahesh, 1988, p. 10) is already largely met because of the small business structure of the industry in most countries (see Chapter 2). Hotels, other accommodation areas, restaurants, retail outlets and attractions are all dominated by small to medium sized enterprises, frequently family or privately owned and managed, and thus fully integrated into their local communities and sensitive to the needs of visitors to these areas.

However, the reality of trends within European tourism and hospitality is such that large, multinational companies are growing in importance in all countries, although the level of market penetration by these businesses has not reached that in North America. Deregulation, the impact of reservations technology and privatization in the airline industry mean that Europe is moving to a situation where dominant control is exercised by a small number of mega-carriers with a global presence, linked to small, regional carriers through part-ownership, franchising and other marketing alliances. British Airways' strategic links to TAT in France, Deutsche BA in Germany as well as Maersk, City Flyer Express and Loganair in the UK are an illustration of this process at work. Likewise, Eastern European airlines are rapidly forging links with Western European partners as a survival strategy. The hotel sector is some way behind the airlines in experiencing the impact of domination by larger companies but the trends are pointing strongly in a similar direction, especially within the rapidly expanding budget sector of the market. Companies such as Accor (Formulae 1, Ibis), Campanile and Forte (Travelodge) are threatening the competitiveness of the traditional small hotel sector in many European countries, but notably in France and the United Kingdom. Budget hotels have all the characteristics of branded products and meet none of the locally focused criteria which Mahesh has advocated. This is true of branding within the middle segment of the hotel market as well, and the growing importance of this trend is strongly supported by central computer reservations systems which are frequently inaccessible to the small operator. A similar picture can be painted with respect to travel agents and tour operators in many European countries.

Ownership of the tourism and hospitality sector by major international companies is not necessarily incompatible with the service-focused approach to business which Mahesh advocates. Ownership by a major company does not necessarily rule out locally sensitive management, marketing and the empowerment of staff to respond individually to local needs. However, the principle of branding, which features increasingly within developments by the multiples, most certainly does eliminate the ability of managers and staff to provide such locally atuned service as the ethos of the product is shifted increasingly towards that of manufacturing production. In many ways, what we have here is a critical human resource dilemma. Locally focused management and staff, responsive and atuned to customer needs, are fully within our notion of sustainable human resource management within tourism and hospitality, but this places considerable emphasis on the requirements of staff selection, training, development, managerial style and general working conditions. Branded tourism and hospitality products, in many but not all respects, fit much more within the traditional human resource management paradigm which, by its nature, reduces the need for training and related support activity by placing an emphasis on the development, implementation and management of systems which are centrally determined and universally applied. The characteristics of what George Ritzer (1993) calls the 'McDonaldization of society' are efficiency, calculability, predictability and control. These features, borrowed and developed from manufacturing operations principles, are making an increasing impact on all sectors concerned with service delivery, but tourism and hospitality in many respects have led the way in their implementation through companies such as McDonald's and Holiday Inn. The role of people working within this model is very different from that outlined in terms of empowerment and managerial support. There is an inherent tension and incompatibility between the move towards standardization and branding on the one hand, and demands for more locally delivered and quality services on the other, and it is not really clear at this point what shape the outcome will take. This managerial paradox is one of a number that in many ways confront the practice of modern business, and the pressures that they pose are part of the concluding discussion in this book in Chapter 10.

In this chapter we have considered the characteristics of the service sector in general and how they impact on the tourism and hospitality industry in particular. We have engaged in a detailed analysis of the implications of these characteristics, especially in terms of what they mean for the management of human resources. It is evident from this discussion that achieving quality service in the tourism and hospitality industries of Europe is a business imperative and is one which will increasingly be the yardstick by which consumers differentiate between airlines, hotels and other facilities which in most other respects will not differ greatly in terms of physical product quality characteristics. Capitalizing on the benefits of the service imperative requires a major human resource focus and one that adopts the features of the sustainable human resource management paradigm.

## REVIEW AND DISCUSSION QUESTIONS

1. Identify company strategies that would fit into the description of relationship marketing. These may be from the tourism and hospitality industry or from other sectors.
2. What are the implications of relationship marketing for the organization, management and marketing of:
   (a) a small mountain hotel in Switzerland;
   (b) a regional commuter airline in France;
   (c) a large airport hotel in Frankfurt;
   (d) one of the big three tour operators in the UK;
   (e) a fast-food restaurant, part of a multinational chain, located at Gatwick Airport, London;
   (f) a bed-and-breakfast establishment in the west of Ireland;
   (g) a beach bar in Corfu;
   (h) a nightclub in Torremolinos.
3. Summarize the characteristics of services that distinguish them from manufactured products. What implications do these characteristics have for the management of human resources?
4. What is meant by a 'moment of truth'?
5. Identify the 'moments of truth' that you encountered during a recent visit to a hotel, restaurant, cinema or other service location. To what extent were these MOTs supervised by management of the establishment?
6. How can a major tour operator control the 'moments of truth' encountered by their clients in contact with various travel intermediaries during their vacation?
7. What do you understand by the term 'empowerment'? What are its constituent parts?
8. What management strategies will be needed in order to empower front-line staff in the tourism and hospitality industry?

9. What are the management implications of inverting the service triangle?
10. Is empowerment compatible with a low-wage, low-status work environment?
11. What are the implications of the critical factors that BA identified (care and concern, spontaneity, problem-solving and recovery) for the management of other tourism and hospitality businesses?
12. Can there be common ground between McDonaldization and the aspiration for quality service delivery via empowerment in the tourism and hospitality industry?

# 6 The dark side of the coin?

## INTRODUCTION

One of the challenges which any discussion of human resources in the European tourism and hospitality industry presents is how to resolve the many contradictions that are evident within the industry. In Chapter 5 we considered the seemingly contradictory tensions between, on the one hand, the demand for greater customization of tourism and hospitality products and services, enabled in part by the process of empowerment, and, on the other, pressure towards standardization and deskilling in the delivery of tourism and hospitality products and services, i.e. the notion of McDonaldization. Also in Chapter 4, reference was made to the high level of turnover within many sectors of the tourism and hospitality industry – for the United Kingdom this is reported to be 19% for managers, 55% for craftspeople, 65% for operatives and 94% for supervisors (HCITB, 1984) – and this was linked to Riley's weak internal labour market characteristics. In interpreting Riley's analysis, do we conclude that the transitory nature of much tourism and hospitality employment is a contributory factor in the creation of a weak internal labour market? Or, alternatively, do we argue that because the internal labour market is weak, conditions are created which lead to short-term and casual relationships between employers and employees? To resort to the use of clichés, this is a classic 'chicken and egg' situation. We will face more in linking Chapter 8, which considers training and development issues, to Chapters 4 and 5 and, indeed, this chapter. One dilemma linking these chapters goes something like this:

1. Quality service requires skilled and well trained service staff.
2. Training and development is an expensive investment in employees.
3. The characteristics of the tourism and hospitality internal labour market are conducive to high labour turnover, especially among those staff in customer contact zones.
4. (a) If staff are going to leave anyway, it does not make sense to invest heavily in their training and development.
   (b) Why give staff enhanced skills which will only go to make them more attractive to other employers and encourage them to leave?

Thus any investment in training will go to benefit the competition.

5. (a) Training and development are strong motivators and can contribute to reducing attrition rates.

(b) Taking pride in the job and being 'empowered' to deliver quality service to the customer, makes it more likely that employees will be happy in the place of work and this will reduce turnover.

Such arguments are the stuff that nightmares are made of and can go on and on without clear resolution. As with many other areas of social policy and practice, one of the roots of this dilemma is how the individual employer and employee behave in the face of wider employment structures and trends, in other words the relationship between the individual (person or company) and society or the wider industry context. If the positive elements of the above analysis are accepted, can an employer afford, or afford not to, go against the macro picture and risk investment in staff, thereby increasing costs and threatening competitiveness by doing so, while faced by the possibility that staff attrition will continue? We could go on and identify a host of further issues to which similar inconclusive analysis could be applied.

This chapter may not directly resolve any of the above problems. What it aims to do, however, is to address a range of what Roy Wood (1992a) calls the 'issues and controversies' of working in the tourism and hospitality industry in Europe. The range of 'issues and controversies' here does not precisely match those of Wood but there is considerable convergence. Inevitably, the 'menu' of issues and controversies that will be addressed may not be exhaustive. However, what discussion of some of the main themes in this area will allow is an attempt at the conclusion to this chapter to synthesize their main implications in the context of the book's underlying theme of sustainability. This analysis will in turn act as a precursor to the final chapter in this book.

Issues and controversies in relation to employment in the tourism and hospitality industry are by no means new. As we saw in Chapter 3, the origin of work in this sector lies firmly in the post-feudal master–servant relationship, bound up with issues of social class and status and a general acceptance of the Malthusian thesis that the hierarchy of social relationships are fixed and permanent. Thus the notion of servitude in the service relationship has its origins in an unquestioning era, at a time when neither partner within the social contract that, for example, bound the English aristocrat and his retinue undertaking the Grand Tour of Europe would have dreamed of debating the rights or wrongs of their relationship. This dimension of the development of tourism and hospitality is generally ignored in both the tourism writing of the time and in subsequent literature. Samuel Johnson, in writing about his travels in Scotland during the seventeenth century, makes little or no reference to those who acted as travel facilitators on his behalf or looked to his comfort en route. In more modern times, Louis

Turner and John Ash (1975), in their wide-ranging and historically detailed discussion of the origins of mass tourism and what they call the 'pleasure periphery' in the later half of the twentieth century, only arrive at a consideration of employment when discussing the economic impact of modern tourism development. It is as if the romanticized picture of the Grand Tour and its nineteenth century precedents which these authors and others such as Buzzard (1993), Steinecke (1993) and Towner (1985) appear to assume did not involve work or the delivery of service.

Saunders (1981), however, gives us a picture of conditions in service during the nineteenth century.

> Although conditions of Elizabethan times, when servants slept on prickling straw, had now passed, it was still customary in most great houses to sleep men in the cellars and women in the attics, often in a long, single dormitory. This practice of 'living in' has later been adopted by hotels, in order to maintain staff requirements in times of acute shortage. Only towards the end of the nineteenth century has the idea that 'anything is good enough for servants' given way to meeting the need of the new scarcity; nor was it usual until that time to give days off or annual holidays, it being considered quite enough to get the occasional afternoon to themselves and to have the opportunity to attend church on Sunday.
>
> (Saunders, 1981, p. 61)

Saunders continues by drawing on further historical links between domestic work and that in the tourism and hospitality industry.

> It will not have escaped attention that some of the practices that have grown up in this century [nineteenth], such as living in and tipping, were carried over into some of the service industries, particularly hotel and catering. Servants suffered also the disadvantage of the scattered nature of their employment, which made it difficult for them to form associations, even at a time when the nineteenth century trade union movements showed how effective combination could become accepted and recognized as part of the social structure. The scattered nature of catering establishments today has been one of the principal reasons why organization for the protection of common interest has proved so difficult to obtain.
>
> (Saunders, 1981, p. 62)

Perhaps the first in-depth picture of aspects of tourism and hospitality work comes from the 1930s and the writing of George Orwell (1933). His description of the work of the plongeur within the working hierarchy of Paris hotels is as perceptive as it is moving and, in many ways, provides a benchmark against which much subsequent sociological discussion of conditions in the tourism and, particularly, hospitality industry can be assessed. Fuller (1971) describes in some detail the sort of work that Orwell would have carried out.

Work in the plonge was hardly an attractive task and labour not easy to obtain, and there was usually a substantial turnover of operatives working in the plonge ... The 'plongeur' (literally one who plunges) is the kitchen porter who has the important task of cleaning the pots and pans. For copper pots, traditional procedure was to have two deep sinks, one fitted with a steam jet to heat water in which the pans were placed, adding soda. The plongeur had a long fish hook to fish out the pans from the hot water and clean them with pickle made from one third salt, one third silver sand and one third flour, mixed with vinegar to paste. Traditionally he did this either with bare hands or with the skins of used lemons, rubbing all over the pan inside and out to bring a shine and effectively removing particles of food. Pans are then rinsed, wiped dry and placed on racks in order of size, each group together and handles pointing all one way. (This operation is still carried out in many plonges today.) (Fuller, 1971, in Saunders, 1981, p. 71)

Orwell's approach is to describe his own experiences of working in Paris hotels and his relationship with colleagues and superiors from the perspective of the foreigner and the 'down and out'. Orwell's objective is to expose the extremes of social deprivation during the depression of the 1930s and, as such, is one of extreme pessimism. He considers the work of the plongeur in its social context.

When one comes to think of it, it is strange that thousands of people in a great, modern city should spend their waking hours swabbing dishes in hot dens underground. The question I am raising is why this life goes on – what purpose it serves, and who wants it to continue, and why I am not taking a more rebellious attitude. I am trying to consider the social significance of the plongeur's life. I think I should start by saying that the plongeur is one of the slaves of the modern world ... he is no freer than if he were bought and sold. His work is servile and without art; he is paid just enough to keep him alive; his only holiday is the sack. He is cut off from marriage or, if he marries his wife must work too. Except by a lucky chance, he has no escape from his life, save into prison ... if plongeurs thought at all, they would long ago have formed a union and gone on strike for better treatment. But they do not think because they have no leisure for it; their life has made slaves of them ... people have a way of taking for granted that all work is done for a sound purpose ... some people must feed in restaurants, and so other people must swab dishes for 80 hours a week. It is the work of civilisation and therefore unquestionable. This point is worth considering. (Orwell, 1933)

Work in supposedly higher status positions in hotels was not necessarily any easier. Page and Kingsford consider the work of the chef.

The cook worked sometimes for fourteen hours or more. The heat from the stoves was immense, and the fumes and smoke drifted round the kitchen, creeping into lungs and eyes of everyone there. The life of those who worked in such kitchens was a hard one. Because of the great heat, the cooks perspired freely and to counteract the thirst this produced, they drank heavily. Beer was always ready at hand, and the more work the cook did, the more he drank, and the more he drank, the less capable he was of doing good work, the more cruel and vulgar he became. Heat and sweat, drunkenness and vulgarity, ill temper through lack of sleep, and constant noise, these were the conditions which caused the young cooks sometimes to be brutally treated by their superiors. The general atmosphere was one of chaos and disorder. The cook had the well-earned reputation of being no better than a vulgar drunkard, who stank most of the time of food, burning fuel, beer and sweat.          (Page and Kingsford, 1971, in Saunders, 1981, p. 71)

Much of what has been written, historically, about the working conditions of workers in the tourism and hospitality industry, notably hotels, is anecdotal and has little by way of empirical corroboration. However, in many respects, the tough reality that is presented in descriptive form as well as the influence of Orwell's analysis can be seen in more recent studies of the industry, which focus on negative aspects of tourism and hospitality work in a comparative social context (Dronfield and Soto, 1982; Byrne, 1986; and Gabriel, 1988). The other side of the coin, equally precise and from the same period as Orwell, are the accounts written between 1937 and 1942 in some five books by Ludwig Bemelmans. However, in complete contrast to Orwell, Bemelmans is the supreme optimist and describes hotel work from the point of view of someone climbing to a senior position in a luxury New York hotel (for example, Bemelmans, 1942).

We are thus already faced with a hint of one of the compelling debates and dilemmas that will be encountered in any analysis of work and its environment in the tourism and hospitality industry. On the one side, there is a very upbeat perspective, stressing challenge, opportunity, variety, mobility and a strong people dimension. This is the image that industry employers and education providers are keen to present. It is a picture that is embellished by the argument that the tourism and hospitality industry provides a broad and heterogeneous working environment, with opportunities and a place for most members of society whether they are disadvantaged on the basis of race, immigrant status or physical disability. On the other hand, there is a picture of drudgery, low pay, anti-social conditions, lack of job security, poor treatment from employers, contempt from customers and the like. Much empirical work, especially into employment at a semi-skilled or unskilled level, has produced conclusions with a focus on these latter issues.

In many respects, there is a realistic prospect that both sides of this argument represent aspects of the truth. The tourism and hospitality industry in Europe is as diverse as it is large, and this in itself means that categorical generalizations about it will be dangerous. The tourism and hospitality industry, as has already been amply demonstrated, consists of an amalgam of subsectors whose work environment and other characteristics are very diverse, melded together only by the common ground of striving to meet the needs of clients, who themselves are seeking an ideal experience which is 'seamless' in the way that service is delivered from travel agent to airport to airline to tour guide to hotel to restaurant to wind surfing instructor to theme park to museum to opera time and time again.

Furthermore, as we have seen in Chapter 3, an additional dimension is provided by the diverse nature of the tourism industry in Europe, a variety born of historical, social, cultural, economic and political factors. Thus even the nature of work and its relationship to the society in which it exists is not the same in all countries of Western Europe. Professional and technical status and all that these concepts imply, for example, have very different historical and contemporary meanings in Germany and Switzerland compared to the United Kingdom. This, in turn, can affect the nature of education and training as well as status and standing in the workplace. If we then extend our discussion to incorporate work in the volatile and rapidly changing environment of Eastern Europe, further complications are immediately in evidence. Sources of security and status in employment which existed under the old regimes may now be despised, undervalued or too costly for the new system to maintain. At the same time, success is much more likely to be measured in conspicuous material terms, frequently the result of entrepreneurial activity on the grey, if not black, market. These represent generic work themes and issues common to all industry sectors in both parts of the new Europe, but form a backcloth to any consideration of work, its context and consequences, within the tourism and hospitality industry.

The purpose of this chapter is to investigate the polarized positions with respect to some of the main 'issues and controversies' and to determine the extent to which they reflect a truly Europe-wide perspective as well as one representative of the tourism and hospitality industry as a whole. The themes that will be addressed in this chapter are by no means exhaustive. Nor are they mutually exclusive. Indeed, it is arguable that any classification of the issues that affect employment in tourism and hospitality in Europe is arbitrary and does not reflect the integration of work within the industry. Such arguments reflect much good common sense. Nevertheless, from an organizational point of view, it is proposed to address themes as follows:

- remuneration for work;
- conditions of work;
- industrial relations and trade unionism in tourism and hospitality work;
- the social composition of employment in the tourism and hospitality industry;

- the status of work;
- professionalism and the managerial function;
- the image of work in the tourism and hospitality industry;
- the future of work in the tourism and hospitality industry.


## REMUNERATION FOR WORK

The popular perception of the tourism and hospitality industry in many Western European countries is that of relatively poor pay or, as Wood puts it, 'most commentators (but few employers) are agreed that the hotel and catering industry is characterized by poor pay' (Wood, 1992a, p. 36). This is a reflection of a number of factors:

- Popular perceptions of the tourism and hospitality industry as synonymous with its largest and, in employment terms, highest profile subsector, that of hotel and catering.
- The low skills intensity within some subsectors, particularly hotel and catering, where, as Riley (1991) points out, some 64% of the workforce fall into the operative or semi-skilled and unskilled category.
- Weak internal labour market characteristics, as we have already discussed in Chapter 4, apply within many subsectors of the industry although by no means all.
- Traditions of high levels of seasonal, part-time, casual and female labour in the industry in many European countries, all of which serve to depress remuneration.
- Traditions of tipping and other forms of ex-gratia or unofficial benefit in kind in some subsectors of the tourism and hospitality industry, which serve to hold down official levels of remuneration.
- Trends towards deskilling within the industry, previously discussed in Chapter 4, have an overall effect of depressing remuneration levels. The process of deskilling, while in evidence throughout Western Europe, is less in evidence in those countries where stronger traditions of professionalism exist, such as Switzerland and France. In the relatively cheap labour environments of most Eastern European countries, deskilling and technology substitution have not had the same impact, except in the case of some foreign-owned businesses.
- Sectors of the tourism and hospitality industry fall readily within the working experiences of a high proportion of the population in many European countries, especially work at an operative level. Much of this work was part-time, casual and seasonal, undertaken when people were school or college students. This exposure to work in the sector is increasing with each generation, as companies such as McDonald's build their human resource policies upon transitory and young staff. Many people, therefore, have a frame of comparison for tourism and hospitality that does not exist with respect to other

industries. Because their experience was of work at the most junior and unskilled level, there is a tendency to extrapolate more generally to the whole industry on the basis of this experience. In a 1981 study, the Hotel and Catering Industry Training Board in the United Kingdom found that experience of work in the industry led respondents to their survey to identify low pay as a negative factor to a significantly greater extent than was the case among respondents with no such experience.

The analysis of the International Labour Office (ILO) leads to similar conclusions as to why there is a tendency towards the depression of wages in the sector. The contributing factors are:

- the preponderance of small establishments;
- fluctuations in the level of business activity;
- cost pressures induced by competition; and
- vulnerable employees, because of contractual status (part-time, youth, etc.) (ILO, 1989, p. 3).

Tourism and hospitality are by no means unique in exhibiting these characteristics in terms of business structure, the skills component and dependence on other than full-time labour. These have similar consequences for pay with respect to other high-contact service industries such as the retail sector.

Initial evidence with respect to developed Western European economies supports the contention that hotel and catering work, if not the full tourism and hospitality industry, employs its unskilled and semi-skilled employees at rates that are lower than those prevailing in other industries. As far back as 1976, a Low Pay Unit study noted that the hotel and catering industry in the United Kingdom had the highest concentration of workers earning poverty wages among all 26 major industrial groups (Low Pay Unit, 1976, p. 1). More recently, Taylor, Airey and Kotas (1983), in a review of evidence, find in support of the view that pay in this sector consistently falls behind that of other industries. Likewise, Byrne (1986) estimated that in 1985 the average wage in the sector fell some £60 per week behind the national average and subsequent reports affirm this situation. Low pay is not confined to unskilled work in the industry. Wood (1992a) notes a British Hotels, Restaurants and Caterers Association report on wages which finds that in 1989 managers in catering earned some 27% below average non-manual wages and that non-manual employees earned 28% less than the average for manual workers. Macaulay and Wood (1992), in the British context, note that of all industrial sectors identified within Department of Employment data for 1991, only agriculture has lower average full-time earnings than hotel and catering and that the average for the sector is over £60 per week less than the national industrial average. The same source also identifies the level and nature of enquiries to the Scottish Low Pay Unit from hotel and catering employees. In

1991/92, 16% of all enquiries were from employees in this subsector and the most common problems reported to the Unit were:

- illegal payment of Wages Council minimum rates;
- no payment or enhanced payment for working overtime hours;
- no paid holidays;
- no written statement of terms and conditions;
- illegal deductions from wages; and
- gratuities from customers that are not passed on to workers (Morag Gillespie in *Forward* to Macaulay and Wood, 1992, pp. v–vi).

Estimates of pay levels tend to focus on basic pay as a relative indicator possibly, but by no means always, with overtime payments included. Mars and Mitchell (1976), however, point to the considerable range of additional components which need to be taken into consideration in calculating true earnings. These include additional elements within the remuneration package such as subsidized lodging, subsidized food, tips or service charges, 'fiddles' and 'knock offs'. The legends within the hotel and catering sector regarding some of these 'grey' sources of supplementary earnings are fantastic but, generally, are not supported by publishable evidence. Other subsectors of the tourism and hospitality industry may benefit from similar additionality, notably airline cabin crew, taxi drivers all over the world and tour guides. These components can be considered in terms of the formal rewards (pay, subsidized food and lodging) which are generally accountable for tax purposes, and informal rewards which have traditionally been outside official scrutiny, although in the case of tips and service charges this situation is changing.

Wood (1992a) argues that there are three key concepts behind the system and levels of rewards that exist within the industry. These are the response to unpredictable demand, resulting in an inability to control the work environment in a systematic manner and consequently a tendency towards a culture of authoritarianism by management as a means of creating the necessary flexibility to cope with the variable demand. The second concept is a response to the first, the forming of individual contracts with key staff governing all aspects of the rewards system. Such contracts operate on a private basis and provide differentiation in remuneration based on local management assessment of the importance of individuals. This leads in turn to the third concept, that of core and periphery workers, which we have already addressed in Chapter 4. In many respects, core workers, especially the operative core, are those staff who benefit substantially from such individual contracts and are seen as key to the effectiveness of the operation. In part, Forte's flexible contracts are designed to counter the flexibility and autonomy that is implicit in Wood's analysis of the rewards system. However, in considering this analysis, we must also be drawn back to Riley and the weak internal labour market which is an ideal bedding ground for such practice.

While much of the published work on low pay in the tourism and hospitality industry has focused on the hotel and catering subsector, other areas of employment can be subjected to similar analysis. Travel agency, airline and tour operations staff, primarily young and female in profile, are frequently offered relatively poor remuneration in return for perceived attractive additional benefits, notably travel opportunities, uniforms and, generally, a pleasant working environment. This situation exists despite the relatively demanding professional and personal qualities which are required for entry. The travel sector is one of considerable disparity in terms of remuneration. Established and larger European airlines, for example, with origins or current status in state ownership have frequently been subject to formal pay negotiations and remuneration in line with public sector norms in their respective countries. By contrast, the growing private sector airlines in Europe, generally much smaller in total size and in the type of aircraft they employ, are much more market-competitive in what they offer by way of remuneration, using perceived glamour as one means by which to depress wages, offer less security and demand more flexible working practices. At the same time, it should not be forgotten that the airline industry includes personnel who are among the highest paid operational staff in the tourism and hospitality industry, namely flight crew, especially those responsible for long-haul operations and employed by major national carriers. One of the major issues facing many larger airlines in Western Europe is that of reducing labour costs in order to eliminate operating losses without injections of state subsidy which would be contrary to European Union free-market trade agreements. In 1994, however, the EU were singularly unsuccessful in applying this principle to, for example, the national airlines of France (Air France), Greece (Olympic) and Ireland (Aer Lingus).

It is impossible to generalize about the issue of remuneration in other subsectors of the European tourism and hospitality industry. Some are subject to similar depressing forces to those we have discussed above, notably in the retail, leisure and entertainments areas where enterprises are frequently small in scale and subject to seasonality and similar factors. Public sector involvement in areas such as cultural and heritage tourism (for example, museums, historic sites and monuments) as well as tourism facilitation (tourist information and marketing) can have a more positive effect on pay levels, but the overall scenario is one where the majority of low skills areas are, in relative terms, poorly remunerated by contrast to the small number of highly skilled technical and administrative support staff who are employed.

As in other respects, the situation with respect to pay in Eastern Europe cannot be analysed in exactly the same terms as have been applied to Western Europe. Under previous systems and planned economies, the majority of employment in tourism and hospitality was on behalf of state enterprises and remuneration was broadly comparable with that in other industrial sectors. It is difficult to fully evaluate the situation in a time of major transition and when the countries of the region are developing in different ways and at varying speeds. Thus any examples used will be subject to rapid dating. In some countries, for example the former German Democratic Republic, many tourism and hospitality enterprises have been privatized and are moving towards operating on the same remuneration principles as apply elsewhere in the country. This, inevitably, will mean greater differentials in pay between skills and status levels than existed under the previous system and a relative depression of wages at the lower end of the skills spectrum. Other countries have been much slower in taking the privatization route. As of 1994, virtually all tourism and hospitality businesses in Romania remain in state hands, although plans for joint venture and partial privatization arrangements are coming to gradual fruition. A number of new private ventures, especially in the hotel and restaurant sector, have opened and this provides a competitive yardstick against which employment in the public sector establishments can be measured. Because of rapid price inflation in Romania, what were secure and relatively well paid jobs in all sectors of the economy, not least tourism and hospitality, have been subject to considerable depression in buying power, and the sector is rapidly becoming one of low pay. At the same time, 'grey' market private enterprise in the industry is thriving with activities such as food service, taxi, bureaux de change and retail enterprises thriving in a totally unregulated environment and providing relatively high pay returns to those involved. However, in Romania as elsewhere in Eastern Europe, it will take some considerable time before the prevailing Western European market structure of employment in tourism and hospitality develops in full.

The evidence with respect to pay levels in the European tourism and hospitality industry therefore is inconclusive. In some subsectors there is little doubt that average pay at unskilled and semi-skilled levels is below that in comparable industrial sectors. At the same time, remuneration is clearly linked to the level of professional tradition that exists in the industry. For example, aspects of hotel and catering work in Switzerland and France have traditions and status which are totally absent in the United Kingdom and this is reflected in the relative remuneration of these jobs. The contribution of statutory minima with regard to wages is a contentious issue. Although, as we have seen, such regulations apply to some areas of tourism and hospitality in all European Union countries with the exception of Ireland and the United Kingdom, there is little evidence that their existence, in itself, overcomes problems of low pay within the industry.

Levels of pay are clearly linked to market demand for the skills on offer and, as Riley's weak internal labour market suggests, the skills required for many tourism and hospitality jobs are relatively easily and cheaply accessible in the marketplace. At the same time, skills shortages in some areas mean that remuneration is highly competitive and attractive, and we should not forget the minority in the industry who are paid at levels which are on a par with or in excess of those available in many other industrial sectors. Low pay will remain an issue in tourism and hospitality until demand for labour increases, although demographic trends in Western Europe combined with measures to reduce the flow of immigration from outside of the European Union are the only likely causes of change in this respect. Poor pay is hardly conducive to fostering a working environment which is customer focused and which supports empowerment in the sense that we discussed in Chapter 5. Whether customer demands for enhanced product and service quality will impose the need for increased service skills on the industry remains to be seen. This represents another conundrum for which there is no immediate resolution.

## CONDITIONS OF WORK

Discussion of remuneration in the context of tourism and hospitality work cannot take place in isolation from the conditions within which such pay is earned. By conditions we mean a wide-ranging array of factors which contribute to the overall working environment and, therefore, to the motivation or demotivation of employees. Thus a discussion of conditions in relation to the tourism and hospitality industry in Europe includes consideration of factors such as the physical working environment and its safety, the physical and mental demands of the job, job security, holiday and other leave entitlements, other rights, entitlements and benefits, hours of work, the nature of work shifts, and the social contribution of work. In most countries, aspects of these conditions are regulated by legislation at a national level and, within the European Union, on the basis of EU law. Such areas normally include paid holiday entitlements, physical working conditions, health and safety matters, maternity rights and equal opportunities. Generally speaking, such conditions operate at a different level, if at all, for part-time, temporary/seasonal and casual employees than is applicable with respect to full-time staff. This differentiation in the levels of entitlement and protection is of particular importance within the tourism and hospitality industry of Europe because of the high and increasing incidence of working patterns other than full-time and permanent. A consideration of conditions, therefore, includes a range of factors which affect work and its appeal and status, as well as the legal framework within which such factors are permitted or restricted.

Popular perception of work in tourism and hospitality is undoubtedly influenced, again, by the situation that pertains in hotels and catering businesses. The 1981 HCITB report in the United Kingdom noted that 43% of the surveyed sample saw 'long and difficult hours' as one of worst features of work in the industry, the highest response to any single attribute, while 34% identified that 'many jobs are dirty', second in the list. Among respondents with experience of the industry, 50% identified work as featuring 'long and difficult hours', although the figure in relation to the dirty nature of work was identified by fewer of those with experience than those without. Other factors identified by the survey which relate to conditions of work included 'very hard work', 'monotonous boring work' and 'on feet a lot'. Orwell's account of aspects of hotel work during the 1930s certainly paints a picture of hard, dirty and poorly paid toil undertaken by casual employees with few rights and no security, and subject to the whims and bullying of the permanent employees.

In common with remuneration, conditions of work are, undoubtedly, influenced by industry characteristics and labour market factors, and there are certainly tendencies in some sectors to respond to this environment by extracting the maximum by way of productivity from the workforce, while giving the minimum in terms of added benefits. The ILO's assessment of this situation is as follows:

> It would not be appropriate to characterize the entire hotel, catering and tourism sector as subject to precarious work arrangements. Many enterprises offer excellent conditions and have been able to find ways to reconcile their needs for flexibility with stable and well-protected forms of employment. There are, however, strong pressures which affect many if not most employers and workers.
>
> (ILO, 1989, p. 3)

However, despite the existence of minimum pay regulations in many European countries, there is increasing pressure for deregulation with respect to remuneration. This situation already pertains in the United Kingdom where rates of pay and associated benefits are left entirely to labour market forces, although the same is not true in relation to other aspects of the wider working environment which are subject to considerable regulation and protection. Legislation concerning conditions of work dates back to child employment regulation in the nineteenth century and has been extended to include a range of entitlements and benefits which are largely unquestioned, in principle, in the working environment of most European countries, although they are matters of concern and exploitation in some developing nations. Where debate and dispute does arise is in relation to the extent of such entitlements and benefits (minima for paid holidays, maxima for working hours per week, etc.) as well as their range and coverage (e.g. whether to include part-time and casual staff).

Certain sectors of the tourism and hospitality industry are subject to the very stringent enforcement of regulations that are specific to the industry, for example working hours per shift and per day. Airline pilots are a good example, although such regulation is born, primarily, out of passenger safety considerations. Other transportation sectors are subject to similar, if perhaps not so stringent, regulation, although such control may be widely abused as it has been with long-distance coach drivers for whom restrictions have only been introduced in response to a number of fatal accidents involving tourists in different countries in Europe. Likewise, specific hygiene legislation affects the working environment and conditions of work of all food workers in the tourism and hospitality industry, although such control is primarily driven at a national level in Europe, with transnational measures relatively weak and ineffectual. The main focus of regulation, in both of these areas, is not on the enhancement of the working lives of those employed in the tourism and hospitality industry but on the health and safety of the consumer. As Lucas (1993) points out, it is interesting that this is the only principle under which the United Kingdom government has supported measures within the European Union's Social Chapter – any measures designed purely to enhance working conditions have been opposed or subject to opt out.

Other aspects affecting conditions of work are subject to general legislative control, for example employment rights which protect employees from race or sexual discrimination, an area of considerable variance between different European countries. Likewise, maternity rights, sick pay entitlements and retirement benefits apply as they would in other industrial sectors. However, the regulation of the working environment beyond that affecting health and safety, especially of the consumer, is a highly contentious issue and the subject of dispute.

On the one hand, there are those subscribing to the liberal tradition emanating from authorities such as the nineteenth century writer Adam Smith, who argue that deregulation of work, in all possible areas, is conducive to more effective competition in the marketplace and will, therefore, force companies to enhance the working environment as a competitive strategy to attract and retain the skills they require in order to carry out work. The liberal argument sees regulation beyond the very minimum necessary to ensure health and safety as restrictive on competitive trade. In the context of tourism and hospitality, in the European Union, for example, provisions of the Social Chapter which address such regulation, will, according to this argument, have the effect of increasing the cost of products and services so that they are no longer price competitive with those provided by destinations outside of the Union, such as north Africa, Turkey and further afield in the Far East and the Caribbean. Alternatively, companies will seek to remain competitive and respond to what are seen as the increased costs of regulation by limiting the numbers that are employed, thus threatening product and service standards and, in turn, international competitiveness.

On the other hand, the counter, social reformist argument seeks to limit exploitation in the workplace, especially of those least able to protect themselves – the least educated, lowest skilled and poorest paid members of the workforce. Given the employment structure of some subsectors of the European tourism and hospitality industry, such protection has direct implications for the working environment in hotels, catering, the retail sector and some travel services, for example. The social reformist argument is founded, primarily, on concerns for social justice and a reduction of what is seen as exploitation in the workplace. Poor management is frequently blamed for failing to develop creative alternatives to the worst excesses of long and unsocial hours, repetitive and unrewarding work routines and related problems. Liberals argue for better conditions in the workplace, certainly, but in their view the impetus for change must be private sector driven, a recognition of the benefits of good employment practices which in turn will reap rewards through enhanced productivity, quality and competitiveness.

Social reformists question the will or ability of, in particular, labour-intensive and low-skills industries such as many sectors of tourism and hospitality to self-regulate and doubt that the workings of the market can provide real workplace solutions. They argue that government regulation is the only means by which to achieve uniform minimum good practice and, eventually, real change. This debate is at the heart of arguments about the Social Chapter within the European Union as well as being central to arguments about the process, pace and outcomes of privatization in Eastern Europe.

The Social Chapter, or as it was originally known the Community Charter of the Fundamental Social Rights of Workers, was designed as a social counterweight to the single European market and the economic deregulation that came in its train. The then Social Charter was agreed by eleven of the twelve members of the then European Community in December 1989, with only the United Kingdom dissenting, and calls for the agreement on minimum standards in major areas of labour law. According to Bridgford and Stirling (1992), the Chapter:

> ... addresses such issues as working conditions; freedom of movement of labour; minimum pay; social welfare schemes; freedom to join a trade union, to engage in collective bargaining and to participate in strike action; vocational training; equal opportunities; information, consultation and participation; health and safety; child labour; pensioners; and the disabled.
>
> (Bridgeford and Stirling, 1992, p. 77)

The Social Chapter itself is not legally binding on member states but was supported by legislative action of 48 proposals, of which 17 were draft directives and 10 were in the field of health and safety. Many of its provisions mirror or extend those already in place at a national level in some member states and the British government has used this argument to justify opting out, that in all areas of major concern national legislation already makes adequate provision.

Two aspects of the Social Chapter have been the object of the most focused opposition by lobbyists representing the tourism and hospitality industry. The first of these relates to working time, in particular the total working week which is proposed at 48 hours per week, and restrictions on unsocial working hours, especially at night. The argument against such provision is that, given demand fluctuation, it is impossible to operate within tourism and hospitality on the basis of such categorical restriction. In highly seasonal tourist destination areas of, for example, northern Norway, the west of Ireland and some Greek Islands, the cycle of business is such that over 80% of turnover may be generated in two to three summer months and it is not realistic or cost effective to guarantee a maximum working week during the short peak period. Increased hours at these times are compensated for by slack periods at other times during the season. Likewise, a tourism and hospitality business needs the facilities to respond to unexpected demand, for example an unplanned coach party staying in a hotel, and to utilize its staff resources to cater for the group accordingly. Such arguments are sustainable but there is evidence that the industry does not always meet its side of the bargain and that, for example, consequent overtime commitments are not met in full. The Social Chapter permits considerable lead time in this area consisting of a seven-year transition period to allow the possibility of adaptation and change by the industry. One response by the tourism and hospitality industry to the threat of regulation in this area has been to increase dependence on part-time labour, who are unaffected by the 'upper ceiling' restriction of 48 hours, although this trend is also motivated by cost factors. In the United Kingdom, for example, the number of part-time workers has increased steadily in all industry sectors since 1980 and such growth is reflected, if anything to a greater extent, in the tourism and hospitality area.

The second aspect of the Social Chapter which has been the focus of considerable attention is the extent to which a range of employment entitlements are extended to apply to part-time and temporary or seasonal staff. Lucas (1993) sees these entitlements resulting in both real and perceived costs to employers.

> 'Real' costs could arise from, among other things, a requirement to pay National Insurance contributions on part-time earnings below the current earnings limit . . ., to afford 14 weeks' maternity leave at a level equivalent to sick pay to all women, regardless of any hours' or service qualifications, and to apply improved terms and conditions of employment to part-time workers, such as the right to a minimum of 4 weeks' annual holiday. Increased 'perceived' costs could arise from the extension of employment protection rights, such as the right to protection against unfair dismissal for becoming pregnant, the right to a daily minimum rest period of 11 hours out of 24 and at least 35 hours uninterrupted rest hours every week, and limitations on night work.  (Lucas, 1993, p. 94)

Extension of employment rights in these areas to part-time employees will have a very significant effect on the conditions under which a substantial proportion of workers in the tourism and hospitality industry of the European Union operate. The extended rights, in themselves, may well have the effect of increasing commitment and loyalty among part-time staff and thus, in part, pay for themselves through a reduction in recruitment and training costs as well as through contributing to improved service and product quality. The United Kingdom, for the moment, remains outside the scope of this aspect of the Social Chapter, although a recent European Court ruling has imposed the extension of maternity rights to part-time staff, while also removing the qualification period. Whether the extension of employment rights to part-time employees will reduce the drift towards this form of employment remains to be seen. One employer response to changes of this nature may be to make greater use of agency staff and other outsourcing strategies, placing the perceived additional employment 'burden' outside of the company. However, as Walsh (1991) shows, the trend in the hotel industry for the moment remains towards increasing use of part-time employment at the cost of both full-time and casual work.

> The employment of part-time, temporary and casual workers, far from being peripheral to productivity, was central to it. Part-time, temporary and casual workers allowed employers to specify labour demands aligned more closely to product demands within the organization than to pressures arising from the external labour market. In this way, labour can be purchased almost on an 'as-needed' or 'just-in-time' basis. (Walsh, 1991, p. 113)

Casual work seems to remain outside some of the provisions of employment protection measures as, for example, in the United Kingdom they are not deemed to hold employees status (Price, 1994). This exclusion, although only tested in the UK courts in relation to the hotel industry (O'Kelly v. Trusthouse Forte – see Price, 1994, pp. 16–17), is of importance because of the very high level of unregulated, casual employment that exists within the tourism and hospitality industry. Much of such work is on what appears to be a self-employed basis but, in fact, may reflect casual, commission-based arrangements. A variety of working activities, all of which service tourists, can fall into this category, including street and beach vendors, timeshare sales persons, unlicensed taxi operatives as well as entertainers and prostitutes. In most countries of Europe, these 'grey' subsectors of the tourism and hospitality economy are of considerable significance in both value and employment terms but people working in these areas are frequently subject to exploitation and do not have any employment rights or protection in legal terms. This area of tourism employment in Eastern European countries such as Romania is growing at a far faster rate than the mainstream, 'legitimate' business sector.

Legislation, whether national or European Union in origin, only addresses matters relating to part of the overall working environment in the tourism and hospitality industry. Working conditions are also affected by a range of formal and informal arrangements within the workplace and many of these stem from the fundamental attitude and commitment of management and owners to the staff that work with them. In Chapter 5, we introduced the concept of internal marketing and addressed the link between using people as a valued resource and the achievement of quality products and excellence in service delivery. If staff are perceived to be assets, as within the sustainable human resource model, as opposed to the traditional view that they are costs, it should follow that the working environment should be designed to facilitate their needs and requirements in so far as this is compatible with maximizing customer satisfaction and achieving general business objectives. Thus working hours and shifts, for example, can be designed to acknowledge personal and lifestyle requirements of staff rather than, as has traditionally been the case, reflecting solely employer needs. Restaurants and other facilities for the internal customer can be designed using the same principles as those which would apply to facilities for the external customer, rather than the practice which is frequently found in the industry. Long-term commitment to staff can be demonstrated by share and profit participation and similar involvement measures.

The issue of conditions in the workplace within European tourism and hospitality is also one where generalizations are difficult to make given the diverse range of traditions and practice at national levels, as well as the wide variety between subsectors. Some areas of work in the industry offer conditions that would be deemed attractive in comparison with many alternative occupational environments, for example providing travel and related benefits that would generally be perceived as compensating for other negative aspects of work. Other jobs are, undoubtedly, repetitive and physically demanding, required at unsocial times and provide little by way of security or opportunity. In considering conditions of work, as with many issues in the human resource arena, we need to avoid sweeping generalizations because of this diversity. However, it is also important to recognize that existing and potential employees in the European tourism and hospitality industry have increasing expectations of the workplace in terms of its rewards and benefits in the widest sense and the industry will need to recognize these expectations in order to compete successfully for labour. Substandard staff accommodation, poor meals, split shifts and dislocated social lives are examples of tangible and intangible manifestations of poor conditions which many businesses in the tourism and hospitality industry need to address. In terms of the underlying theme of this book, acceptance and perpetuation of such poor conditions represent the traditional or non-sustainable human resource management model. The needs and expectations of employees, especially young people, will only be met through human resource practices which are in accord with the sustainable paradigm. Linney and Teare summarize the argument about changing expectations effectively.

Staff expect better pay and conditions of service as their lifestyle and standard of living expectations are influenced by societal patterns and trends. These sources of expectation have in common the need to devise systems and methods which will facilitate improvements in productivity. The enabling mechanism for productivity improvements is a well motivated workforce. This means that the employee expects the employer to provide opportunities to grow and develop, to be trained and to be promoted within the organization.                    (Linney and Teare, 1991, p. iii)

## INDUSTRIAL RELATIONS AND TRADE UNIONISM IN TOURISM AND HOSPITALITY WORK

In part, the industrial relations climate in the European tourism and hospitality industry is governed by the legislative framework within which it operates. Thus laws relating to health and safety, the employment of children, the physical working environment and, increasingly, other areas as well, provide the framework within which many of the relationships between companies, management and their employees are formalized and in most European countries are not overtly abused. However, even this framework is subject to extreme pressure in some tourism and hospitality businesses, especially those of a highly seasonal nature operating to tight profit margins and, increasingly, those in Eastern Europe.

The counterweight in industrial relations to the effects of poor pay and conditions in the tourism and hospitality industry is the role played by trade unions. As in other areas within the human resource environment in European tourism and hospitality, it is difficult to generalize when discussing the level of trade union membership and the impact that such organization has on a pan-European or cross-sectoral basis. Certainly in the tourism industry in the United Kingdom in general, and in the hotel industry in particular, trade union membership is put at as low as 6% of the total workforce (Wood, 1992a). A number of other sectors are not unionized to any significant degree at all, notably fast food and non-hotel accommodation. However, airlines and other transport staff from what remains or used to be within the public sector have a much stronger tradition of union representation. By contrast, the hotel industry in Germany has a much stronger tradition of union membership and the relationship between employers and unions, especially in their partnership in support of education and training, is testimony to this. In those parts of Europe where public ownership of tourism and hospitality concerns remains significant, trade union membership is likely to be greater. Airlines such as Air France, Aer Lingus and Olympic Airways all have union representation that, traditionally, has been relatively effective in its support for membership rights, and changes and restructuring have been underwritten to a considerable extent by public funding as a result of trade union pressure. Likewise, Great Southern Hotels in Ireland, a state-owned company, has operated with reasonable protection, in part because of the recognition of its trade union.

In the UK context, Aslan and Wood (1993) identify four main

reasons for the low level of trade union membership in the hotel industry:

- employee conservatism and reluctance to join trade unions which, in part, is engendered because 'hotel and catering workers to some extent assume the values of their social superiors (managers and guests), values which are highly individualistic and hostile to trade unionism' (Aslan and Wood, 1993, p. 61);
- high labour turnover which means that few workers remain in a job long enough to join;
- the active hostility of employers and managers to union membership;
- inter-union conflict and competition for membership.

To these four, it is worth adding a number of additional factors which militate against high levels of trade union membership in the industry:

- the geographical dispersement and fragmentation of the sector, which makes organization difficult;
- the importance of part-time, casual and seasonal labour in the industry, groupings of the workforce which traditionally have been of little interest to trade unions and whose conditions probably demand the most urgent address;
- the high level of female employment in the industry, a group that has traditionally not been active in trade unions;
- the importance of ethnic minority and immigrant groups to the industry, especially at low or unskilled levels. These groups are low in union participation but may also be under some pressure regarding their status and thus be reluctant to 'get involved' in protecting rights and enhancing conditions.

Riley (1985) explores two additional what he calls background barriers to active union participation within the tourism and hospitality industry:

- the historical isolation of employees in the sector from the mainstream of the labour movement. By this, Riley means isolation from traditional union values of solidarity, opposition to management and possibly a dichotomous class view of society. However, isolation goes beyond attitudinal factors to include removal from industrial environments that show propensity to labour organization and action;
- the notion of service being incompatible with the ethos of traditional trade unionism. At the root of this distinction is the notion of servitude and the implicit devaluation of personal worth that is attached to it, or what Riley calls 'the distance of serfdom'. Thus trade unions, far more used to working in the production sector, find service jobs difficult to comprehend and even accept.

Within this environment, trade unionism has had major problems in making significant headway in terms of membership or support in many areas of the European tourism and hospitality industry. At the same time, a general erosion of trade union influence in many European countries since the early 1980s has not been a good backcloth against which to alter this situation. It is reasonable speculation to suggest that in those areas of the European tourism and hospitality industry where trade unions remain relatively strong, notably in the airlines, this strength is likely to be challenged as a result of privatization, competition from the non-union sector, the enlarged statutory base with respect to pay and conditions provided by instruments such as the Social Chapter reducing the need for union representation, and a growing recognition among forward-looking employers that there are direct benefits to providing more than a minimum by way of pay and conditions in return for enhanced productivity and service.

## THE SOCIAL COMPOSITION OF EMPLOYMENT IN THE TOURISM AND HOSPITALITY INDUSTRY

The tourism and hospitality industry is frequently portrayed as a young person's industry and this projection is used to create the image of vibrancy, energy and fun. Companies such as TGIF (Thank God Its Friday) restaurants and Club Meditteranée resorts specifically focus on this image in their recruitment and look for employees, male and female, who match the environment they seek to project, that of youth and fun. They are also seeking to match their staff image to that of that client profile of the restaurants or resorts and, by doing so, to reduce the social distance between guest and employee in a way that reflects our earlier discussion in Chapter 3. Other tourism and hospitality companies also seek to project a youth image but in a different context than that of energy and fun, the 'adrenalin factor', which drives the above examples. Singapore Airlines, for example, uses the image of the 'Singapore Girl' in order to project quality, caring and, to some extent, sensuous service. The image, of course, is gender-specific but the client will find that in reality the airline's services are provided by a mixed gender cabin crew. To a large extent, however, youth is the image of fun and frivolity in the tourism and hospitality industry. Where employment legislation and social attitudes permit, this image is perpetuated by the termination of employment contracts when female staff reach a certain age – in the case of some Asian airlines this is in the early 30s. The end to marriage bans, whereby women were required to give up employment on marriage, is only a thing of the relatively recent past in many European airlines. However, when an image is required to convey issues of safety, security and, in general, confidence, a more mature model is portrayed. Thus the airline pilot or hotel manager in advertising and promotion tends to be portrayed by a slightly greying more mature male with the obligatory good looks!

In reality the composition of the tourism and hospitality industry does confirm the image of youth, but it is possible to identify other specific groups within society beyond just age, both in work areas that have a strong glamour appeal and in the more routine and humdrum aspects of employment in the industry. In purely numerical terms, it is a sector that in northwestern Europe is dominated by young and female labour with in some countries a strong representation of ethnic minorities and migrant workers. However, particularly in relation to women, the situation may be rather different in some southern and eastern European countries, where a strong male presence in all service or customer contact areas is much more common. This structure is strongly linked to the hierarchy in the industry in that the representation not only of youth (not surprisingly) but also, women, ethnic minorities and non-nationals reduces significantly at supervisory and management levels in most sectors of the industry. Walsh and McKenna (1990), in a study of women in the tourism and hospitality industry, address this issue is terms of the differing expectations of employees but also, more importantly, of employers.

> Throughout all sectors of tourism where there is customer contact, women predominate – as front office and dining room personnel; as airline staff; as tourist office personnel; as tour guides – to mention but the most obvious. However, when it comes to the more senior positions in these same areas, where the jobs have less customer contact but a greater management and decision-making role, the situation is usually reversed. Employers in these situations either announce that women operate so well at their existing levels that it is impossible to replace them or else cite the perceived negative traits of women – their inability to gain authority and respect, their timidity and indecisiveness as barriers to promotion.
> (Walsh and McKenna, 1990, p. 163)

A study by Hicks (1990) sought to examine the possible processes occurring in organizations that appear to work against women fulfilling their management potential. The perceived reality of respondents in this study was that females' presence in the industry was only temporary. Instead of playing the 'game' that the male managers are playing (including accepting the long unsocial hours and fostering a sense of managerial camaraderie), the females are seen to be playing a different sort of game with different values and assumptions. Christensen (1987) argues along similar lines in noting that many supervisors have perceptions of female entrants which can thwart their progress, seeing them as not conforming to the leadership image.

In a similar vein, a study of the United Kingdom's hotel industry by the Commission for Racial Equality (1991) found that ethnic minorities were disproportionately concentrated in unskilled grades such as cleaners, waiters and porters, with only minimal representation at management levels. The management of cultural diversity in the tourism and hospitality industry is the subject of separate consideration in Chapter 7.

Walsh and McKenna, Hicks, and Christensen all postulate reasons for the failure of women to achieve promotion and higher status positions on an equal basis with men in the tourism and hospitality industry. Similar arguments can be presented with respect to the position of ethnic minorities and migrant workers in the industry. The high proportion of young people within the workforce has linked but independent causes. The truth is that the social structure of the industry in Europe reflects a complex amalgam of social, economic, cultural and historical factors, many of which are closely interrelated. These include the following:

- the skills structure of many subsectors, with a preponderance of positions at operative, unskilled or semi-skilled levels;
- the nature of the labour market in many tourism and hospitality subsectors (see Chapter 4), which enables flexible access and attrition, in particular to operative positions, by those with varied or no formal qualifications or experience;
- deskilling in some subsectors, especially food production and service, which allows much more general access to positions previously protected by specific skills requirements;
- variable demand, especially seasonality, which reduces the security and permanence of employment in many areas. One response to this is the active promotion of, in particular, seasonal work, for example of positions as tour operator representatives in Mediterranean resorts to the young. The low skills demands of many jobs in the industry also attracts young people to make use of the consequent flexibility of access and departure in order to support travel and mobility within Europe and beyond. A high proportion of young Australians and New Zealanders in Europe for perhaps a year work in a number of tourism and hospitality related jobs for this reason;
- contraction of core employment opportunities and the growth in peripheral part-time and casual work, especially in northwestern Europe;
- recruitment strategies and conditions in some companies which are designed to attract those interested in short- and medium-term commitments only and do not appeal to those seeking permanent and long-term employment or career opportunities;
- levels of pay and conditions in some subsectors of the industry which are only acceptable to immigrant or otherwise marginalized members of society;
- restructuring of tourism and hospitality related employment in Eastern Europe includes growing levels of foreign investment, frequently through major international hotel groups, restaurants and

airlines. Their employment policies frequently focus on the recruitment of young school and college leavers with no previous experience. At the same time, established local businesses are having to downsize their labour forces of older workers significantly (by about 50% in Bucharest, Romania) in order to survive and compete in the new marketplace.

The demographic structure of most countries in Western Europe is already a major force for change in the social composition of the tourism and hospitality workforce. The decline in the youth population means that the tourism and hospitality industry's traditional source of relatively cheap and flexible unskilled labour is declining in size and the competition for labour is likely to intensify on a national and European Union level. Parsons (1990) notes that relatively few businesses have really taken the implications of demographic change aboard and acted as a consequence of them by raising the wage levels and benefits payable to young recruits or by looking to alternative sources of labour. Parsons advocates strategies which focus on the recruitment process and, subsequently, on how employees are treated at work in order to attract young people in a competitive and shrinking labour market. These strategies include:

- improving liaison between schools, colleges and employers;
- improving youth training programmes;
- adapting recruitment and working practices to alternative sources of labour, notably women returners and mature workers;
- identifying and tapping under-utilized skills potential, including people with disabilities, those from ethnic minorities and the longer-term unemployed;
- reducing staff turnover; and
- placing less emphasis on meeting new skill or knowledge needs from the external labour market by making much more use of the existing workforce (Parsons, 1990, p. 65).

Given that the main requirement for labour in most Western European countries is likely to be at the unskilled and semi-skilled levels where women and ethnic minorities are already over-represented, Parson's alternative source strategies will only serve to increase this imbalance while making only a limited contribution over the longer term to redressing the imbalance at more senior levels.

## THE STATUS OF WORK

The status of work in the European tourism and hospitality industry is clearly linked to the social composition of employment within the sector. In this, some subsectors of the industry have much in common with other, highly labour-intensive and low-skills areas of the service economy. In many respects, we are once again faced with an unbroken circle. The perceived low status of work in the industry in many European countries means that employers fail to attract the level of skills and ambition that they desire and, as we have seen, employ workers from social groupings that are frequently perceived to be low status and marginalized within that society. This employee profile in turn fuels external perceptions of the status of work within the industry as an environment of poor conditions, remuneration and limited opportunity. We must, of course, treat this generalization with some caution because there are areas of work in tourism and hospitality that carry perceptions of high status in relation to professional and skills criteria as well as in terms of glamour and excitement. In addition, perceptions are by no means homogeneous throughout Europe. In some countries, notably in southern Europe, certain activities such as restaurant service carry kudos and considerably higher status than is the case in northern Europe.

Status is affected both by the subsector of the industry in which work is undertaken and by the nature of the responsibilities held. The airline business, *per se*, has higher employment status attributes than restaurant or retail work, and this differentiation applies to the relative status of comparable roles and skill areas between the various subsectors. For example, airline cabin crew generally have higher status in terms of general public perception than service staff on trains, long-distance coaches or in family-style restaurants, although arguably a substantial proportion of their work requires very similar technical and social skills. Admittedly, there are what are seen as glamour attributes and attendant benefits attached to cabin crew work which is denied to the other groupings but this alone cannot account for the relative gap in perceived status. The differentiation in status of different areas of tourism and hospitality employment was confirmed by a study of public perception in this area carried out by Baum (1991a). This study asked visitors to a number of tourist attractions in Buckinghamshire, England, to identify the desirability of employment in various subsectors of the tourism and hospitality industry. The ranking of the choices from a sample of 384 visitors is shown in Table 6.1.

Wood (1993) considers relative status within the hotel and catering industry and provides a typological classification which is useful in considering the determinants of status or lack of status within the tourism and hospitality industry in general. Wood's typology identifies three 'status markers', which place work activities in categories according to their perceived status.

> First, *symbolic status markers* include such considerations as whether workers were uniformed, which normally accorded lower status ... or were engaged in 'dirty work', which also conferred lower status ... Second, *locational status markers* include whether workers were, by virtue of their job, in a position to gain direct

**Table 6.1** Perceptions of the status of tourism employment

| Rank order | Subsector | Selected by |
|---|---|---|
| 1 | Travel company/airline | 75% |
| 2 | Travel agents | 61% |
| 3 | Hotels (supervisory/ management) | 50% |
| 4 | Sports/leisure | 47% |
| 5 = | Restaurant (supervisory/ management) | 39% |
| 5 = | Entertainment/clubs | 39% |
| 7 | Historic/heritage/attraction site | 38% |
| 8 | Hotels (operational) | 32% |
| 9 | Souvenir/gift shop | 27% |
| 10 | Restaurant (operational) | 26% |
| 11 | Fast food (supervisory/ management) | 22% |
| 12 | Coach/bus transport | 21% |

*Source*: Baum (1991a).

access to clients. This position was important in procuring informal rewards such as tips, or determining whether workers occupy positions that gave them the chances to obtain other illicit rewards by petty theft of monies and commodities. The degree of access to such rewards was likely to influence status; the higher the access or reward, the higher the status ... Finally, there were *skill status markers*. Jobs perceived as entailing low levels of technical skills were generally accorded lower status – a commonplace social phenomenon made curious in the hospitality industry context by the fact that the corollary (i.e. that comparatively more highly skilled jobs attracted higher status) appeared to be true only when considered relative to the wider occupational structure.

(Wood, 1993)

Wood's final point about skill status markers requires some further elaboration. He continues the discussion by pointing out the relative higher status of skilled employees who have transferable skills, such as front-office staff, to those with hospitality industry-specific skills, such as serving staff or chefs. This leads him to subdivide the skill status marker category into general skill markers and industry-specific skill markers. This principle probably extends to other sectors of the tourism and hospitality industry. Engineers with generic and transferable skills will attract higher status than those whose skills are specific to aircraft maintenance alone.

The status of employment in different subsectors of the tourism and hospitality industry as well as the relative status of specific jobs within subsectors varies between cultures and countries. Such variation is related to a number of factors, including:

- the importance of tourism and hospitality to the overall economy of the country or region and the consequent significance of the industry's employment generating capacity. Where such dependence is high, as it is in countries of the Mediterranean, for example, and alternative employment opportunities are limited, relative status to that of other economic sectors is likely to be enhanced;
- the extent to which the personal service nature of much tourism and hospitality work is associated with the issue of servility in a particular culture will also impact upon its status. There is a tension in the interpretation of this issue:

> The low external status of hotel work is seen as a result of its personal service nature. This is regarded as a subservient role by people outside whilst those within it see the personal service element as important and fundamental.
>
> (Commission on Industrial Relations, 1971, p. 39)

- tourism and hospitality work is also likely to attract higher status in societies where participation levels by males are high and that of women, minorities and migrant labour are low;
- the participation rate in post-compulsory education is also a factor that can impact upon the status of work in tourism and hospitality. Where such participation is high, the low skills demands of much employment in the industry are such that for a significant proportion of young people they are over-qualified for such work and this contributes to the overall perception of status. Where post-compulsory education participation rates are lower, a significantly higher proportion of the school leaving population will see tourism and hospitality as a career option and thus the relative status of the industry will be higher;
- perceived skills levels are a further influencing factor. In countries and localities where traditional and frequently labour-intensive skills are still practised to their full, the status of employment in areas such as the hotel kitchen is likely to remain higher than it is in environments where the process of deskilling has reduced the technical and creative demands and, as a consequence, the status of such work;
- status is also influenced by the extent to which regulation is imposed upon access to work in the industry. Switzerland, for example, requires specific qualifications in order to work in certain management and skills areas in the hotel industry and this contributes to the status of such work;
- traditions and culture are also important status determinants. France, for example, accords superstar status to leading chefs and represents a society where some traditional areas of employment in the industry have high status in the popular perception and in the level of rewards they can attract.

These status markers in many respects accord with Riley's differentiation of strong and weak internal labour markets which we introduced in Chapter 4. High status, therefore, can in part be associated with the relative strength of the internal labour market, whereas any measures or trends which weaken the internal labour market will in turn serve to reduce the status of the work area in question.

## PROFESSIONALISM AND THE MANAGERIAL FUNCTION

The notion of professionalism in the European hospitality and tourism industry is one that is closely allied to that of status. The term 'professional' in most uses implies a certain status association, although in some uses such as in sport it may also have somewhat pejorative connotations. In this regard, then, the extent to which work is deemed 'professional' will be linked to Riley's labour market characteristics – a strong internal labour market such as that found in medicine is likely to have definite associations with high professional status. This in turn has links to issues of remuneration, conditions of employment and the nature of the work carried out and also to the ability of the industry to compete for scarce skills at a managerial and senior technical level. In the United States, the National Labor Relations Board define a 'professional employee' as:

> any employee engaged in work (i) predominantly intellectual and varied in character as opposed to routine mental, manual, mechanical or physical work; (ii) involving the consistent exercise of discretion and judgement in its performance; (iii) of such character that the output produced or the result accomplished cannot be standardized in relation to a given period of time; (iv) requiring knowledge of an advanced type in a field of science or learning customarily acquired by a long course of specialized intellectual instruction and study in an institution of higher learning or a hospital, as distinguished from a general academic education or from an apprenticeship or from training in their performance of routine mental, manual, or physical processes.
>
> (Keiser and Swinton, 1988, p. 24)

In the context of the tourism and hospitality industry in Europe, professionalism goes further than the issue of status. At the level of management and skilled technicians, it includes consideration of a wide range of associated matters such as aspirations and career progression, training and development opportunities, adherence to collective norms and codes of behaviour, and role and attitudes in relation to front-line and operative staff. Thus professionalism can be taken to include personal attributes, those of the grouping of employees in the collective sense, and behaviourial factors in the way that managers in particular relate to others. In what appears to be one of the few detailed studies of professionalism across the tourism and hospitality industry, Sheldon (1989) identifies twelve dimensions of professionalism based on a review of published literature sources, primarily American in origin. These dimensions focus mainly on the personal and collective aspects of professionalism although behaviourial considerations may be implicit in them. In the order of importance, based on literature references, they are:

- long training/education (university, college);
- code of ethics (for those within the professional grouping);
- organized (through a professional association such as HCIMA or the Tourism Society in the United Kingdom);
- complex occupation (the level and range of tasks required);
- altruistic service (customer service needs focused);
- body or corpus of knowledge (such as that prepared by the HCIMA for hotel management);
- people orientated (in terms of job descriptions and other overt manifestations of people as opposed to product orientation);
- licensed (requirement to obtain a specific licence to practise);
- high prestige (the most obvious link to status);
- competence tested (formal skills and competence testing as a requirement for practice or for promotion);
- self-employed;
- high income (relative to other professional occupations) (Sheldon (1989), p. 494).

These dimensions reflect attributes which are close to Riley's strong labour internal market features and, as a consequence, absence of professionalism can be linked to a weak internal labour market. On this basis, professionalism could be added as a further dimension to the labour market model. Sheldon applied these dimensions, through a survey of the tourism and hospitality industry in Hawaii, to five discrete subsectors. The outcomes of this study are shown in Table 6.2.

Sheldon concludes that in Hawaii the accommodation and transportation sectors are perceived to be the most professional and the food service sector the least professional. Such conclusions may well not be directly transferable to the European context where factors such as the size of many businesses in the accommodation/hotel sector and established traditions in food production and service may result in somewhat different outcomes as well as some variation between different European countries. It is unlikely that some aspects of professionalism which Sheldon identifies will apply to the same extent in some countries of Europe although others, especially in countries such as France, Germany and Switzerland, may if anything be rather more applicable than in Hawaii. However, Sheldon's dimensions provide a useful framework by which we may consider professionalism in the tourism and hospitality industry.

Sheldon's analysis of professionalism takes a perspective which includes all positions or jobs within the various subsectors. While it may be meaningful to discuss the professional execution of work at the operative, semi-skilled and unskilled levels in the industry, and even at

**Table 6.2** Tourism industry sectors' achievement of professional characteristics

| Characteristics | Accommodation | Food service | Transportation | Attraction/ entertainment | Travel agent/Tour operator |
|---|---|---|---|---|---|
| Long training | + | .. | + | .. | + |
| Code of ethics | + | + | ? | .. | .. |
| Organized | + | + | + | .. | + |
| Complex occupation | ? | ? | ? | ? | ? |
| Altruistic service | + | + | + | + | + |
| Body of knowledge | + | + | + | .. | + |
| People-orientated | + | + | + | + | + |
| Licensed | .. | .. | + | .. | .. |
| High prestige | .. | .. | .. | .. | .. |
| Competence tested | + | .. | + | .. | + |
| Self-employed | .. | + | .. | + | + |
| High income | .. | .. | + | .. | .. |
| Total | 7 | 6 | 8 | 3 | 7 |

+ True for majority of occupations in this sector.
.. Untrue for majority of occupations in this sector.
? Insufficient data available to make a judgement

*Source*: Sheldon (1989), p. 494.

skilled craft level, in reality her criteria are more likely to have application at management and senior technical/master craftsperson level. The professional execution of work at other levels in Europe is not generally associated with the institutional framework for professionalism which features in the twelve dimensions. Thus Sheldon's notion of professionalism has relevance in terms of various management areas within tourism and hospitality as well as with respect to such areas as airline pilots, chefs, sommeliers and museum curators. The formal vestiges of professionalism vary from area to area and by country, and in most cases active commitment to the implications of professionalism is a matter for a minority of those eligible for involvement. The various associations which represent groupings of those employed in the industry are generally speaking limited in impact. In this respect, the attributes and consequences of the weak labour market operate against effective collective, professional identity. A lack of formally recognized professionalism in many subsectors of the industry in turn serves to perpetuate the recruitment difficulties that the industry experiences in competition with opportunities in other professions.

One possible dimension of professionalism which Sheldon does not consider and which appears to have relevance in the context of European tourism and hospitality management relates to the extent to which managers perceive their role overlaping with operational functions and allocate time to their work in reflection of this. This is an aspect of functional flexibility but also has links to traditions in some subsectors of the industry, notably hotels and restaurants, whereby the education, training and early career paths of managers have included considerable exposure to craft and operational work. Wood (1992a) describes this process as a form of 'pre-entry socialization into the occupation of hotel management', which is justified 'in terms of the need for managers in the hospitality industry to possess vital technical skills, particularly in the field of food and beverage management, that allows them the opportunity to control other powerful work groups such as chefs' (p. 80).

The traditions of hotel and restaurant management education and training in France, Germany and Switzerland, among other European countries, demonstrate the importance accorded to the development of practical skills. This issue of the place of craft skills within management education, and the counter-argument which is more prevalent in the Netherlands and the United Kingdom, will be addressed more fully in Chapter 8. There is also a tendency for managers to seek solace in the operational aspects of work. In a study of hotel managers in Ireland, Baum (1989b) found that many of the sample placed considerable emphasis on both their visibility and 'mine host' responsibilities and on their ability to pull their weight in areas such as the kitchen, banqueting room or front desk as required. The small business nature of much work in the tourism and hospitality industry in Europe is such that management, in many operations, must be eclectic and multi-functional, and the attraction of the practical is, in part, a reflection of this. In terms of professionalism, the facility for seamless movement between operational and managerial functions reflects weak internal labour market characteristics. The absence of such functional mobility and clear job demarcation between operational and managerial tasks is much more akin to the strong internal labour market.

However, execution of practical skills is not now a priority competence for hotels recruiting newly qualified graduates, at least not among larger establishments. Baum (1991b) shows these priority competencies to be in the area of what might be called 'soft competencies', or generic, transferable skills relating to areas such as guest and employee relations, communications and IT. These findings are significant in the context of Wood's (1993) argument that higher status is given to those with transferable as opposed to specific skills, and status here can be taken to have similar attributes to Sheldon's 'high prestige' dimension. This therefore suggests that there are greater professional tendencies among managers in larger businesses and this generalization would appear to be applicable across the whole tourism and hospitality industry.

A number of key trends may contribute to the undermining of what professionalism does exist in the tourism and hospitality industry of the

future. In Chapter 4, we considered the impact of deskilling and standardization upon work in the tourism and hospitality industry. These
are closely allied trends which are likely to contribute to further weakening of the internal labour market at skilled technical and management levels in the industry which in turn will weaken the professional
attributes of such work. Both processes reduce the educational and
training requirements for such work in the sector and allow companies
to recruit from a much wider labour market base in order to fill
vacancies. Branding, as a response to standardization, can reduce the
range and level of decision-making involved in work at a technical and
management level. Although many hotel companies, for example, have
delegated aspects of greater authority to the unit and departmental
level, branding and standardization act to define and 'ring fence' this
authority to an increasing extent. These trends are tourism and hospitality specific. In a wider sense, there are clear moves towards a weakening of a number of professional labour markets. For example,
exclusivity limitations on the execution of a number of legal functions
in the United Kingdom have been removed so as to allow para-legal
executives to undertake such work. Similar trends are evident in medicine, education and other professional areas. The deprofessionalization
of work, in the wider context, can only weaken aspirations for professional status among groups in the tourism and hospitality
industry.

## THE IMAGE OF WORK IN THE TOURISM AND HOSPITALITY INDUSTRY

The image of work in the tourism and hospitality industry is of
considerable importance to the management of human resources
within the sector in its attempts to recruit new entrants at all levels and
to retain those that are already employed. Image and reality are not,
necessarily, the same thing and while the real situation may reflect
diversity in working conditions, remuneration, status and professionalism, the image that is projected of employment in the industry may
well be based upon the lowest denominator, the worst-case employer
or area of work.

It is clear that the image of work in tourism and hospitality within
subsectors, between sectors and in different countries is varied. As we
have seen in the discussion above about the relative status of work in
the tourism and hospitality industry, the popular image in the United
Kingdom places travel and airline companies at the top in terms of
their desirability for employment and fast food and coach/bus transportation as the least attractive. In relation to all of the identified
subsectors, however, those with experience of working in the area were
significantly more positive about such employment than those without
such first-hand knowledge (Baum, 1991a). The gap in attitude is widest

in the case of hotel and restaurant management and work in the historic/heritage and attractions subsector. In the case of the former, hotel and restaurant management, the gap is likely to be linked to a merging of work at operational and management level in the minds of respondents. This study points to possible disparity between image and reality but also emphasizes the value of exposure to the industry as a key means to overcome negative perceptions that may be held about the sector. At the same, it is that very exposure to which students on industrial placement are subjected that may be a contributory cause of the high level of drop-out from the industry after graduation.

The image of work in the European tourism and hospitality industry is generated by the reality of the pay, conditions, social structure, status and level of professionalism within each sector and within the industry as a whole. The relative position of tourism and hospitality measured against these criteria, along with other labour intensive service sectors, is generally unfavourable in Western Europe and this results in a broadly poor image. Prior to political and economic change, tourism and hospitality was also viewed unfavourably in comparison to productive industries in Eastern Europe. However, change has undermined the primacy of what are now seen as inefficient and uncompetitive manufacturing and agricultural sectors and service work has risen in status. It is also one of the few areas of growth and new employment in countries such as Russia and Hungary and work is now seen in rather different terms. Thus new hotels and restaurants in these countries frequently attract applications from job seekers with a wide variety of professional and technical qualifications and experience (Vikhanski and Puffer, 1993).

In addition to countering the effect of contemporary image problems relating to the range of factors addressed in this chapter, the tourism and hospitality industry is also faced with perceptions derived from the historical relationship between the guest and the server. We have already considered this in relation to the origin and nature of work in the tourism and hospitality industry in Chapters 3 and 4. At the root of this problem in contemporary society is the relationship between service and servility. Service in the United Kingdom and some other Western European countries originated in a relationship that was based on servility on the part of those serving to their social, economic and political 'betters'. By contrast, in France, for example, the notion of service has a more honourable tradition, perhaps reflecting the earlier effects of the idea that all people are equal in their social and political rights. The democratization of travel and the utilization of tourism and hospitality products and services has all but eliminated the outward manifestations of this servility relationship in western, developed countries. Eastern Europe is, in some ways, experiencing a re-emergence of a large gap between the status and economic resources of foreign guests, on the one hand, and those serving them on the other. The shadow of servility remains at the root of the image that work, especially in the hotel and restaurant sector, has in the minds of potential employees and their families in many European countries. This acts as a barrier to many as they evaluate, in particular, longer-term career and education/training options. Interestingly it is reasonable to speculate that those work areas which are of relatively recent origin in tourism and hospitality, notably airlines, tour operators and travel agents, do not face the same problems with image, and, consequently, in their recruitment and staff turnover levels, in part because their large-scale origins postdate the era of servility.

From a human resource perspective, the public perception or image that the tourism and hospitality industry projects is critical. It can be a problem which, at times of labour shortage, leads to the industry competing, unsuccessfully, with other industries for scarce labour resources. It also means that many university and college entrants and graduates look to tourism and hospitality as a low priority resort, to be considered if other, better image areas of work fail to deliver desired opportunities. Finally, it can also mean that those studying for and working in the industry look elsewhere and use their transferable skills in other service and related industries. Tourism and hospitality's weak internal labour market, while beneficial to employers in many respects, can act to the detriment of the industry in relation to these issues. There is considerable awareness of these problems but few realistic and collective attempts to act in order to enhance poor image perceptions. As long as there are employers, even a small minority, who are happy to perpetuate the reality of poor pay, conditions and related problems, the poor image will remain.

## THE FUTURE OF WORK IN THE TOURISM AND HOSPITALITY INDUSTRY

The title of this chapter poses the question as to whether, in areas of pay, conditions, social composition, status, professionalism and overall image, the tourism and hospitality industry in Europe represents the 'dark side' of the employment coin. It is clear from the preceding discussion that the evidence is mixed and any conclusions cannot be other than tentative. In some geographical and subsector areas, tourism and hospitality provides an attractive, high-status working environment with competitive pay and conditions, which is in high demand in the labour force and benefits from low staff turnover. The image of the industry, consequently, is good. The other side of the coin is one of poor conditions, low pay, high staff turnover, problems in recruiting skills in a number of key areas, a high level of labour drawn from socially disadvantaged groups, poor status and the virtual absence of professionalism. Where this environment is manifest, the industry suffers from a poor image, with all its attendant problems. Both pictures represent a widespread reality and this leaves the case 'not proven' either way.

In Chapter 5, we considered the delivery of quality service in the tourism and hospitality industry and the contribution that effective human resource management can make towards its attainment. The idea of empowerment, which is central to this argument, demands employees who are committed in the long term to the objectives of the organization through effective internal marketing and are able to deliver quality service to customers without close and constant supervision and control. This environment is only achievable in a climate where the front-line workforce is highly motivated and are supported by technical and management staff who recognize their enabling role in the provision of good service. This environment can only be achieved when both the reality and the perception of pay, conditions and related factors are consistent with the expectations that the organization has of its employees. In short, it is unrealistic to expect quality service from employees who perceive their pay, conditions and status to be poor. Addressing this issue is a multifaceted challenge, one where adoption of the sustainable model of human resource management outlined in Chapter 1 can make a significant contribution.

The sustainability route is one scenario for the future. It is an optimistic, perhaps somewhat idealistic route and one that will certainly not be followed by all tourism and hospitality organizations in Europe. It is a route that Ritz Carlton and Marriott in the hotel sector have followed with considerable success. The Hong Kong Marriott's insistence on operating a five-day working week, in the face of stern opposition from other hotel companies and the Hong Kong Hotels Association, is one example of this approach. However, there are considerable pressures, notably short-term financial performance, which may persuade companies to use alternative, less sustainable approaches while, at the same time, paying public lip-service to the aspiration of quality service and employee empowerment.

As we have discussed previously, perhaps the most compelling pressure against empowerment is the movement towards standardization, or McDonaldization to use George Ritzer's rather more broad-ranging term. It is also a process that, while generally providing a perfectly adequate physical working environment, tends to be equated with pressures towards low pay, part-time employment, low status, limited professionalism and an image that depicts the industry as a poor career option. Deskilling and technological substitution are at the heart of McDonaldization and the logic of future developments, in this respect, is one that will see further movements in these directions.

## REVIEW AND DISCUSSION QUESTIONS

1. Consider the dilemma posed at the start of the chapter. As an aspiring manager in the tourism and hospitability industry, how would you respond to it?

2. Why have writers about the history of tourism and hospitality largely ignored work and working conditions?
3. How does use of Riley's labour market model assist in understanding pay and conditions in the tourism and hospitality industry?
4. Based on your own working experience what is your assessment of the level of pay and the nature of conditions in the tourism and hospitality industry?
5. What are the origins of the popular perception of work in the tourism and hospitality industry?
6. What are the opposing positions taken by liberal and social reformist traditions with respect to working conditions in the tourism and hospitality industry?
7. What are the benefits and losses which may result from opting in or out of the EU's Social Chapter?
8. Why has the level of part-time work increased in the tourism and hospitality industry?
9. Why is the level of trade unionism so low in many subsectors of the tourism and hospitality industry?
10. Is the tourism and hospitality industry really a young people's industry?
11. Account for the variations in status suggested for sectors of the tourism and hospitality industry in Table 6.1.
12. Are Sheldon's criteria for professionalism (Table 6.2) applicable to the European tourism and hospitality industry?
13. Is there a resolution to the customization/empowerment–McDonaldization debate? What is likely to be the long-term outcome?

# 7 Managing cultural diversity in the European tourism and hospitality industry

This chapter considers the implications of providing for, on the one hand, demand created as a result of the multinational and varied cultural origins of Europe's tourism and hospitality marketplace and, on the other, managing a workforce that needs the skills and knowledge to respond to this customer diversity and, in itself, reflects heterogeneity in its composition and origins. In Chapter 6, we considered the social structure of the tourism and hospitality workforce and noted the over-representation of ethnic minorities, immigrant and migrant workers among the least skilled groups in the industry. In this chapter, we will consider the implications of managing a multicultural environment, guest and employee, from a broad and wide-ranging perspective.

In addressing the twin dimensions of multiculturalism (markets and workforce) in the tourism and hospitality industry in Europe, it is important to consider them as dependent variables. They do not operate in isolation of each other. It is the immediacy and directness of interaction between multicultural markets and a multicultural workforce which places the tourism and hospitality industry in a relatively unique position and presents managers with challenges that they might not face in other industries. We can present these two dimensions in the form of a matrix and then plot businesses with high or low levels of multiculturalism on either or both axes. High and low should not be taken to imply 100% or 0% – the model is not based on precise quantification. Figure 7.1 represents this two-dimensional model, and provides examples of business contexts plotted against it.

It is possible to extend this model so that it operates at a three-dimensional level by incorporating the extent of cultural distance between the parent corporation and the local community in which the hotel, travel agent or restaurant is located. The model and its three-dimensional extension provide the basis for assessing the extent to which management needs to incorporate the implications of multiculturalism into its guest and human resource management policies, practices and systems. Before this is undertaken, it is important to

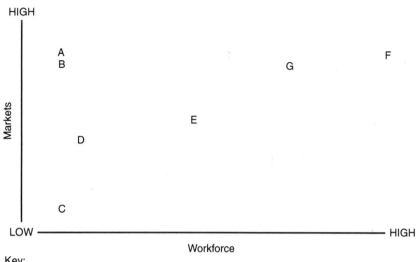

Key:
A – European 'flag carrier' international airline (Olympic, Tarom).
B – Cultural show for tourists – Greece, Ireland or Spain.
C – Blackpool guesthouse.
D – German internal airline (Deutsche BA).
E – EuroDisney.
F – Large four-star hotel in London.
G – Middle Eastern Airline (Gulf, Emirates, Royal Jordanian).

**Figure 7.1** Multiculturalism in the tourism and hospitality industry.

understand the origins and nature of cultural, national and ethnic diversity in the markets and workforce of the European tourism and hospitality industry.

## A MULTICULTURAL MARKETPLACE

It is almost axiomatic to say that the international tourism and hospitality industry caters for diversity in its clientele, whether such variation reflects different circumstances, interests, economic resources or cultural and national traditions. Such variety is reflected in differing tourism products, whether hotels which range from the budget to the luxury or in the range of sporting, leisure and entertainment options that are available to visitors in most tourist destinations. Traditional product development and marketing strategies sought to cater for the variety in visitor interests by gradually extending the menu of facilities provided and thus aiming to cater for as wide a range of potential visitors as possible. However, such change and responsiveness was, largely, slow and reactive rather than proactive, avoiding change in so far as was possible and employing the Fordian axiom that, for example, the guesthouse visitor can have dinner at any time, provided that it is between 6.00 and 6.30. Thus, evolving English resorts such as Blackpool, Bournemouth and Brighton developed facilities and attractions from the mid-nineteenth century onwards in response to the demands of a widening market base and without any specific and targeted market focus to direct such growth.

In common with more general marketing trends which have increasingly recognized the segmented nature of demand for most products and services, this 'catch-all' approach has been replaced by much more focused niche development and marketing, a strategy which recognizes that an attraction, hotel or destination cannot cater for all types of potential visitors and is likely to be much more effective if it targets well-defined groups and designs facilities to meet their identified needs. The outcome of niche development and marketing has been a considerable sharpening of the focus and image projected by individual businesses within the European tourism and hospitality industry, as well as by resorts, regions and, to some extent, countries as well.

The consequences of this change include increasingly sophisticated packaging of products and attendant marketing on the basis of demographic or lifestyle factors – vacations for the 18–30s or over 55s (Saga Holidays), resorts for these specific markets (Club Med), golf, tennis and other sporting hotels, couples-only resorts, family-focused facilities, eco-tourism products, bridge or educational cruises, and a wide range of other examples. In the transportation arena, some airlines have targeted their product and pricing at specific markets in contrast to the more widespread approach in international aviation which seeks to cater for a wide range of market needs within the one schedule and system. Taking a lead from carriers in the United States, Ryanair, the low-cost Irish airline, competes on Ireland–UK routes by offering a cheap, no-frills service, primarily designed for the leisure traveller. The pricing structure is simple, on-board service is minimal, timings frequently avoid peak periods when airport slots are more expensive and airports are used where ground costs are lower than some of the main gateways – for example, Prestwick near Glasgow as well as Gatwick, Luton and Stansted in the London region. On a larger scale, while the market focus of a region is largely dictated by the range of natural, historic and related attractions available (mountains, sea, monuments), specific destinations have developed and promoted reputations that reflect the management of the main focus of their products – for example, Ibiza as a location for young visitors seeking extensive nightlife options.

Such segmentation is relatively self-evident and can be identified through a wide range of examples within the European tourism and hospitality industry. Segmentation and product service design in order to cater for cultural and national differentiation is also a strategy that is employed but is not so clearly identifiable as part of conscious marketing or product development approaches. The relative homogeneity of Western European markets in tourism and hospitality terms means that many companies and destinations have played down the dimension of national diversity and concentrated on demographic and lifestyle considerations. There are obvious exceptions. Specialist coach tour packaging for American, Canadian and Australian visitors is well established in most European countries and has developed in response to more recent demand from Japan and other Asian countries. Some beach resorts in Spain and Greece have developed facilities in response to main market demands and the consequence is a range of restaurants, bars and shops which cater, primarily, for British, German or Scandinavian visitors. This process may be self-perpetuating as the presence of such facilities acts as a magnet to increase visitor numbers from the specific national markets. Newly found freedom of travel rights for citizens of Eastern European countries have prompted some resorts in Spain, for example, to develop specific, budget products in order to cater for this potentially significant market. Likewise, conspicuous among the diverse range of goods available to travellers at Shannon Duty Free in Ireland is a specialist Lada accessories shop, reflecting the importance to the airport of Aeroflot and other Eastern European transit traffic.

Probably the most sophisticated packaging of tourism and hospitality products and services by European countries and individual businesses has been in response to cultural and national expectations and demands from the Middle Eastern and Far-East Asian markets. Hotels in many major tourist centres have responded to the specific culinary and accommodation needs of groups and individuals from these parts of the world through the development of new restaurant facilities or the provision of dedicated menu items. Some London hotels respond to the large-scale exodus of wealthy families from the Middle East during July and August by reorganizing their room service and related facilities in response to a family market that makes relatively little use of public restaurants. Published information is widely provided on a multilingual basis. Likewise, airlines make specific provision for the requirements of these markets, through menu options, alternative movies or soundtracks and multi-lingual information and publication services. For example, when American Airlines extended their international route system, Robert Crandell, the company's CEO, recognized the need to adjust services in order to cater for national preferences, because:

> German passengers, for example, are very particular about the use of formal titles like 'Herr Doktor' when addressed by attendants. Japanese fliers abhor being touched. On flights carrying a lot of Latin American passengers, the main course is likely to be beef, and the wines had better be French.
>
> (Labich, 1990, pp. 42, 44)

Product and marketing response is important in catering for this diversity but, probably, of even greater significance is the ability of the company's personnel to respond flexibly and with understanding to the diversity of needs displayed by customers from different cultures and nations. This provides a major human resource and, in particular, training challenge for tourism and hospitality companies seeking to operate effectively in the multicultural marketplace. The requirements go beyond language skills, although of course these are important, to a close understanding of the culture and expectations of different groups and an ability to empathize with the perspective of guests, whatever their cultural origins.

Responses to this particular challenge are diverse among European tourism and hospitality companies. At a minimum level, limited language competencies are sought among as many customer contact or front-line staff as is possible in order to cater for key market requirements, generally in major European languages such as English, French, German and Italian. In a relatively monolingual country such as England, even achieving a limited level of provision presents considerable problems to tourism and hospitality companies and, in addition to recruiting staff with language capabilities locally, there is an increasing tendency, among major firms such as British Airways to seek multilingual staff from other European countries. Similar practices are adopted with respect to other, major overseas markets and the presence of, for example, Japanese staff among cabin crew of airlines serving the Far East as well as in the hotels of major cities in Europe exemplifies this. In addition to providing language proficiency, this approach is designed to ensure the presence of at least a minimum core staff who have understanding for and empathy with the expectations and demands of customers from these countries. As well as providing services directly to the guests, such expatriate staff have an important role to play in the training of their colleagues to enable them to provide a better and more customized service in response to particular cultural demand.

This latter point, the training of a wider staff to understand and respond to the needs of particular cultural, ethnic and national visitor groups, is a very important human resource requirement in a Europe in which the guest profile is becoming increasingly diverse. While domestic and other European markets remain very important to most countries and regions, new growth is, largely, coming from emerging markets in Asia and elsewhere. Outbound international travel from countries such as Korea, Malaysia, Singapore and Taiwan continues to grow at rates that far outstrip growth from other markets and, although much of such travel is inter-regional, the concentric expansion of the horizons of travel, which were discussed in Chapter 3, means that an increasing proportion of travellers from these markets will include Europe on their itinerary. The demand for travel from these originating markets as well as from China and other countries in the region means that this trend is likely to remain a major influence on the European tourism and hospitality industry for the foreseeable future. While 'honeypot' destinations such as London, Paris and Venice will remain the prime objectives for many of these new visitors, considerable dispersement is also likely, with the result that the impact of the new markets may well be felt in the periphery tourist regions of Europe as well as at the core. As a result, there is a strong case to be made that all tourism and hospitality staff in Europe would benefit from greater understanding of the practical implications of cultural and ethnic diversity in the context of the need for greater guest sensitivity in general. Chapter 5 considered the role of human resources in the provision of enhanced service quality, especially through empowerment. A key to this process is a keen understanding of guest demands. Without insight and understanding of the guest's background and culture, empowerment and enhanced service quality become somewhat elusive objectives.

Expectations on the basis of cultural variation among European guests are not perceived to show the same level of diversity that is exhibited between European and Asian visitors. Therefore, once language considerations have been addressed, few tourism and hospitality businesses address this matter in product terms or undertake any dedicated staff development or familiarization in response to the needs of specific European markets. There is a case to be made that such implicit assumptions about homogeneity in culture and expectations within Europe, as well as between Europe and North America and Australia/New Zealand, are misguided. In product terms, Accor appear to have assumed that French and British market expectations were similar when introducing the Formulae 1 budget hotel product into the UK. As a result, the standard arrangement of shared bathroom facilities between four rooms was included on the basis that low price would create demand. However, this was quickly revoked when customer non-acceptance and dissatisfaction became evident. Likewise, Disney made broad assumptions about common eating patterns in the United States and Europe and designed their food and beverage facilities at EuroDisney, near Paris, on the basis of such assumptions. In the United States' Disney properties, consumption of food and drinks is continuous with no dramatic peak at any one particular point in the day. Thus excessive queuing is avoided because consumption is staggered. European eating habits were found, in practice, to be very different, with a strong midday concentration and a demand for 'proper' meals as opposed to snacks. As a result, in the initial period after opening, guests at EuroDisney faced extensive peak-period waiting at food and beverage outlets and provision had to be rapidly reviewed. This change, in turn, had significant implications for the utilization and rostering of human resources.

This far, we have illustrated some of the issues that are raised in relation to the tourism and hospitality industry's multicultural marketplace. In many ways, this ground is not entirely new, although the management and human resource implications of this dimension of multiculturalism are not widely addressed in personnel and human resource management texts. Similar cultural 'gaps' faced the tourism and hospitality industry in Europe in the post-1945 period, as the number of visitors from, in particular, the United States grew very rapidly. Many of these visitors had personal or historical motivations to visit some of the more remote parts of Europe, such as Connemara in Ireland, Calabria in Italy or the Scottish islands, as well as the main 'honeypot' destinations. The provision of tourism and hospitality services in these areas was considerably at variance with experience engendered at home and even with expectations modified in response to the popular, media-induced image of the regions in question. Visitor expectations of Ireland, for example, have been greatly influenced by images presented in films such as *The Quiet Man* and, more recently, *Ryan's Daughter* and the reality is frequently at variance with such images. At the same time, those providing the services had little basis from which to comprehend the needs and expectations, as well as the social and cultural norms, of their guests from overseas. Problems of this kind have gradually reduced over time, as familiarity between the two cultures has grown. Visitors grew more tolerant of European service and facilities but, at the same time, Europeans travelled more extensively themselves and, even in relatively peripheral regions, developed facilities and levels of service to international standards. The globalization of the tourism and hospitality product has made a significant contribution to this process but the change has not been without some cost to the authenticity and uniqueness of local communities and cultures in many parts of Europe.

Where the situation today differs from that in the 1950s and 1960s is in the scale and speed of change. Tourism and hospitality businesses today cannot afford the twenty-five to thirty year 'honeymoon' or 'incubation' period which has closed the gap, in part, between European and North American perceptions. Market growth and change is much more rapid and many of the new markets have no intrinsic loyalty to one destination in the way traditionally exhibited by 'returning Yanks'. If the expectations and needs of the traveller' of the future, especially from the affluent Asia-Pacific Rim, are not met, they will exercise their portable loyalty and go elsewhere, maybe in Europe but probably to other parts of the world. On this basis, effective management in the multicultural marketplace becomes an imperative in a wider sense, not least of which are the human resource considerations. We will return to this theme at a later point in this chapter.

## A MULTICULTURAL WORKFORCE

Cultural, national and ethnic diversity has long been a feature of the workforce in the European tourism and hospitality industry. As early as the thirteenth century, some of the first commercial hotels in Europe, licensed by the city of Florence in Italy, were run by expatriate Germans. In the eighteenth century, travelling participants in the Grand Tour of Europe took their own servants with them and, as this tour became popularized and placed on a more commercial footing, those catering for the needs of travellers in France, Germany and Italy frequently included staff drawn from the country of origin of the visitors, particularly Britain. In relation to the nineteenth century, Berry (1992) considers the growth and nature of British tourism to the French and Italian Rivieras and notes the significant number of expatiate-run businesses and services which emerged in order to cater for the visitors.

As we have previously discussed in some detail (in Chapters 4 and 6), the nature of work in many areas of the tourism and hospitality industry is low skilled and low status and frequently on the margins of the formal and regularized labour market, and thus includes work which is not in great demand among local populations in more affluent countries. These attributes allowed George Orwell, an Englishman, to work as a casual in the Parisian hotel industry of the early 1930s. Likewise, these conditions, combined with seasonality and related demand factors, also facilitated considerable labour mobility within the tourism and hospitality industry of Europe prior to the institution of free labour movement within the European Union.

General labour mobility within the European Union has certain features which are broadly reproduced within the tourism and hospitality industry. The Commission of the European Communities (1990) point to a general movement from the external parts of the Union to the centre and suggest a typology of intra-union labour exchanges, from which three particular migratory situations can be identified. These are:

- member states which are preponderantly countries of departure: Ireland, Italy, Portugal, Greece, Spain;
- member states which are preponderantly countries of reception (host countries): Luxembourg, France, Germany, Belgium, United Kingdom; and
- member states with balanced exchanges: The Netherlands, Denmark.

Within the host country group, France has the highest number of non-national EU citizens resident (at 2.6% of the total population, of whom 48% are Portuguese, 21% are Italian and 20% are Spanish); Germany is next (2.4% of total population of whom 40% are Italian, 21% are Greek, 11% are Spanish and 8% are Dutch); and the United Kingdom is third (1.4% of total population of whom 72% are Irish) (CEC, 1990).

Baum (1993b) parallels this analysis and considers the specific mobility of tourism and hospitality labour in terms of 'core' and 'peripheral' regions of Western Europe. The 'core' regions include the industrial and economic heart of the region, notably Germany, the Netherlands, Belgium, northern France, the south-east of England, Switzerland, Austria and northern Italy, where shortages, especially in low skills areas, creates a 'vacuum' which draws in labour from the periphery, traditionally the countries of southern Europe (Greece, southern France, southern Italy, Spain, Portugal, Cyprus) as well as the western margins of Europe (Brittany, northern and western regions of England, Ireland, Scotland and Wales). These 'peripheral' areas have tourism and hospitality industries with somewhat different structural characteristics to those at the 'core' notably more pronounced seasonality, small businesses and lower impact of major multinational investment in the industry. As a consequence, traditional labour movements have seen tourism and hospitality labour move from the 'periphery' to the 'core' in search of work, at the same time creating a mixed, multicultural workforce not found in other industrial sectors. Examples of 'periphery' to 'core' movements which have had considerable impact on the character of the tourism and hospitality industries in some areas include Irish immigration to London and the movement of Italian, Spanish and Portuguese workers to London as well as major cities in France and Germany. Some of this movement has been of a seasonal nature but the large number of Italian-owned hospitality enterprises (restaurants, fish and chip shops and ice-cream manufacturers and distributors) in Britain, for example, also points to the greater permanence of some migration. The majority of European immigrant workers in the industry have worked at the lowest skills levels and largely continue to do so. At the same time, it is possible to point to Lord Forte as, perhaps, the most visible success story of an Italian immigrant in the British tourism and hospitality industry. The irony of the 'periphery' to 'core' movement of labour within Western Europe is that it is in precisely the reverse direction to that of the main tourism flows, from north to south and to the western fringes. Interestingly, in some cases the development of tourism in 'periphery' regions has contributed to reducing the overall level of emigration. Valenzuela (1991) notes that 'partly due to tourism, the 1960s flow of emigrants to Europe has been stemmed' (p. 41).

Overall south–north labour migration within Europe in its recent main phase was considerable. The Commission of the European Communities (CEC) estimate that, between 1955 and 1974, 730 000 Greeks, 3.8 million Italians, 1 million Yugoslavs, 1 million Portuguese and approximately 2 million Spaniards emigrated to the northwest of Europe in order to find employment, mainly in service sectors and manufacturing industries (CEC, 1991b, pp. 20–1).

Trans-European labour mobility within the tourism and hospitality industry preceded and in some cases paralleled the large-scale immigration of, generally, low skilled labour from the colonies and former colonies of a number of European countries. Key migration routes have been to Belgium from central Africa; to Britain from, in particular, the Caribbean, Hong Kong and South Asia (India, Pakistan and, latterly, Bangladesh); to France from the Caribbean, west and north Africa and Indo-China; to the Netherlands from Caribbean colonies (Aruba, Bonaire, Curaçao, St Eustacius, St Martaan and Saba), Indonesia and Surinam; and to Portugal from Angola, Macao, Mozambique and Goa. In the case of Portugal and some other countries such as France, the process of decolonization led to a return of a substantial number of settlers, frequently with little in common with the Europe that their ancestors left. Thus in a very real sense they can be described as immigrants, although their ethnic origins may be common to the majority of the receiving population. Lewis and Williams (1991) note the tendency for migrants returning to Portugal to invest their savings in tourism and hospitality-related businesses. Other European countries without the colonial tradition looked to other parts of the world in order to meet labour shortages, notably as in the case of Germany, which attracted a large number of migrant workers or *Gastarbeiter* from Turkey and the former Yugoslavia, who work on a 'permanent temporary' basis with no citizenship rights. In addition to these 'main' sources of migrant workers, political and economic refugee status has permitted a significant number of immigrants from a wide variety of countries to settle in Scandinavian countries and elsewhere in Western Europe. Since 1989, the flow of migrants from Eastern Europe to the West has also been very significant, both on a legal and illegal basis. Prior to 1989, the then German Democratic Republic faced labour shortages in a number of industrial sectors and, as a result, met these shortages by accepting migrant workers from elsewhere in Eastern Europe as well as from Vietnam.

The reasons for such large-scale migration within and to Europe can be summarized into 'push' and 'pull' factors. 'Push' factors reflect economic, social and political conditions in the home country or region which 'push' people to leave. In many cases, these were countries of the developing world or Eastern Europe undergoing slow reconstruction, offering limited employment or economic opportunities. Thus the chance to work at whatever level in industrialized Western Europe was seen to be much more attractive than remaining at home. This remains a major factor, especially in the continuing legal and illegal movement of people from Eastern to Western Europe. 'Pull' factors refer to conditions in the receiving country, frequently rapid growth, with a consequent shortage of relatively cheap, generally unskilled labour in certain sectors of the economy. Britain in the 1950s faced this growth situation and turned to the New Commonwealth countries of the Caribbean and south Asia in order to fill employment vacancies in transport, the Health Service as well the hospitality sector, especially in non-commercial areas. Knight (1971, in Wood, 1992a) found that of all foreign (and he does not distinguish between migrant and immigrant status) workers employed in catering, some three-quarters entered the industry as their first job in Britain and more than one quarter had catering experience prior to arriving in the country. Wood concludes that

> Whatever the relative position of overseas workers in the British catering industry *vis-à-vis* their countries of origin, the majority come to occupy positions in the industry that are among the worst paid.
> (Wood, 1992a, p. 34)

The consequence of the various levels of migration between and to European countries has been the creation of multicultural and multi-ethnic societies, especially in larger urban, industrialized centres. This reality is not accepted by all political persuasions and right-wing racist reaction has been strong in a number of European countries in attempts to undermine the position of ethnic minority groups within the wider community. Estimates of the total number of non-nationals living within member states of the European Union are subject to considerable unreliability because of the considerable level of illegal residence in some countries. Although the 'official' number of foreigners living in Italy was 541 000 in 1987, other estimates put this figure at anything between 750 000 and 1.65 million and growing (CEC, 1991b, p. 14). A similar issue of illegal immigration can be found in other southern European states, notably Spain, Greece and Portugal, primarily from other Mediterranean countries but increasingly from further afield as well. Within these four countries, it is estimated that approximately two-thirds of an estimated 1.85 million foreigners are irregular (CEC, 1991b, p. 37). The total numbers of documented non-nationals living in European Union countries is presented in Table 7.1.

Such figures give a sense but little more of the extent of cultural, national and ethnic mix in Europe today. Even with the assistance of figures relating to non-national presence in the population, it is almost impossible to put an accurate figure on the level of cultural mix within any one country, largely because definitions of ethnic groupings are somewhat restrictive and information collected is subject to considerable error. Non-nationals data, for example, give no indication of the ethnic or cultural mix of the national population. In Switzerland, for example, it is estimated that approximately 20% of positions in the

**Table 7.1** Estimate of the number of non-nationals who are documented or regularly residing in EU member states, 1985–87

| Country | | Population of non-nationals | % of total population | Nationals of EEC countries | Percentage of EEC nationals |
|---|---|---|---|---|---|
| Belgium | 1987 | 898 000 | 9.0 | 518 000 | 57.7 |
| Denmark | 1985 | 108 000 | 2.3 | 25 000 | 23.1 |
| France | 1985 | 3 680 000 | 6.8 | 1 578 000 | 42.9 |
| Germany Fed. Rep. | 1987 | 4 630 000 | 7.6 | 1 380 000 | 29.8 |
| Greece | 1985 | 87 000 | 0.8 | 27 000 | 31.0 |
| Ireland | 1985 | 88 000 | 2.5 | 67 000 | 76.1 |
| Italy | 1987 | 541 000 | 0.9 | 150 000 | 27.7 |
| Luxembourg | 1985 | 96 000 | 26.3 | 92 700 | 96.6 |
| Netherlands | 1985 | 559 000 | 3.9 | 173 000 | 30.9 |
| Portugal | 1985 | 80 000 | 0.7 | 21 000 | 26.3 |
| Spain | 1987 | 335 000 | 0.6 | 195 000 | 58.2 |
| United Kingdom | 1985 | 1 700 000 | 3.8 | 729 000 | 42.9 |
| | | 12 802 000 | | 4 955 700 | 38.7 |

*Source*: Migrations Sociètè, in CEC (1991b), p. 29a.

total workforce are held by non-Swiss nationals, but because of severe restrictions to the taking out of Swiss citizenship, this figure incorporates many long-time residents of a wide variety of ethnic, national and cultural origins. In the tourism and hospitality industry, Gilg (1991) notes that:

> Foreign workers account for one worker in three in the hotel and restaurant sectors. This is largely because few Swiss want to work in jobs which are seen as poorly paid and offering poor career status, and also because Switzerland has a very low unemployment rate.
>
> (Gilg, 1991, p. 141)

Gilg also points to consistent increases in the number of foreign workers employed in the industry in Switzerland, especially among those holding permanent jobs. The impact of migrant workers, however, must also be taken to include a substantial number of students, in work as part of their training programmes.

In Britain, the Commission for Racial Equality (1991) quote figures which suggest that approximately 4% of economically active persons of working age are from ethnic minority groups. CRE figures also suggest that there is considerable geographical variation in the distribution of the non-white population in Britain. Using a different criterion (a good example of the need for extreme caution in dealing with ethnic and cultural diversity statistics), that of head of household born in the New Commonwealth and Pakistan, CRE note figures of 21.7% for Leicester, 21% for Slough, 19.4% for Inner London, 15.2% for Birmingham, 11.2% for Bradford, and, within other urban centres, 1.6% for Edinburgh and 2.1% for Glasgow. The implication is that the presence of ethnic minorities in rural and 'peripheral' regions of the United Kingdom is very limited. With respect to the hotel industry, the CRE study suggested considerable geographical variation in the proportions of workers employed from ethnic minority groups but not with exactly the same distribution as that suggested across households. Table 7.2 reproduces the regional distribution of hotel employees by sex and ethnic origin from the CRE study.

Although limited survey data of this kind must be treated with considerable caution and the data in Table 7.2 is not directly comparable with that referred to earlier, the disparity in ethnic minority employment in the hotel industry in London (where we can see considerable over-representation) and Leicester and Bradford (with marked under-representation) is noteworthy. The religious composition of ethnic minority groups in Leicester and Bradford, largely Muslim, may account in part for the variance, but a combination of factors with their origins in the prejudice of the majority population may also in part be responsible.

Accurate figures with respect to the impact of migrant labour in other European countries are difficult to ascertain. There are indicators, however. King (1991) refers to the employment impact of tourism and hospitality in Italy and notes 'illegally hired hotel and restaurant

**Table 7.2** Regional distribution of employees by sex and ethnic origin

| | Ethnic minority | | | | | | White | | | | | |
|---|---|---|---|---|---|---|---|---|---|---|---|---|
| | Male | | Female | | Total | | Male | | Female | | Total | |
| | No. | % | No. | % | No. | % | No. | % | No. | % | No. | % |
| Birmingham | 100 | 7.0 | 161 | 11.0 | 261 | 17.0 | 508 | 33.0 | 756 | 49.0 | 1264 | 83.0 |
| Bradford | 0 | 0 | 0 | 0 | 0 | 0 | 24 | 44.0 | 30 | 56.0 | 54 | 100.0 |
| Bristol | 11 | 2.0 | 9 | 1.0 | 20 | 3.0 | 247 | 41.0 | 339 | 56.0 | 586 | 97.0 |
| Cardiff | 4 | 1.0 | 6 | 1.0 | 10 | 2.0 | 178 | 37.0 | 289 | 61.0 | 467 | 98.0 |
| Edinburgh | 4 | 0.5 | 7 | 1.0 | 11 | 1.0 | 361 | 44.0 | 443 | 54.0 | 804 | 99.0 |
| Glasgow | 0 | 0 | 4 | 0.5 | 4 | 0.5 | 288 | 43.0 | 382 | 56.5 | 670 | 99.5 |
| Heathrow | 233 | 10.0 | 274 | 11.0 | 507 | 21.0 | 820 | 34.0 | 1114 | 45.0 | 1934 | 79.0 |
| Leeds | 8 | 1.0 | 22 | 3.0 | 30 | 4.5 | 260 | 40.0 | 354 | 55.0 | 614 | 95.0 |
| Leicester | 29 | 6.0 | 23 | 5.0 | 52 | 11.0 | 165 | 35.0 | 248 | 54.0 | 413 | 89.0 |
| Liverpool | 10 | 3.0 | 8 | 2.0 | 18 | 5.0 | 143 | 36.0 | 233 | 59.0 | 376 | 95.0 |
| London | 714 | 17.0 | 591 | 14.0 | 1305 | 31.0 | 1528 | 37.0 | 1341 | 32.0 | 2869 | 69.0 |
| Manchester | 20 | 2.5 | 15 | 2.0 | 35 | 4.5 | 356 | 45.5 | 389 | 50.0 | 745 | 95.5 |
| Nottingham | 7 | 3.0 | 5 | 2.0 | 12 | 5.0 | 101 | 44.5 | 114 | 50.0 | 215 | 95.0 |
| Plymouth | 0 | 0 | 1 | 0 | 1 | 0 | 99 | 43.0 | 132 | 57.0 | 231 | 100.0 |
| Sheffield | 4 | 1.0 | 8 | 3.0 | 12 | 4.0 | 125 | 47.0 | 131 | 49.0 | 256 | 96.0 |

*Source*: CRE (1991), p. 11.

workers, many from Third World countries such as Ethiopia and the Philippines (these clandestine immigrants are particularly important in Rome and other big cities)' (p. 137).

A number of other sources note that tourism growth in some regions has not been matched by the creation of employment opportunities for the local population. Williams and Shaw (1991) note cases in the French Alps and the Algarve where tourism development has either confined the local community to lower skills employment or, because of its scale, drawn in additional labour from outside of the locality. While these examples point in all probability to labour mobility that is intra-national, the sociocultural impact of this form of migration to the character and management of the workplace cannot be ignored. The Republic of Cyprus represents a country where rapid tourism and hospitality development and a small indigenous population has led to labour shortages in lower skills areas. Prior to partition, the economic structure of the island was such that the minority Turkish population tended to meet demand for unskilled labour. This source of labour is no longer available and Cyprus now relies on immigrants from the Balkan states, especially Bulgaria, and Russia to meet requirements in the tourism and hospitality industry. This practice, of course, has major human resource management implications in terms of our discussions in Chapter 5 in that tourism and hospitality businesses may well be providing services to customers with a front-line team who speak neither the languages of their guests or their management.

However, most data with respect to the level of immigrant labour in the tourism and hospitality industries of Europe, only go some way towards explaining the extent of cultural, national and ethnic diversity within the workforce. The British figures ignore immigrants from Europe, especially Ireland, within the British workforce and in part neglect the presence of members of ethnic minorities who were born in the United Kingdom as well as those born outside of the New Commonwealth. In terms of the tourism and hospitality industry, the figures also neglect a substantial number of workers who are in the country on a temporary basis, students and others from, for example, Europe, Australia and New Zealand. Byrne (1986) estimates that approximately 115 000 workers in the United Kingdom hospitality industry are migrants and that a substantial number more are members of ethnic minorities indigenous to the population. However, these figures again do not reflect cultural diversity in the workforce in its widest interpretation.

One aspect of tourism and hospitality labour mobility that has not, traditionally, been associated with Europe on a significant scale is that at a management and senior technical level. The use of expatriate labour in tourism and hospitality is an issue of considerable political, social and economic significance in many parts of the developing world. For example, in Jamaica, under the Manley government of the 1970s, the issue became one of considerable political and subsequently economic significance when the government required hotel companies to replace overseas managers with local expertise. This policy created considerable problems because of the lack of lead time and the tourism and hospitality sector suffered considerably as a result. Limited movement of expatriate labour has a long-standing tradition in Europe, with French chefs as well as German and Swiss chefs and managers featuring in the London hotel industry since the early years of this century. The growth of multinational companies has further developed this trend. However, perhaps the most significant trend in this respect at the present time and one that is likely to continue into the next century relates to the development of the tourism and hospitality industry in Eastern European countries. Much development investment and operational control is foreign and this brings – understandable – requirements for the protection of that investment and reputation through the employment of Western European and North American expertise in key positions. This expertise, represented on the ground by significant numbers of managers, chefs and other personnel, is further supported by the importation of management and working cultures which are largely alien to the experience of the local working population. The practice of expatriatism can only be justified and will only be sustainable in the long term provided that local staff are trained and given the opportunity to progress to positions of senior responsibility in the companies in question. The experience of many developing countries is that the development of such practice is by no means universal.

To conclude this section, the European tourism and hospitality industry is by no means unique in operating within a multicultural, multinational and multi-ethnic working environment. Where the industry does differ from the environment found in other sectors is in the extent to which this diversity in the workplace interacts with the high level of variety within the customer base in situations of high contact and association. The potential for situations of misunderstanding but also for enlightenment is considerable. Our next task is to consider the implications of the work of key theorists in understanding cultural diversity.

## THE CONTRIBUTION OF THEORY TO AN UNDERSTANDING OF CULTURAL DIVERSITY

An understanding of cultural diversity is clearly important to managers and employees in the European tourism and hospitality industry in the context of both a workforce and a customer marketplace that is multi-cultural, multi national and multi-ethnic in origin. Understanding of culture and its variation is provided in the main by the work of anthropologists and sociologists and a brief consideration of some of these theoretical sources can be of value to a discussion of the management implications of working within a multicultural environment. Leeds, Kirkbride and Durcan (1994) provide a clear analysis of a number of these theories, all of which contribute different cultural dimensions or aspects to our understanding. This leads Leeds *et al.* to propose a typology of European culture clusters. In our discussion, we will follow and develop their analysis by focusing on three of the main theoretical models that are used in formulating their typology. The other research models are also of relevance but will not be dealt with in any detail here.

Perhaps the best known researcher in this field is Geert Hofstede, who through his work based on factor analysis of data from a major empirical study was able to identify four major dimensions as the key to cultural differences (Hofstede, 1980). Hofstede applied his dimensions to some forty countries worldwide, with a strong concentration in Europe. Interestingly, the only Eastern European country included was the former Yugoslavia. The four dimensions are as follows.

- **Power distance**, defined as 'the extent to which the members of a society accept that power in institutions and organizations is distributed unequally' (Hofstede, 1985, p. 347), is a measure of the interpersonal power or influence between two people, as perceived by the less powerful of the two. Power distance in Hofstede's studies was found to be small in northern European countries and, relatively speaking, higher in southern Europe. Attributes of high power distance organizations include steep hierarchies; autocratic, directive or paternalistic management; special status symbols and privileges for senior staff; and ambivalent attitudes of employees to management (Leeds *et al.*, 1994, p. 15). High power distance in many respects reflects traditional management–subordinate relationships in the tourism and hospitality industry, especially hotel and catering. It is

difficult, however, to reconcile this with the concept of empowerment which we considered in Chapter 5, and the wider notion of
sustainability in human resource management which we introduced
in Chapter 1, although cultural acceptance of a high power distance
relationship by both parties may make such reconciliation somewhat
easier. Power distance measurement is also an interesting tool by
which to compare the cultural climates of different industries across
national boundaries. Hofstede found that lower-education, lower-
status occupations tend to produce high power distance values while
higher-education, higher-status occupations tend to produce low
power distance values, with education the dominant factor in determining this split. This, in part, may account for the traditions of
authoritarian management and its acceptance in low skills subsectors
of the tourism and hospitality industry in Europe, notably hotel and
catering.

- **Uncertainty avoidance** reflects a society's fear of the unknown and
  the extent to which uncertainty generates comfort or discomfort in
  its members and is thus important to avoid. Low uncertainty avoidance societies include Denmark, the Netherlands, Ireland and the
  United Kingdom which are characterized by tolerance of diverse
  views, informality, limited impact of experts, few formal rules and
  emotional self-control. By contrast, high uncertainty avoidance is
  characteristic in Germany and in all southern European countries
  which feature an emphasis on laws and rules to cover all contingen-
  cies maintaining careers within the same organization over a long
  timespan and a focus on formal procedures at work and in leisure.
  High uncertainty avoidance places greater stress on intellectual and
  reflective approaches to problem-solving as opposed to the pragmatic and action-focused strategies adopted in low uncertainty
  avoidance societies. The nature of many tourism and hospitality
  businesses, with highly fluctuating demand cycles and propensity for
  change in the product and market environment, would seem to demand management that is relatively low in uncertainty avoidance.
  However, Hofstede found no specific occupational links with uncertainty avoidance tendencies.
- **Individualism/collectivism** is Hofstede's third dimension. Individualistic societies are those in which ties are loose, where all members of
  society are expected to care for themselves and their immediate
  family only, and where emphasis is placed on individual achievement, identity and decision-making. Managers prefer to maintain
  social and professional distance from their subordinates (Leeds *et
  al.*, 1994, p. 16). By contrast, collectivist societies reflect close and
  extended family units and, in the work situation, the need to form
  strong groups through alliances, seeking harmony at work, consen-
  sus at meetings, face-saving strategies and group decision-making.
  On Hofstede's research, only Portugal and Greece among European
  countries were identified as collectivist in focus. Given the teamwork

emphasis of much activity within the tourism and hospitality industry, an extreme individualistic culture may be problematic and not in the interests of customers. Again, however, Hofstede found no occupational correlations within his individualism data.

- **Masculinity–feminity** is Hofstede's final dimension though the use of these terms is open to criticism in that they appear to assume innate gender characteristics against which to plot national cultures. Alternative terms might be assertive–nurturing. In masculine countries, characteristics include male stereotypes such as competitiveness, individual advancement, materialism, profit, assertiveness, strength, action-focus and considerable distance between male and female roles in society. Countries representing these traits include Germany, Greece, Italy, Spain and the UK. By contrast, feminine attributes include cooperation, warm relationships, caring and nurturing, life quality factors and a merging of male and female roles in society. Feminine countries are Denmark, Finland, Norway, Portugal and Sweden. Hofstede links the masculinity or femininity of an occupation to the level of female work participation in that sector and their influence in the industry. In this sense, tourism and hospitality exhibits some tendency towards female values and the caring culture of the guest–employee relationship in many situations would seem to bear this out. It is hardly surprising, therefore, that some hotels in Russia are seeking to employ former care workers as the most suited to hospitality work. In some respects, however, traditional management demands in tourism and hospitality, especially the hotel industry, focus on masculine traits and this is supported by the dominance of males in positions of authority and power within the industry, despite their minority status.

As with all other analysis of this kind, Hofstede's theoretical model must be treated with some caution as an analytical framework and not as a precise programme for the management of staff from different countries. Table 7.3 gives a summary of the scores that he attributed to the four dimensions for a range of European countries.

The second theoretical position to be considered is that of context and time. The work in this field is associated with Hall, who identified and drew attention to what he described as high and low context societies (Hall and Hall, 1990). Context is a communicational concept, indicating the extent to which the message, given by a person, is explicit, as in the form of specific instructions or computer programs (low context) or is coded in the sense that little is actually written down or said but much is implied in what is said (high context). According to Leeds *et al.* (1994):

> Low context people, such as Americans, Germans, Swiss, Scandinavians and other Northern Europeans, appreciate explicit, clear, written forms of communication as provided by computers, books, reports and letters. In contrast, high context peoples, such as the Japanese, Arabs and Southern Europeans, divulge less information

**Table 7.3** Scores of European countries on Hofstede's cultural dimensions

| Country | Power distance | Uncertainty avoidance | Individualism/ collectivism | Masculine/ feminine |
|---|---|---|---|---|
| Denmark | 18 | 23 | 74 | 16 |
| Finland | 33 | 59 | 63 | 25 |
| France | 68 | 86 | 71 | 43 |
| Greece | 60 | 112 | 35 | 57 |
| Ireland | 28 | 35 | 70 | 68 |
| Italy | 50 | 75 | 76 | 70 |
| Norway | 31 | 50 | 69 | 8 |
| Portugal | 63 | 104 | 27 | 31 |
| Spain | 57 | 86 | 51 | 42 |
| Sweden | 31 | 29 | 71 | 5 |
| Turkey | 66 | 85 | 37 | 45 |
| UK | 35 | 35 | 89 | 66 |
| Mean | 51 | 64 | 51 | 51 |

*Source*: Leeds *et al.* (1994), p. 15.

officially in written forms, but tend to be better informed than low context people, since they develop extensive informal networks for exchanging information verbally face to face or by telephone.

(p. 12)

Hall's concept of high or low context, therefore, has significant implications for the conduct of business and other forms of negotiation. Low context people tend to be specifically focused on the requirements of the current item on the agenda and to avoid any merging of issues and concerns. They move straight into the reason for the meeting or negotiations while high context people may well have a number of explicit and implicit agenda items in mind and are happy to merge these into the same meeting or series of encounters. Time to get to know each other is important to negotiations in the high context culture and problems and deadlocks will not be sorted out unless interpersonal relationships are permitted to develop. Therefore work and social topics, in particular, are permitted to merge and are not kept separate as in the low context society.

Differences are also evident with respect to an understanding of time and punctuality in particular. Low context people tend to be very precise about things like punctuality. Time for low context people is defined in very short 'chunks' and lateness, therefore, applies in a matter of a few minutes. High context people, by contrast, are much more relaxed about time and define lateness in terms of much longer timespans. The Swiss and German railways represent the precision of the low context culture and are legendary in this respect, but it is also interesting to note the precision of American airline timetabling, where flights are due to arrive and depart at, for example, 7.03 am or 5.24 pm, suggesting a predictive accuracy which other parts of the world do not attempt.

Hall mapped levels of context and, in Europe, placed northern European countries such as Germany, the Netherlands and Scandinavia in the low context camp and southern Europeans as high context countries. Britain and France are placed in an intermediate position between the two. The Irish would certainly appear to be more high context than their British neighbours and, here, the influence of dominant religion may play some part. Most religions in general, but the symbolism of Catholicism in particular, exude a strong sense of high context and this may well provide a link between countries such as Ireland, Italy, Spain, southern Germany and Austria as well as Poland to the east. Interestingly, Eastern European countries are not placed within Hall's framework, although Russians, for example, appear to have many high context attributes.

The potential for misunderstanding between high and low context people is considerable at a business and social level. High context people will not necessarily divulge information in an entirely explicit manner and may assume that an agreement contains rather more than is stated on paper. Low context people will see the formal contract or written document as the totality of the agreement and will not expect to move outside what is in black and white. They will give and expect quick decisions and will see delay as suggesting a lack of interest while the reverse will be in the case in the high context society. The American way of doing business, which has considerable influence within the globalization of tourism and hospitality, is clearly low context while, by contrast, that of the Japanese is high context.

Hall's context framework, which has been tested empirically on a number of occasions, has considerable implications for the management of businesses and people in the tourism and hospitality industry, especially where the two meet. For example, the nature of the distribution of tourism movements is such that tour operators, from low context countries in northern Europe, are required to negotiate contracts for services with colleagues from southern countries in Europe and the potential for misunderstanding is considerable. Likewise, the high context Japanese, Koreans and Taiwanese are increasingly important markets for low context northern Europe. The critical requirement to understand the needs of customers from these countries discussed earlier is, perhaps, made clearer by considering it in terms of Hall's framework.

The migratory trends of labour within Europe, as we have also seen, have brought peoples from high context countries to work in subservient positions in the tourism and hospitality industries of low context countries. Low context management, therefore, are dealing with a higher context workforce and this dichotomy has the potential to create considerable misunderstanding unless both parties, but especially management, are sensitive to the differences. Providing written instructions or notification on how to do a job or on new approaches to customer service may make eminent sense and be a very efficient form of communication to a low context manager but may be seen as remote and threatening by workers who operate by high context codes. Considering empowerment in the context of Hall's framework is also interesting in that true empowerment can only be achieved within a workforce that is known and fully trusted by management and where front-line staff in particular also feel that they are viewed with a sense of trust and worth by their managers. Such relationships may be much more achievable in the high context, informal society. However, if we reintroduce Hofstede here, we find that many high context societies in Europe are also masculine in character and rate high on uncertainty avoidance, dimensions that are incompatible with empowerment. Hall's framework also has considerable implications for important supervisory and management functions such as coaching, correction and censure. Such measures can be relatively explicit and direct in the low context environment, where they will be compartmentalized and have few consequences for relationships beyond the specific situation to which they relate. By contrast, the interrelationship of a diversity of agenda items, business and social, in high context societies means that it may be difficult to isolate the circumstances of one correction or censure from the wider relationship environment of the individuals or groups concerned.

Hall's work would also be interesting in terms of the comparative cultural norms of specific industries although such work has not been undertaken with respect to the tourism and hospitality sector. Certain structural and traditional factors within the industry may influence its positioning on the high–low context continuum. Small businesses (which dominate tourism and hospitality in Europe) are more informal in the way that they operate than larger organizations and thus aspects of high context practice may be more prevalent as a result. The demand cycle and attributes of the industry which we have already considered may also predispose towards high context relationships, in that the management of hotels, for example, is often seen as a reactive, multi-functional, verbal and non-paper activity.

Leeds *et al.* (1994) introduce what they call the systematic–organic dimension as the third approach to understanding cultural variation in Europe and link this to leadership style in order to create a matrix in which to place different European cultures. The systematic–organic dimension relates to the extent to which people believe that rational or systematic order should be applied regarding human behaviour and organizations. Rationality and systems lead to the view that the organization is rather like a machine and loyalty is to the organization rather than to its individual members. Consequent behaviour has many similarities to Hall's low context dimension – careful planning, keeping to schedules and agendas and precise job definitions. Managerial authority is largely derived from competence and professionalism within a particular field of responsibility. By contrast, the organic situation is much more high context in that the organization is seen in social terms and operates to rather more informal and unwritten behaviour codes. Features include vague job definitions, informal communication and management behaviour, implicit group relationships based on loyalty and trust to the group and the minimization of red tape.

> In 'organic' societies order and control tends to be based on personal influence and power, the latter coming less from a person's competence or role, but from his position in the hierarchy. Managers have a high standing in society and it is accepted that they might offer advice outside their particular function. People are status conscious, use power for personal ends and compete through outmanoeuvring others. (Leeds *et al.*, 1994, p. 17)

Mole (1990) adds the concept of leadership to this dimension in order to create what he calls a cultural map of Europe.

> The leadership dimension is based on the extent to which it is believed that power is given by groups to individuals. This form of words was carefully chosen to reflect that a leader's authority, at least in a European business organization, can only be exercised with the consent of the people who are being managed. The values associated with followship are identical to those associated with leadership. The spectrum of belief about leadership ranges from individual to group. (Mole, 1990, p. 167)

On this basis, Leeds *et al.* describe individual leadership as authoritarian, directive, top-down and autocratic, with power a right to be directed by superiors at their subordinates. By contrast, group leadership is egalitarian, participative, bottom-up and democratic in style, with all employees having a right to be heard and to make a valued contribution to their work unit or to the organization. Using the systematic–organic and the leadership dimensions, Mole created a cultural map of Europe, as represented in Figure 7.2. Again, a north–south divide becomes evident in European terms, with the former

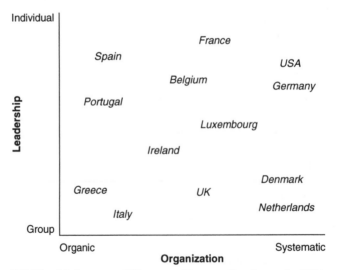

**Figure 7.2** The Mole map of Europe. (Source: Leeds *et al.*, 1994, p. 18.)

more inclined towards the systematic and the south to the informal. The individual–group leadership dimension, however, cuts across the other dimension and thus two-dimensionality provides a rather more culturally sensitive instrument than that provided by Hall. Again, it would be interesting to consider an industry sector analysis on the basis of Mole's map.

Leeds *et al.* consider a number of further theories of cultural variation in their analysis. These include the universal–particular dimension diffuseness–specificity and neutrality–affectivity. The outcome of their work, however, is the proposal of what they call 'European country clusters', based on loose factor analysis from the various cultural analysis studies that they address. They identify seven clusters, as follows:

1. **Scandinavian**: Denmark, Finland, Norway and Sweden;
2. **Anglo**: Ireland and the United Kingdom in Europe but also other English speaking countries elsewhere;
3. **Germanic**: Austria, Germany and Switzerland;
4. **Latin and Metatherian**: Italy, Portugal and Spain;
5. **Near Eastern**: Greece and Turkey, a group which also has Latin characteristics;
6. **Northern (quasi) Latin**: France and Belgium (part) – but France, especially in the south, has many Latin features;
7. **Miscellaneous**: a grouping that includes Alsace, in France; Flemish and German Belgium and Luxembourg (from Leeds *et al.*, 1994, p. 23).

It is easy to criticize any of the models that we have considered here because they attempt to impose generalizations upon diverse and heterogeneous national, cultural and business environments. This typology could be faulted in that it fails to accommodate French-speaking Switzerland as well as common characteristics found at the Celtic fringe. It also neglects Eastern Europe and this is a deficiency that will need to be addressed by further studies. However, what the typology as well as the specific theoretical models from which it is derived do allow is assistance in identifying some sense of the requirements and sensitivities that are necessary for multicultural market and workforce management within the tourism and hospitality industries of Europe. This is the focus of the final section in this chapter.

## MANAGEMENT IN A MULTICULTURAL ENVIRONMENT

So far in this chapter we have given consideration to the multicultural background of the tourism and hospitality marketplace in Europe as well as to the diverse origins of the industry's workforce. We have complemented these diversities with an introduction to some of the theoretical classifications or typologies that have been developed as a means of explaining cultural differences, particularly from a business and working environment point of view. However, Hall, Hofstede and Mole may also be of assistance in an understanding of guest needs and priorities and this is, perhaps, a neglected aspect in the consideration of these theories. For example, an understanding of Hall's time dimension within low and high context societies is of considerable importance in managing a hotel's services in support of a conference attended by delegates from one particular country or representing a multinational mix. A predominantly low context group is likely to expect services at times precisely agreed on the programme while the hotel may need to be much more flexible in its time response for a high context group.

It is important to emphasize that the generalizations which are derived from any classifications and typologies must be treated with extreme caution in order to avoid their use in support of stereotyping and, ultimately, the promotion of racist attitudes. This is especially true in the classification of cultures. They provide guidelines and identify the fact of cultural variation in the way that groups and people behave and respond to different situations. However, each guest and employee/colleague is, first and foremost, an individual who may or may not fit into the general attributes identified for his or her cultural, national or ethnic group. The management of these dimensions of diversity in the tourism and hospitality industry must at all times be sensitive to individual behaviour and needs as well as to the norms of a group.

From the point of view of a manager in the European tourism and hospitality industry, multiculturalism, multinationalism and multi-ethnicity present different challenges, depending upon the context in which they occur. The multiculturalism model that we discussed earlier in this chapter (Figure 7.1) illustrates the diversity of interrelationships that can be found when the two main dimensions are brought together. As we have already implied, there are a number of common situations where practical awareness is important of the influence that an individual or group's origins and background can have on the way that they perceive a situation and behave in response to it. These include the following:

- Where a business in the tourism and hospitality industry receives guests from countries, cultures and ethnic backgrounds that are different from that of the dominant culture in which the business is located, for example Japanese visitors staying in a Paris hotel.
- Where guests are from different cultures, nationality or ethnic origin to that of the workforce, for example in a Chinese restaurant staffed by immigrant Chinese staff and catering for local demand in, say, Bucharest, Oslo or Rome.
- Where a varying proportion of the workforce in a business or department are of different cultural, national or ethnic origins to that of the dominant local culture. This is a very common situation in certain departments in the hotel industry of large European cities

in particular. In some situations, ethnic diversity may mean that people from a wide range of nationalities and cultures are employed – this would be common in London. In others, cultural diversity is reflected in one, or perhaps two, major cultural, national or ethnic groups – the strong presence of Irish employees in the hotels of the Channel Islands is one example of this. In both situations, it would be common for management staff, especially at senior levels, to be drawn from the dominant local cultural, national or ethnic groups. As we have seen in Chapter 6, migrant workers and ethnic minorities are generally under-represented at supervisory and management grades in the tourism and hospitality industry.

• Where the management of the tourism/hospitality business represents a different culture or ethnic background to that of the majority of the workforce. This is a common model where expatriate management is used and is applicable in the case of the hotel industry in many parts of Europe, but especially in the developing industry of Eastern Europe. It is also a model widely employed by airlines, where local station management tend to be expatriate. EuroDisney, at start-up, employed American management and expertise in a number of key posts but the objective of these postings was always short term and, it could be argued, was important in order to ensure the transfer of what is essentially American culture and systems to Europe.

• Where the corporate culture of the tourism/hospitality business is significantly different to that normally prevailing in the country or community in which it is based. In human resource terms, this may mean that although there is little or no distance between the management and operational staff in terms of their original culture, corporate norms create new divides which must be addressed.

Any of these situations as well as variants of them has the potential to produce misunderstanding, conflict and discriminatory behaviour in the relationships between managers, staff and, indeed, guests. Such tensions, whether overt or part of a hidden agenda, can only undermine guest and working environment within the tourism and hospitality business and, ultimately, detrimentally affect the quality of service that is delivered to guests. Anticipating potential problems in the interrelationships of different customer and employee groups and instituting positive measures to avoid their occurrence is called multicultural management. The term normally applies to the management of human resources within an organization, but is a concept that is equally applicable to the management of the wider guest and employee environment. According to Tanke (1990), writing from an American perspective:

> Multicultural Management is the application of general human resource management principles and strategies within the context of the ethnic and cultural diversity found in your hospitality operation. This approach to human resource management operates on

the premise that both the managers' and employees' ethnic identities and cultural orientations, backgrounds and experiences are important influences that affect how both behave in the work place. Multicultural Management also assumes that work habits and attitudes are influenced by culture. Thus, culture matters when managing a work populace that is ethnically and culturally pluralistic. Increasingly, today's hospitality managers are expected to manage cultural diversity, for it is a part of the daily life of both their role functions in the industry, and the hospitality industry itself.

(p. 43)

Working and managing in a multicultural, multinational and multi-ethnic environment does not necessarily require skills and capabilities that are intrinsically different from those demanded of work in mono-cultural environments, with the possible exception of additional languages capabilities. The principles of sustainable human resource management, which we addressed in Chapter 1 and developed in subsequent discussion in the book thus far, are entirely compatible with meeting the needs of diversity among guests and within the workforce.

That said, however, there are a number of critical issues to do with cultural, national and ethnic heterogeneity which those working in the tourism and hospitality industry in Europe at all levels will benefit from addressing. These include the following:

- The need to recognize and respect diversity within the guest and workforce populations and thus to avoid imposing dominant values and practices upon either group. In guest terms, the tendency to impose rules which determine, for example, what, where and when they eat is much less pronounced in many European countries than it was in the past and this change permits greater flexibility in meeting specific cultural or ethnic requirements. It also means reviewing a range of guest handling procedures and systems in order to ensure that they are not designed on the basis of implicit assumptions about the dominant (generally local) culture. For example, different cultures have different ways in expressing dissatisfaction with service and it may be fair to assume that American guests will utilize guest comment cards or address problems directly to staff or management. Lack of complaints via this route from Japanese tourists does not necessarily mean total guest satisfaction but may imply discomfort with direct or confrontational methods of expressing complaints or other comments.

  In relation to the workforce, the recognition of diversity and its potential implications for a variety of workplace practices is also of considerable importance and both the explicit dimensions of the working culture (rules, regulations, etc.) and those which are implicit but not formally stated need to be reviewed in the light of the cultural, national and ethnic composition of those employed or those who may potentially join the workforce.

- Recognition and respect, however, are only part of the process. The next and critical step is one of learning and understanding and this involves far greater investment. Language is an important aspect of this but is rarely sufficient in itself. The ability to communicate with guests in their own language is widely recognized as important in the tourism and hospitality industry and both major and small companies have taken significant steps to enhance employee capabilities in this direction, both by employing staff with multilingual skills and by instituting specific language training programmes for their front-line staff. Rarely, however, is the importance of intra-staff communication recognized to the extent that language skills are provided in order to enhance communication within the operational workforce or between staff and management. Front-line staff are, generally, not employed unless they speak the main language of the locality and in other, generally low-skills areas such as cleaning in airports or housekeeping in hotels, inability to communicate in the local language is overcome by the employment of bilingual supervisors. Thus it is quite frequent for managers to have no direct means of communicating with their staff except through an intermediary. The 'normal' assumption is that it is the responsibility of the frequently poorly educated and low-skilled staff concerned to learn English, French or German. An alternative viewpoint is that managers and supervisors, personnel with higher educational levels, should be the ones to learn at least the rudiments of the main languages which their colleagues and staff employ, whether it is Spanish, Bengali or Turkish. Recognition of this alternative is quite widespread in the United States where Spanish classes and self-study texts for the hospitality industry are widely available for monolingual, non-Hispanic managers.

- Mention has already been made of the employment of, for example, Japanese and Indian staff by British Airways to service routes to and from those countries. This is an important step in ensuring that guest needs and expectations are understood by key front-line personnel and it is likely that aspects of the approach adopted by these staff will 'rub off' on their working colleagues, thus enhancing the wider sense of understanding of cultural needs. A similar principle can be effective in relation to a workforce that is multicultural or multi-ethnic. Token steps have already been mentioned such as providing interpretive intermediaries to overcome language barriers. However, far more effective and compatible with the concept of sustainability is to invest in the training and development of staff from cultural, national or ethnic minority groups. In Chapter 6, significant under-representation of ethnic minorities in positions of responsibility in the hotel industry was noted. Policies which are designed to support and facilitate the promotion aspirations of staff from minority groups so that, eventually, they can take responsibilities as supervisors and managers is, probably, the most effective strategy to overcome cultural and ethnic divisions and a lack of mutual understanding and respect. This approach is supported by the Commission for Racial Equality in Britain, which, in a report on hotels, advocates that employers should 'target training towards ethnic minority employees who have either expressed interest in promotion to supervisory posts or who have been identified through staff appraisals as having career potential. The aim of the training ... should be to equip trainees with the necessary skills, experience and confidence to compete on equal terms for promotion' (CRE, 1991, p. 35).

- Explicit as well as less overt forms of racism are widespread in all European societies and examples of the extreme and violent expression of such attitudes has been seen in a number of countries in recent years. Some European countries, such as Britain, have specific legislation which is designed to outlaw discriminatory practice on grounds of race in the workplace and in other areas of society. Such legislation is by no means universal in Europe nor is its application entirely effective where it is in place. However, it is an important principle for employers to view their human resources in a way which allows them to maximize the potential and actual capabilities of each and every member of staff and also to recruit those who will be able to offer the most to the organization. This is an essential step in seeking to offer quality service to guests and in the application of the principles of empowerment within the workforce. Discriminatory practice, at any level, patently does not meet these objectives. The Commission for Racial Equality report advocates that companies should have clear statements of policy with respect to equal opportunities, supported by a programme of action to ensure general awareness and specific training in relation to its implications. Colleges and universities, offering tourism and hospitality programmes could readily support learning in this area by providing greater focus within their curricula to legal and other aspects of multiculturalism and multi-ethnicity.

- Implicit racist attitudes and behaviour are much more difficult to legislate against than direct discriminatory practice and, therefore, is rather more insidious. It is also a major problem in European society and, consequently, in the tourism and hospitality industry. This form of racism can operate at a number of levels:

  - from guests/customers to employees;
  - from guests/customers to other guests/customers;
  - from employees to guests/customers;
  - from employees to other employees;
  - from management to employees.

The manifestation of racist attitudes from guests to other guests and from guests to employees has, of necessity, to be treated with some care and caution. In extreme form, neither behaviour can and should be tolerated and should be actioned in the same way as any other form of abuse or disruptive action by guests or customers. At other levels, complaints by fellow guests cannot be ignored and discreet action may be required by senior management. In relation to employees, it is an important principle to protect and support members of staff against abuse and mistreatment of any kind, whether from guests or fellow employees. Racism may well become part of wider problems of service and servility and this needs to be addressed in the context of wider empowerment development. However, in situations where the guests are predominantly from one cultural or ethnic group and those serving them are from another, there is a clear danger that assumptions about status and the superiority of one group over another may be drawn from these respective roles. The responsibility lies with management to ensure that such perceptions are not perpetuated, either explicitly or implicitly and do not detract from the level and quality of service that is provided to guests.

Racism, in any form, in the way in which employees relate to their guests must be totally unacceptable to tourism and hospitality businesses in any sector. Such racism may manifest itself in the form of apparent humour out of the sight, hearing or language comprehension of guests but may also show in favoured or differential treatment of one group of guests over others. It is a management responsibility to demonstrate clearly that such behaviour is totally unacceptable. Punitive measures alone, however, are insufficient to deal with problems of this nature. Training and development programmes, designed to enhance understanding and tolerance of cultural and ethnic diversity may also be necessary.

Such training programmes can also contribute to overcoming racial tensions within the staff body. Given the cultural and ethnic diversity of the workforce of many tourism and hospitality businesses, there is considerable potential for inter-group rivalry on the basis of culture or ethnic origin. At times of contracting employment, for example due to recession, what Weber described as 'group closure' may take place, with the dominant group excluding and even scapegoating minorities in order to protect their own position. Racist behaviour, whether perpetuated by groups or individuals, must be actioned with all seriousness and early in order to avoid the development of overt and possibly violent responses.

Finally, the manifestation of racist attitudes or behaviour by managers to their staff cannot be acceptable within a reputable tourism and hospitality business. Training, again, can make some contribution to overcoming tendencies in this direction but the most effective strategy lies in managers becoming familiar with their subordinates as individuals in order to enhance understanding of their background and needs in the workplace.

- Racism, prejudice and intolerance of customs and practices other than the 'norm' are often the result of ignorance and a lack of contact with people from different cultural or ethnic origins. Given the diversity both in the origins of guests/customers and the workforce of the industry in Europe, the college and university education and training of those aspiring to work in tourism and hospitality at all levels will be enhanced through formal consideration of the implications of this diversity. It is a theme which can be introduced into the curriculum in a number of ways, within, for example, a consideration of marketing, human resource management and the tourism and hospitality industry structure. The theme can be reinforced through discussion and analysis prior to and following work placements. Among the most effective means of breaking down barriers and assisting students to enter the tourism and hospitality industry with an open mind and without the baggage of prejudicial ignorance is to include a period of study or work within a different cultural, national or ethnic environment. In the European context, therefore, programmes that specifically include periods of study or working placements in other countries can make a major contribution to overcoming the barriers of ignorance and prejudice. Many courses in the European Union at a variety of levels include such components and in time this practice may also spread more widely throughout the rest of Europe.

Bringing together the cultural, national and ethnic diversity of the European tourism and hospitality industry in terms of its markets and its workforce has the potential to be one of its prime strengths. The intensity of the relationship between customers and front-line staff is such that effective management, training and development in the area of multiculturalism can make a significant contribution in the area of relationship marketing and provide a real competitive advantage to companies. Likewise, recognizing and addressing the issue of multiculturalism in the workforce has the potential to offer opportunities for effective team building and can contribute to enhanced customer service quality by improving staff commitment and facilitating real empowerment.

At the same time, mismanagement of a multicultural, multinational and ethnically diverse environment in the tourism and hospitality industry has the potential to be very destructive. Tensions derived from this source are difficult to defuse or control and can lead to a situation where all management decisions are assessed and questioned against cultural and ethnic criteria.

REVIEW AND DISCUSSION QUESTIONS

1. Add additional situations to the multicultural matrix (Figure 7.1).
2. Consider situations that you might have experienced where tourism and hospitality businesses have provided specialist services for particular cultural, ethnic or national market segments.

3. What steps might a traveller take in order to prepare him/herself for a visit to an unfamiliar culture or country?

4. Why do tourists seek out products and services that are familiar when they are away from home? What might host countries do in order to encourage greater patronage of local and authentic tourism and hospitality products and services?

5. What are the main benefits of working in a new environment, in a different culture or country?

6. How can the level of migration within the European tourism and hospitality industry be explained?

7. Why does the European tourism and hospitality industry attract a significant level of illegal immigrant labour?

8. What concerns might Eastern European countries have about the employment of expatriate labour by foreign tourism and hospitality countries?

9. What use can a tourism and hospitality manager make of the work of:
   - Hofstede;
   - Hall;
   - Leeds *et al.*;
   in understanding the needs of a multicultural workforce?

10. What are the potential dangers in classifying cultural, ethnic and national groups according to broad characteristics?

# 8 | Education, training and development

## INTRODUCTION

The education, training and development of employees of all levels within European tourism and hospitality is a vital component in maintaining the industry's competitiveness in the international arena. In essence, education, training and development are the means by which a number of the key outcomes which we have considered in preceding chapters can be achieved.

These include the following.

- The attainment of true service quality should be the aim within tourism and hospitality businesses. This is a function of effective education and training practices both within the companies themselves but also within the preceding educational experience of those recruited.
- Consequent moves towards employee empowerment a strategy which can only be effective in the context of well trained and, indeed, educated staff at all levels.
- Effective relationship marketing, a key feature of a service focused company, depends heavily upon empowerment concepts and thus on education and training inputs.
- The nature of the tourism and hospitality labour markets should be recognized and the implications that Riley's model has for education and training within the sector. While it must be understood that there is no real identifiable and unitary tourism and hospitality labour market but rather an amalgam of a number of subsectoral markets, Riley's concept of the weak internal labour market and its consequences for vocational education and training is of particular relevance to our discussion here. This issue will be further considered during the course of this chapter.
- Achieving harmony and effective cooperation and teamwork within a multicultural and, frequently, a multilingual workforce depends on effective training of the team themselves as well as of their supervisors and managers.
- College students and employees within tourism and hospitality businesses need to be prepared for vocational mobility within Europe, either in support of personal aspirations or of company requirements. Some parts of Europe have invested more in this than others

and the very differing language skills of the Dutch, on the one hand, and the British on the other, bears testimony to this. Education and training have a major part to play in this preparatory process.

- The upgrading of tourism and hospitality operating standards, especially in service delivery, in Eastern Europe must be built upon sound education and training principles if it is to succeed but, even before that, creating recognition of the need for educational and training input is required.
- Addressing some of the worst excesses in terms of conditions, rewards and benefits, within European tourism and hospitality has a major educational component at its heart, focused primarily on those in authority within the industry to learn from their more enlightened peers.
- In a sense subsuming all the above, the underlying theme of this book – that of recognizing the importance of sustainability within human resource policies for tourism – has a particular focus on education and training as a key plank within its strategies.

As well as drawing on the concepts of previous chapters of this book, our consideration of education and training for tourism and hospitality will also act as a precursor for the final two chapters. These address issues of macro planning, development and social responsibility with respect to human resource development for tourism and hospitality in Europe. Clearly, education and training form a major component within this framework.

## EDUCATION AND TRAINING – THE CONCEPTS

The exact distinction between education and training has taxed philosophers and thinkers for centuries. Notable contributions include those by Whitehead and Dewey. John Dewey, the American philosopher, writing in 1916, defines education thus:

> It is that reconstruction or reorganization of experience which adds to the meaning of experience, and which increases ability to direct the course of subsequent experience.    (Dewey, 1916, pp. 89–90)

Bertrand Russell (1926) enters the education–training debate by considering the contrast between that which is 'ornamental' in education – in his terms this refers to a classical education – and that which is 'useful', which includes the sciences and applied vocational areas, some of which may well fall into rather more contemporary definitions of training. He disposes of the issue of utility in fairly strong terms.

> Nevertheless, I believe the whole controversy to be unreal. As soon as the terms are defined, it melts away. If we interpret 'useful' broadly and 'ornamental' narrowly, the one side has it; in the contrary interpretations, the other side has it. In the widest and most correct sense of the word, an activity is 'useful' when it has good

results. And these results must be good in some other sense than merely 'useful', or else we have no true definition. We cannot say that a useful activity is one that has useful results. The essence of what is 'useful' is that it ministers to some result which is not merely useful. Sometimes a long chain of results is necessary before the final result is reached which can be called simply 'good'. A plough is useful because it breaks up the ground. But breaking up the ground is not good on its own account; it is in turn merely useful because it enables seed to be sown. This is useful because it produces grain, which is useful because it produces bread, which is useful because it preserves life.     (Russell, 1926/1960, pp. 15–16)

Such a debate may appear to be primarily semantic and Russell certainly develops the discussion considerably further in order to demonstrate that the ornamental and utilitarian have little useful distinction when the logic of their definitions is dissected and analysed. On this basis, it is sufficient to say, as we do conclude here, that the distinction between education and training is spurious and unhelpful in the context of human resource management for tourism and hospitality.

However, some of the definitions that have emerged from very extensive discussion of the distinction have tended to polarize the two concepts. In addition, a veneer of relative status and a class dimension is frequently introduced when separating the two terms, in that education is perceived to be that which is of a general and developmental nature while training is deemed to be vocationally specific and often the precursor of trade or craft positions. So for example, with regard to the law in England, students are educated within the university context but frequently complete their vocational training for careers as solicitors in an entirely different, specialist college. Likewise, the learning of foreign languages is the educational concern of universities while the application of this learning, for example in preparation for a bilingual secretarial career, is a training matter for different institutes.

Such absolutist distinctions are not really helpful in understanding the role of both education and training in the context of the tourism and hospitality industry. The nature of much work within the sector is that it requires a contribution from a number of sections of what is more appropriately thought of as a continuum between on the one hand Pavlovian response training and very specific, limited skills development, and on the other the extremes of philosophical, mathematical and creative speculation processes without evident application.

In hospitality and tourism there is little dispute that entrants at all levels require inputs of both an educational and training kind, although traditional practice tends to focus primarily on the latter in preparing students and employees for what are perceived to be the lower skills positions in the industry, especially within hotel and catering. Even here, skills training builds upon a number of years of education within the school system and many formal programmes, primarily training in focus, include what might be deemed a broader educational dimension within the curriculum. Indeed, the German apprenticeship schemes which prepare school leavers for careers in the various tourism and hospitality sectors operates the so-called 'dual system' whereby developing the specific skills requirement of the job is the task of industry working to clearly stipulated curricula and guidelines, while local colleges take responsibility for the continuing general education of the apprentices (Holloway, 1993). Other examples of a combination process, with a somewhat different and less academic educational focus, can be found in Ireland, where a complementary Lifeskills programme (now known as Personal Skills) was designed to complement specific craft skills training (Baum and McLoughlin, 1984). Likewise, within General National Vocational Qualifications (GNVQ) and Scottish Vocational Qualifications (SVQ) in the United Kingdom, programmes in both Leisure and Tourism and Hospitality and Catering require study of the core skills of communications, number and information technology as well as assessing work on the basis of the processes of planning, research and evaluation.

In considering the respective roles of education and training (if it is of value and meaning to separate them) we are faced, once more, with the consequences of operating within a very diffuse and variegated sector. There are few generalizations that can be made with respect to the sector as a whole. The labour market characteristics, the initial education and training requirements, the cost of this training and its subsequent updating, the levels of remuneration and reward, as well as vocational and social status, vary dramatically between a hotel kitchen porter and a beach vendor on the one hand, and a senior Boeing 747 pilot or director of a national tourism office on the other. The only common denominator is that they all work within tourism and that as a result the tourist in some part depends on their skills and knowledge for the enjoyment of her or his vacation experience.

## TRAINING IS FOR SKILLS AND EDUCATION IS FOR LIFE?

The conscious separation of education and training as distinct processes has strong historical origins. It is a popular misrepresentation, simplification and throw-away distinction to argue that training is for a skill and education is for life. However, historically, this distinction has had a degree of validity. In pre-Industrial Revolution times, when training for a craft took place in an environment where the skills and traditions of those skills did not change significantly over long periods of time, training really was designed to equip the apprentice with skills which he would use throughout his working career. Master status within the context of the trade guilds in England, for example, implied that the craftsman (and, historically, we are only talking about men in this context) had acquired all the necessary skills and knowledge for the independent execution of his craft. There was no more to learn and, while the skill may have been honed with experience, there was no expectation that the demands of the job would alter during the working life of that craftsman. Thus the cup of skills, empty at the start of the training process, was now full with everything that was available by way of skills in that society to the master carpenter, physician, lawyer, stonemason, baker or goldsmith.

The concept of education at this time, by contrast, was rather more fluid. While the rudiments of European education in medieval society had many features in common with skills training within the crafts, in that students were taught the fundamental skills necessary to internalize classical and religious orthodoxy, the assumption was that the process would continue throughout life as part of a search for increased wisdom, provided that the rules and obligations of prevailing orthodoxy were observed. Of course, it is important to emphasize that the benefits of both models, skills training and learning as part of education, were accessible to but a very small minority of the population in Europe. Education was, by and large, a carefully guarded perogative of the Church until the time of the Reformation while access to the skills of the guilds was equally jealously protected and controlled.

To say that the fixed skills model, the filling of the cup, altered as a result of the Industrial Revolution is only partially accurate. What the industrialization process did was to divide and simplify the work in many craft areas, so that in partial form tasks could now be performed by less skilled workers at much lower cost and using the machinery of a factory rather than in the workshop of the craftsman.

The profit motive of industrial capitalism, the division of labour upon which it depended and, above all, the technology that it employed created a further and entirely new factor within the workplace, that of ongoing and incessant change. From the certainty and stability of the craft guilds, where skills, literally, remained the same from generation to generation, the working world, at least within the industrial sector, was rapidly plunged into a constant process of change, with machinery rapidly becoming redundant and newer technology replacing both earlier generations of machines as well as the age-old craft skills. Ironically, the world of education was much slower to respond to this process of change sparked off by the Industrial Revolution. Classical study, a model derived from some two thousand years earlier and refined through the influence of the Church over that same time period, remained the dominant educational model, largely impervious to the impact of science and technology until the twentieth century. The classical model was deemed to be a suitable education by which to prepare entrants for careers in government, the arts and the professions and no compromise to the needs of vocationalism were made except in the specific cases of medicine and law.

The process of change has remained the one constant in the world of work since the mid-eighteenth century and has accelerated with each succeeding generation. As a result, the currency of skills taught by technical institutes and in the workplace has become shorter and shorter with the consequent need either to retrain staff or to replace them with newer generations of employees. The impact of change was, perhaps, not fully recognized within each generation of workers until the post-1945 period but comparison between generations, between mother and daughter and father and son, would have highlighted changes in the machinery employed and the procedures followed. Up to this point, the only incentive to change in the individual was to meet the requirements of promotion and greater responsibility, and even that change was readily assimilated and finite in its demands. The advent of computer- and, latterly, microprocessor-based information technology has reduced the lifecycle of some jobs to within the working career of most employees. The punchcard operator, so important to computer operations during the 1960s and early 1970s, probably only existed as a significant employment designation for fifteen to twenty years before tape, disk and chip technology made the skills and the jobs obsolete.

The process of change in other non-industrial sectors of the economy has, apparently, been much slower. Agriculture was for a long time immune to the level of changes which were taking place within the industrial sector but the introduction of technology and chemicals as well as work and management systems has revolutionized work in even this sector. The numbers employed on the land in most Western European countries is just a fraction of what it was forty years ago yet the total agricultural output has increased to levels of surplus. Likewise in the service sector, for example banking, the impact of change in the workplace has taken time to be felt but now has taken hold in a major way as technology replaces human skills and financial institutions dispense with old routines and procedures in the workplace.

What has this potted history of work to do with the mass tourism and hospitality industry which, after all, was only in its infancy at the dawn of the computer age? In the context of some work areas in tourism and hospitality, the answer is quite clear. For example, the skills and knowledge requirements for airline pilots has gone through massive change in the past forty years, as aviation moved from using the relatively straightforward technology of the DC3, with its high dependence on pilot skill and judgement, to the high technology sophistication of the new generation fly-by-wire, computer-controlled Airbus, Boeing and McDonald Douglas airliners. Likewise, the impact of developments with respect to both technology and markets have significantly changed the work routines of travel agency employees, airline check-in clerks, hotel receptionists, food and beverage operatives in fast-food restaurants and a host of other areas.

However, it is possible to argue that the fundamentals of many, lower skilled, customer-contact positions in the tourism and hospitality industry remain the same as they were forty years ago and, on the face of it, may continue to do so for the foreseeable future. On the basis of this argument, therefore, change is not as significant a factor in many parts of the tourism and hospitality workplace as it is in other business sectors. As a consequence, according to this analysis, skills once learnt should be adequate to meet the needs of the tourism and hospitality working environment without further enhancement during an employee's career. Such beliefs, characteristic of the non-sustainable model of human resource development considered in Chapter 1, remain implicitly prevalent within many sectors of the industry in Europe, particularly hotels and catering. A good, but by no means unique, example of this attitude was expressed recently to the author by the general manager of a large hotel in Bucharest, Romania. Noting that all his staff had been recruited, fully trained, from colleges when the hotel first opened eight years previously, and none had left in the interim, he stated that the hotel had no need to implement further training programmes as 'all the staff are fully trained' – a good example of what has earlier been described as the 'full cup' concept of training. Even if this analysis was to be accepted on technical grounds (and this would be a highly contentious conclusion), it is fundamentally flawed for two further reasons.

Firstly, while change may not impact on the specific technical tasks undertaken by many tourism and hospitality employees, the social and market context in which they are working has altered dramatically over the timeframe in question and continues to change inexorably. In Chapter 3, we considered the way in which the social context of work in the tourism industry has altered in response to mass participation and the democratization of the industry. In Chapter 5, discussion focused on the ever-changing expectations of the tourism marketplace and how this impacts on the role of employees in responding to what Balmer and Baum (1993) described as the true motivating factor for tourists, service quality, as opposed to those aspects which are increasingly taken for granted, the physical product 'hygiene factors'. Thus tourism and hospitality employees are working in a customer environment which is constantly changing and, unless they themselves are able to comprehend these changes and respond to them, their skills will be as redundant as if they were coopers operating in an age of aluminium barrels or flag carriers who walked ahead of early locomotives in the era of the TGV and Bullet train.

The second problem which an analysis which seeks to separate tourism and hospitality skills from those in other sectors faces is related precisely to the fact that the industry cannot exist in isolation or in a vacuum, insulated from the wider world of work. Vocational training and preparation for the world of work, in general, places increasing emphasis on preparing young people for working lives that will not be single track, in the one job and with the same employer, over a forty-year cycle. Expectations are, increasingly, built around mobility and change and the anticipation that an individual may move between companies and sectors at a number of points within a working life. Each of these stages will, in all probability, require training and the acquisition of additional qualifications. As a result, the labour market brings expectations to the workplace that emphasize the opportunity to change and to face new challenges, through rotation between different functional areas but also through enhancement and promotion. The tourism and hospitality industry cannot isolate itself from this environment and pretend that such aspirations do not and should not exist within it. Thus training has a role to play at all levels within the tourism workforce, as an ongoing and continuous process designed to enable employees to meet changes in their working environment but also, and of equal importance, to cater for their own personal and career needs and aspirations.

It is no coincidence, therefore, that employers in most industry sectors in Western Europe are giving increasing priority to the acquisition of generic and transferable skills during the initial college and university phase of a young person's development, while recognizing that specific technical competencies can readily be acquired in the workplace. This conclusion is confirmed by research into the expectations that hotel managers have of graduate entrants to the industry in the United Kingdom (Baum, 1990). This study identified the following competencies as among the eight most important, from the point of view of employers:

- management of guest problems with understanding and sensitivity;
- effective communication in both written and oral form;
- achievement of positive working relationships with employees;
- professional appearance and poise;
- development of positive customer relations;
- motivation of employees to achieve desired performance (Baum, 1990, p. 15).

It is clear that those competencies which are most in demand are what might be called 'soft' skills, personal and communicational capabilities which have equal value in tourism and hospitality as they do in a wide variety of vocational settings. This transferability of generic skills is confirmed by the substantial number of tourism and hospitality graduates in the United Kingdom who rapidly at or soon after graduation opt for careers outside these vocational fields. There is also the possibility that, having 'tasted' the industry through industrial placement, a significant number are put off by exposure to the 'dark side of the coin' that we addressed in Chapter 6.

Where does this discussion take consideration of education and training, one as a finite and terminal activity and the other as an ongoing, non-terminal process? What it certainly does do is to blur and confuse any absolute distinction between the two concepts, or at least confound the notion that there is any value in perceiving the two as independent processes, carried out with respect to different cadres of people and in separate learning and training institutions. So much of the preparatory process that young people undergo in anticipation of a working career fuses the specific and the generic in a way that is impossible to separate and this process is not exclusive to the formal school, college or training centre environment. It can hold true of work-based learning as well. Vikhanski and Puffer (1993) point to this in the context of McDonald's and the foundation for working life that even part-time working exposure to the yellow arches provides for many young people.

> In the United States, McDonald's is often the first job that young people take, and the company's training practices are a solid foundation that can serve a person well in any type of employment. Many American employers value prospective candidates who have excelled at McDonald's because they recognize that these people have acquired good work habits.
>
> (Vikhanski and Puffer, 1993, p. 105)

It is interesting that, despite this important observation which appears to blur the distinction between the two concepts, Vikhanski and Puffer present their paper as a discussion of management **education** and employee **training** and do not appear to recognize the inherent contradiction in what they are saying. In doing so, they re-emphasize the traditional status division between the concepts, that education is for professionals and training for the artisan and the unskilled.

The reality is that, within the contemporary working environment in many tourism and hospitality enterprises in Western Europe, most employees at all levels have a need for attributes that, on the basis of traditional distinctions, could be described as both educational and training in nature. Managers require the skills that are developed as a result of training in accounting and finance and may even need the ability to demonstrate the benefits of training in specific technical skills – in small hotels, for example, managers will frequently substitute for the absent breakfast chef or function waiter if required. Likewise, as was argued in Chapter 5, front-line staff in all tourism sectors require empowerment and a real understanding of marketing and their customers in addition to the technical attributes of their jobs, and such understanding can only be derived from exposure to educational as well as training processes. It is, perhaps, because of this overlap and the evident lack of clear-cut distinctions between the separate concepts of education and training that a unifying term, that of development, is frequently employed.

Development has the advantage of being a term which has equal applicability to skills and knowledge and is one which is more generally understood. It is also a term which does not have terminal or absolute connotations but can be seen to have a role to play at all stages of a person's formal development (while at school, college or university), their vocational development (at vocational school, training centre or in the workplace) and their informal development (in any of the above situations as well as at home and during social and leisure situations). The three types of development are also not mutually exclusive in that the same context can contribute to more than one. In the situation of a management development programme which is set in an outwardbound context, we may learn about our ability as leaders in a way that has applicability in the workplace but, at the same time, may also develop in a personal sense in our relationships with colleagues and friends. Likewise, a work placement from college in another country may help us develop skills with respect to the preparation of French or Russian cuisine but, in all probability, it will also assist in the development of personal resilience in our ability to cope away from home and will contribute to our understanding of other cultures and traditions.

Furthermore, there are no time constraints or problems of sequencing inherent in the concept of development. It is a process of which any component can occur at any time and in any order during a person's working or non-working life. Individuals can, within certain constraints, respond to changing personal, vocational or other requirements by availing themselves of any form of development at any point of their lives.

Recognizing an individual's infinite potential for development throughout their life is a critical responsibility for managers in all sectors of the economy but has particular relevance within the tourism and hospitality industry. This is not the same as saying that all people can become nuclear physicists or Nobel laureate mathematicians given the appropriate development opportunity. What it does imply, however, is that all people have the potential to learn new things at all stages in their lives and negative assumptions about their interest or capacity to learn should not be made by others on their behalf. As we have seen, the tourism industry is characterized by its breadth in terms of subsectors, its labour intensity, its small business structure in many countries and its geographical dispersion (it is truly an industry of every parish). As a result, tourism and hospitality can provide working opportunities for an incredibly wide range of people in terms of their ability, their interests, their aspirations and their availability – career focused professionals; craftspersons, technicians, housewives/husbands seeking flexible employment opportunities, students seeking temporary employment, school students seeking their first jobs, as well as those who, for a variety of social and physical reasons cannot find employment in other areas, in particular the physically disabled or the mentally handicapped. Given this diversity in its workforce, it is easy to make assumptions about an individual's capability and potential based on the tasks and responsibilities that they currently have and, thus, to deny some the opportunity to avail themselves of development chances. Furthermore, given the change factor which is inherent within tourism and hospitality today, employers require a workforce that can adapt to new technologies, systems and markets and it is far more cost and socially effective as well as sustainable to invest in this change through internal development rather than to replace labour already employed with new staff. To do so requires recognizing both the potential and the limitations of the whole workforce.

## THE CONTEXT OF DEVELOPMENT

It is implicit in the above discussion that development is a process which can take place at any time and is not constrained by formal parameters at specified points within an individual's childhood, adolescence or working life. The same flexibilty applies to other contextual dimensions such as the reasons/motivation for the development, location of development, its duration and timing, how it is carried out, its assessment and the recognition accorded to the outcome. Development is not something that is confined to the classroom, laboratory or training room nor is it, in situational terms, restricted to planned and formalized group sessions in college or the workplace. Development activities may consist of a brief half-hour session or a full year's programme and they may or may not be assessed in academic or practical terms. The outcomes may lead to formal recognition through certification, promotion within the company, enhanced remuneration or none of these. It is important to recognize the potential for such diversity within development and here we are only talking about what might be described as planned or structured development.

In the vocational context of tourism and hospitality it is realistic to consider development in terms of a planned process, and thus to put to one side unplanned and unstructured learning which we have included implicitly in our discussion up to this point. Planned and structured development is a process over which management, as well as the individual, has control and where both parties may anticipate what will occur, prepare for the occasion and evaluate the outcomes. Therefore it is possible to identify the main contexts in which such development takes place in relation to the tourism industry:

- time;
- place;
- reason/motivation;
- meeting the costs;
- method;
- measurement of outcomes; and
- recognition of outcomes.

Table 8.1 lists these in rather more detail, though the elements of this contextual map are by no means mutually exclusive or, for that matter, entirely comprehensive as the purpose of developing such a contextual map is to demonstrate the wide range of situations in which development within tourism and hospitality can take place.

**Table 8.1** Development in context

---

**Time**

*Macro*
- Compulsory education age
- Optional schooling
- Post-secondary school
- Postgraduate
- Post experience/mid-career
- Return to education/new career
- Post-redundancy
- Pre-retirement
- Post-retirement

*Micro*
- During 'normal' school/college hours
- Evenings
- Weekends
- Day release
- Block release
- During 'normal' working hours
- During 'normal' leisure time
- Summer school

**Place**

*School/college/university/training centre*
- Classroom
- Lecture theatre
- Seminar room
- Tutor's office
- Laboratory (science, kitchen)
- Simulated work environment (kitchen, restaurant, travel agency)
- Real work environment (kitchen for public restaurant, travel shop)
- Computer laboratory
- Language laboratory
- Library
- Audio-visual room
- Field trip/site visit
- Independent learning suite
- At home (open learning, homework, assignments)
- On bus, train, in cafe, etc.

*Workplace*
- Classroom/training suite
- Seminar room
- Manager's/supervisor's office
- Simulated work environment (flight simulator, restaurant)
- Real work environment (no customers)
- Real work environment (customers)
- Company training centre
- Site visit
- Open learning facilities
- At home (open learning, assignments, practice)
- On bus, train, in cafe, etc.

**Reason/motivation**

*Personally motivated*
- Career opportunity

- Career enhancement
- Career change
- Advance in pay/benefits
- Job protection
- Up-dating of skills
- Personal development
- Interest in subject
- To re-enter workforce

*Employer motivated*
- Enable promotion
- Fill skills gap
- Keep employee
- Personal development
- Reward performance

## Meeting the costs
- State
- Individual
- Individual's family
- Employer
- Potential employer
- Trust/foundation
- Shared between any of above

## Method
- Lecture
- Seminar
- Tutorial
- Discussion
- Demonstration
- Laboratory practical
- Simulated real situation practical
- Controlled real situation practical
- Sit-by-Neil/Nellie
- Simulation
- Case study
- Group activity/project
- Individual project
- Research project
- Computer-based assignment
- Field-trip/visit
- Counselling

## Measurement of outcomes
*Type*
- Closed book examination
- Open book examination
- Paper assignments/project
- Thesis
- Multiple choice type test
- Practical text
- Practical project
- Simulated real situation
- Observed real situation
- Progress in the workplace

*Management/authority*
- Public authority (education ministry)
- Private agency – local/international (AHMA, HCIMA)
- Professional body
- School/college/university
- Employer/company
- Manager/supervisor
- Training/personnel department

**Recognition of outcomes**
- Award of diploma/degree
- Professional/Guild accreditation
- Certificate of attendance/participation
- Increased/changed responsibilities
- Promotion
- Career opportunities with new company
- Career opportunities in new area
- Enhanced pay/benefits
- Commendation from supervisors/peers
- Enhanced self-esteem

---

Placing development activities in their approriate context is an important activity for both the individuals concerned and for tourism and hospitality industry employers. It can, for example, assist in determining the respective roles of both parties if they are involved, who pays the costs and what are the terms of such payment, and how the outcomes are to be evaluated and acted upon.

It is important to recognize, however, that any contextual combination from Table 8.1 represents legitimate development activities for the individual, the employer or society, and all combinations do in all probability take place within European tourism and hospitality at some point.

## EDUCATION, TRAINING AND DEVELOPMENT AND THE TOURISM AND HOSPITALITY LABOUR MARKET

Chapter 4 addressed the structure of the labour market with respect to the tourism and hospitality industry in Europe. It was difficult to reach generalized conclusions about tourism labour markets primarily because of the heterogeneous nature of the industry. The discussion drew quite heavily on the work of Michael Riley (1991 and 1993) but his model, while suitable to some of the main subsectors within tourism, notably hotels and catering, retail and aspects of attractions work, does not have universal application. The internal labour markets with respect to, for example, travel management, transportation, notably in the airline sector, and heritage management, among other areas, have characteristics which make them much 'stronger'. They do exhibit many of the structural features which Riley associates with a strong internal labour market, such as specified hiring standards, single or limited ports of entry, high skills specificity, continuous on-the-job training, fixed promotion and transfer criteria, strong workplace customs and fixed pay differentials.

Thus applying labour market models to a consideration of vocational education in tourism, as Riley does, has certain inherent problems. However, given the size and importance of the weak internal labour market sectors within tourism as a whole, it is useful to consider Riley's analysis in some detail here.

Riley's analysis of the contrasting internal labour market leads to the presentation of a model which attempts to describe the relationship between type of work, labour markets and mode of human resource management. This model is reproduced in Figure 8.1.

This model is dynamic in that it proposes a two-way influence of labour market characteristics, mode of human resource management and qualitative demands that are made upon vocational education. This model leads Riley to certain propositions with respect to vocational education. These are discussed in Table 8.2 along with analysis in italic of their applicability, as well as illustrative examples.

Riley's labour market model provides us with a useful tool with which to analyse the relationship between tourism companies and the providers of vocational education and training. It also points to the dominant contexts within which education, training and development are likely to occur with respect to the various sectors of the tourism and hospitality industry. However, it is a model and thus does not provide a universal explanation as to how labour markets and vocational education relate within European tourism and hospitality. Some

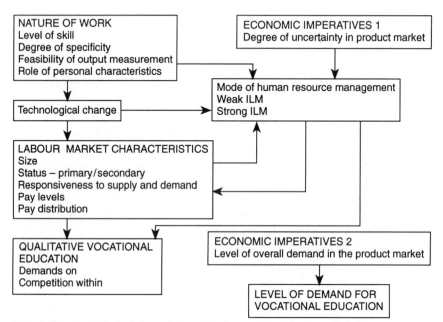

**Figure 8.1** A model of the relationship between type of work, labour markets and mode of human resource management. (Source: Riley, 1993, p. 50.)

of the possible areas of difficulty are elaborated within Table 8.2. The next section will consider models of education, training and development for tourism and hospitality in Europe to illustrate the various approaches that exist within this environment.

**Table 8.2** Relationship of weak and strong internal labour markets to vocational education

---

*The weaker the internal labour markets . . .*
- The lower pay levels will be and the attraction of specific, preparatory vocational education will be reduced as a result.
  *This analysis is certainly born out by experience in Ireland where fully-funded pre-entry training programmes for entry-level careers in food and beverage service and accommodation services/housekeeping regularly fail to attract sufficient applicants because, on the one hand, work in these areas is perceived to be low status and, on the other, graduates of the training programmes are recruited into the same positions in industry as those without the formal training.*

- The greater will be the dependence of the industry on vocational education to provide skills.
  *This is because resources allocated to in-house training will be limited as a result of high labour turnover, creating an inherent contradiction between low demand for vocational education and great dependence upon its services. One response to this dilemma is to apply the principles implicit in the sustainable tourism human resource model presented in Chapter 1. This should reduce the pressure of high labour turnover, even in the low skills areas, and justify increased spending on in-house development programmes.*

- The greater will be the range of skills required from vocational education.
  *This characteristic has a certain logic to it in that skills demands from industry are likely to be very specific, designed to fill clearly identified gaps or needs in the workforce, i.e. for a coffee shop station waiter or junior travel agency clerk, because establishments will not wish to or do not have the capability to invest in their own specific training. However, there are some indicators within vocational training in Europe which run contrary to this analysis and others which support it. Specific job-related vocational training is, in some instances, being replaced by the development of more general and transferable skills. General National Vocational Qualifications (GNVQ) in England, Wales and Northern Ireland provide a broad-based introduction to the skills needs of, on the one hand, leisure and tourism and, on the other, hospitality and catering. Original intentions had been to combine these areas into one training programme. At the same time, very specific, competency-based training towards National Vocational Qualifications (NVQ) are also offered but have less prospects of providing educational and vocational progression to participants. Likewise, in Ireland, there have been strong moves away from vocationally specific training programmes to courses which emphasize multi-skills development in tourism and hospitality areas (Baum and Reid, 1986; Baum, 1987). By contrast, the German dual system remains very skills-specific in its training focus but depends heavily on the industry to provide much of the training.*

- The harder it will be to match courses with jobs and careers.
  *If the initial skills and training demands made on vocational education by*

---

**Table 8.2** Continued

*the tourism industry are highly specific, squaring these with the longer-term aspirations and ambitions of young people may prove difficult. We have already suggested that course and career choice factors are much more broadly based than was previously the case and, in providing this breadth, GNVQs, for example, are responding to student market demand. However, as a consequence, graduates of these courses cannot be slotted into precise industry positions and grades without additional training and without clear indications of career structure in front of them. In this sense, the weak internal labour market can benefit the employer in that vocational education will provide a flexible and mobile recruit, able and expecting to undertake a variety of tasks in different functional areas of the business. However, recruiting course graduates with the expectations of filling a specific slot on a permanent basis becomes a rather more unlikely prospect.*

*The stronger the internal labour markets are . . .*
- The more specific and qualitative will be the demands on vocational education.
  *This is clearly true with respect to the strong internal labour market areas within tourism and hospitality in jobs such as museum curator or airline pilot. At the same time, sectors of the weak internal market industry are placing increased emphasis on specific general or generic skills – the 'soft' competencies (an apparent contradiction) – as their training priority. This suggests a strengthening of these internal labour markets but in a somewhat unusual manner.*

- The easier it will be to match courses with jobs.
  *This follows with respect to both types of strong internal labour market, discussed above.*

After Riley (1993), p. 50. *Italic* print indicates discussion by this author.

## MODELS OF EDUCATION, TRAINING AND DEVELOPMENT FOR TOURISM IN EUROPE

Essentially, the provision of educational, training and development opportunities in Europe is a partnership between the tourism industry, primarily in the private sector, and the education and training system, mainly within the public sector. Of course, there are exceptions to this generalization. As we saw in Chapter 2, the public sector within the European tourism and hospitality industry remains substantial, especially in Eastern Europe but also in Western Europe through the many fully or partly state-owned national airlines as well as in the hotel sector (Great Southern Hotels in Ireland, for example) and through tourism information and promotion companies. Likewise, many countries have seen the entry of private education and training organizations into the market of providing courses for those entering the tourism industry – the Swiss hotel school sector is a good example as are private colleges specializing in courses leading to the granting of professional IATA qualifications. In the United Kingdom, the independent University of Buckingham provides undergraduate and post-graduate degree programmes in tourism and hospitality studies.

Despite Riley's assertion that the inherently weak nature of tourism labour markets inevitably creates a high level of dependence on the vocational education system for the tourism industry, there is substantial evidence that the successful and large companies of European tourism and hospitality are investing increasingly in their own training and development capabilities, especially those which are predominently internationally focused corporations. This is, in part, a response to perceived weaknesses in the external college training system but also allows what is seen as greater focus and control within both initial training programmes and those provided as part of in-company development. It may also reflect the move towards stronger, branded images within some companies and the consequent desire to employ those trained specifically within the culture of the organization. This approach is important to companies that are placing increasing emphasis on branded and standardized products and services. Control is very important to the development ideology of a company like EuroDisney and was a major plank within the pre-opening strategy of the theme park in 1993. Likewise, major training-based market reorientation programmes, such as the British Airways *Putting People First* initiative must, inevitably, be carried out in-house because of their specialism and the scale of the project. Many larger tourism and hospitality companies in Europe make their own provision to run training schools independently of the public system. Forte Hotels in the UK ran their own 'Academy' in west London until recently as well as a management training centre in a more rural setting. The German retail travel company Hapag Lloyd has a training school near Bremen while EuroDisney and Club Mediterraneé prefer to meet their own training requirements in-house. In addition, training organized through industry associations is also quite common, especially in the travel agency sector in Norway and France, for example.

At the same time, it must be recognized that in all Western European countries, and probably within the tourism industry of the future in Eastern Europe, the dominent business structure in terms of the number of units is the small to medium-sized enterprise (SME). It is in this sector that Riley's analysis does have validity because smaller businesses are less able to provide the infrastructure and support for in-house training and development activities and have, traditionally, depended to a great extent on the external training system. Many Swiss hotels, for example, most of which are small family businesses, have probably the highest level of dependence on students on college placement (*stagiers*) anywhere in the world and include the expectation of an ongoing supply of these students within their normal staffing establishments. In the United Kingdom and Ireland, for example, SMEs have traditionally been the main beneficiaries of the free and subsidized training offered by the industrial training boards (the former Hotel and Catering Industry Training Board (HCITB), now the Hotel and Catering Training Company in the UK and CERT in Ireland). They have also been the main sufferers as a result of the withdrawl of the major part of government support for such training and development activity.

The training and development provided within tourism and hospitality companies is also of very variable quality and focus. There are plenty of examples from large as well as small businesses where the approach to training is typified by attitudes that mirror those within the non-sustainable human resource development model outlined in Chapter 1. Training in these companies is conducted on a limited and specifically 'needs must' basis in order to meet the short-term skills requirements of the company or unit. Such training rarely leads to formal recognition for the newly acquired skills and thus is not of great value to the individual within the context of their career development. In some situations, such an approach may be entirely justified. McDonald's, for example, recruit young people, many still at school or college, in the sure knowledge that they are providing short-term, part-time working opportunities for people who have no longer-term aspirations with the company. Thus, rapid emersion training, designed to allow the new recruit to undertake the required tasks as quickly and as efficiently as possible, can be justified. As a general rule, this model of training and development is both short-sighted and ineffective.

However, tourism and hospitality businesses increasingly recognize the importance of education, training and development as important components within the wider strategic development of the company and its markets. In Chapter 5, we considered the link between service quality and the attributes of the human resources which a company employs, particularly in relation to the concept of empowerment. Staff, at all levels, do not become 'empowered' at the dictate of a senior management decision but can only move in that direction with the support, training and development of the company and as a result of total confidence in the new corporate culture. As we have discussed in Chapter 5, Cook Johnson (1991) points to the complex links that appear to exist between perceived good service, staff empowerment and supportive human resource policies. Specifically, she points out that empowerment manifests itself in the way that companies:

- are highly focused and consistent in everything they do and say in relation to employees;
- have managers who communicate with employees;
- facilitate, rather than regulate, their employees' response to customers;
- solicit employee feedback about how they can do things better;
- stress the importance of teamwork at each level of the organization; and
- plan carefully the organization's recruitment and training needs (Cook Johnson, 1991).

Recognition of the place of the training and development process at a company level is strongly fostered by governments and their various agencies. Spending of companies in this area relative to turnover is carefully monitored as one means of understanding other indices of industrial (and service) output and productivity. However, such data is difficult to compare accurately on a transnational basis in Europe because of the differences in starting points relative to initial education and training, differences within the external education system, and the problems of quantifying the outputs of this investment as opposed to the inputs. It is relatively easy to identify the number of hours of formal training that each employee receives within a company, even if this quantification does neglect the impact of the wide range of informal learning opportunities that exist. However, measuring the return on this investment is much more difficult and, frequently, cannot be undertaken in a clear-cut and quantifiable manner. Lauermann (1992), for example, discusses the impact of a particular approach to interculturalism at British Airways which was designed to put all senior managers through a training programme:

> ... a major component of which was an explanation of the Hofstede model for understanding the cultures of different nationalities. A diagnosis of the training need had been rigorously conducted and it was generally agreed that understanding of cultural differences was a significant need driven by business strategy.
>
> (Lauermann, 1992, p. 85)

She goes on to assess the impact of this programme in purely qualitative terms.

> However, 18 months later, it is quite hard to find people whose thinking was affected by it. A major reason would seem to be that although people understand the general need, they personally had no real hunger for the education or immediate requirement.
>
> (Lauermann, 1992, p. 85)

However, despite the problems inherent in evaluating the outcomes of specific training and development initiatives, difficulties that can be used to detract from the value and purpose of the whole notion of committing resources to this area, it is difficult to dispute the principle that investing in human resources has tangible and market competitive benefits to most companies within the tourism sector. For this reason, participation by major tourism and hospitality companies in the British government's *Investors in People* scheme is relatively high. IIP is, in many respects, the application of sustainable human resource practices within a company and provides 'a public statement that we have satisfied national criteria as a company which invests wisely in its people; ensures each individual gets access to training and development; and links its training spend with the business goals' (McIntosh, 1994, p. 24).

IIP involves companies in a thorough and public overhaul of their human resource systems and practices, not just in the development area but also covering areas such as the management of employee records, ensuring widespread awareness of and access to training and development opportunities, conducting employee attitude surveys, formally evaluating each training course, and seeking to assess the impact of training and development interventions over time. IIP involves external scrutiny and validation and thus ensures public accountability. Companies flying the blue IIP flag are making a public statement about their attitude and commitment to staff and this is utilized as a major marketing platform for those who achieve the required and demanding standards.

The reality in the tourism and hospitality industries of most countries in Europe, however, is that education, training and development are partnership processes between the tourism industry and its amalgam of public and private sector operations on the one hand, and the specialist providers of courses and development activities, again both public and private sector, on the other. Brotherton (1993) notes the variety of formats through which such partnerships may operate, through official structures as in Germany or Switzerland or on the basis of *ad hoc* arrangements as in France and Britain. Thus it is a partnership that operates according to a number of different models and with differing centres of control and influence. These models include the following, although the examples are simplifications and do not necessarily apply in total within any national system.

### The total separation model

In this model there are few links between training and development within the two areas. The industry depends upon the external education and training system as the main source for its new recruits but contributes nothing to the education and training process and is not consulted by education and training providers in terms of curriculum, teaching methods, etc. Until recent reforms, Romanian tourism education and training operated relatively closely to this model. The main providers of education and training for tourism, the National University, the National Institute for Tourism Management and Training and tourism high schools had little formal contact with what was an exclusively publicly owned tourism and hospitality industry. The parties were so remote that the industry did not contribute to training through work experience placement, taking the view that those on formal courses did not have the skills to work in the professional environment. On graduation, students were placed in jobs within the industry, where industry found it necessary to apply its own training input, but up to that point the two parties maintained no links. Changes are now in place that will ensure the start of dialogue but contacts are still fairly remote and their benefits not fully understood. The new private sector in tourism and hospitality is reluctant to participate in any official structures initiated by the government and so, for example, manpower data collection and participation in attempts by the Romanian Hoteliers Association to establish formal training committees have received no private sector support.

Airey (1994) notes similar problems with respect to tourism and hospitality education in Poland. The work of the European Union's aid programme to Eastern Europe (PHARE) in Poland was developed to respond to four key indicators of successful vocational education and training, which are in fact useful measuring tools for the analysis of any tourism and hospitality education and training system. They are:

- sufficient and effective education/industry links;
- up-to-date, best standards and practice;
- adequte provision for all levels, subsectors and employment groups;
- sufficient breadth, understanding and challenge.

Airey's analysis with respect to the first pointer leads to the following conclusion:

> Links with industry are poorly developed in Polish education. For example, employers are rarely involved in courses or curriculum design; few teachers have recent or any experience of industry and industrial secondment for teachers is virtually unknown; case studies based on industry rarely form part of teaching; while most courses include industrial placements for students these are rarely well integrated into the courses. (Airey, 1994, p. 8)

Airey also notes difficulties with respect to the other three pointers, notably inadequate and out-of-date resources; outmoded curricula, especially in business and customer-focused areas; insufficient breadth to reflect the range of the modern tourism and hospitality industry; and courses that do not challenge students in the way that is relatively commonplace in Western Europe, especially with respect to the development of responsibility and independence in the workplace which is an essential educational precursor to work in an empowered industry environment.

## Long-standing education/training and industry partnerships

Examples of this model are those in place in Germany within the dual system which focus on an apprenticeship model in all trade areas. Under this system, all young people leaving school at sixteen continue in education through a combination of training in the workplace and attendance on a part-time basis at local training colleges or *Berufsschule*. Programme content in the workplace is decided through a nationally agreed training code, determined through extensive consultation between educational, employer and trade union interests. Educational curricula are also decided nationally. Hotel and catering trades are well provided for within the German dual system but the importance of the model in the travel and leisure sectors is much less pronounced, perhaps because of the extent of formal training organized and run by that sector in its own right. In Holloway's view:

> The German 'dual system' apprenticeship scheme has much to commend it. It is distinguished by the extent to which it is employer led, employer controlled . . . and in part employer delivered by staff trained and qualified to do so. However, it has the added advantage of drawing not only on those who have left school before the age of 18, but also many in their late teens and twenties, who wish to top up their formal education with vocational training for specific jobs.
> (Holloway, 1993, p. 106)

### The British partnership model

This model operates at two levels. On the one hand, *ad hoc* and very variable links exist between individual education and training providers and the tourism and hospitality industry at a local, national and, increasingly, international level. These partnerships frequently work very effectively. On the other hand, the mainstream system is much more government-led than is the case in Germany. Traditionally apprenticeship schemes did operate, especially in the hotel and catering sector, but without the strength and organization of its German counterpart. The system collapsed owing to a lack of control and incentive to participate as well as through the impact of economic downturn during the 1980s. The model which has replaced it is unique in Europe in that it focuses on the outcomes of training, in other words the skills and competencies which employees can demonstrate regardless of where they were acquired, rather than on the formal programme designed to assist students and trainees to acquire those skills. National Vocational Qualifications are designed to give recognition to the attainment of specified skills and competencies at levels ranging from very basic (Level 1) through to complex supervisory and management tasks (Level 5). Where those skills were acquired is immaterial to the award, provided that the employee or student can demonstrate the necessary level in that skill.

This model allows experienced tourism and hospitality staff who have received no formal and certified training during their career to demonstrate and claim their competencies and offer these towards nationally recognized awards. This process is known as the Accreditation of Prior Learning (APL). In practice, most NVQs are obtained either through the college system or within a formal training context in industry. Teachers and trainers are formally recognized as verifiers, able to accredit competency in the requisite skills areas and, in turn, have their assessments monitored by external verifiers, appointed by bodies approved by the government's managing agency, the National Council for Vocational Qualifications (NCVQ). While an element of partnership exists within this system, it is also true to say that, in part, the tourism and hospitality industry and the education/training system are now in competition within this system, competing for the right to train young people and to access public funding in order to do so. One of the main benefits in providing formal recognition for the training and skills development which occurs in the tourism and hospitality industry is that it allows those who are able to claim recognition for their skills to use the NVQs as stepping stones onto the ladder for further training and development, both within the industry and back within the formal education system. The model will also help to plug what is a very worrying training and skills deficiency within the tourism and hospitality industry in Britain, especially in certain sectors. A very high proportion of the two million plus workforce in the hotel and catering sector have received no formal training for the work they are undertaking. This issue applies at management as well as at skilled and unskilled levels. Battersby (1990) refers to a Hotel and Catering Training Company study which suggests that of 460 000 supervisors and managers in the industry, 300 000 have no formal management qualifications (Battersby, 1990). Clearly, the British model has the potential to cope with this problem.

### The Irish model

This model also operates at two levels in that the *ad hoc* and informal level exists, as in Britain, between colleges and industry at local, national and international level, especially in relation to the provision of work placement opportunities. The other level is managed through a unique coordinating agency, an Irish semi-state body, responsible to the Minister of Tourism (formerly the Minister of Labour) and known as CERT. CERT was founded in 1963 and operates under the authority of a board which is representative of employers, trade unions, educational institutions as well as government agencies and departments. Its brief is to coordinate all aspects of the planning of manpower needs within tourism at a macro level through research and the determination of training/development priorities as well as through the design and implementation of courses through the agency of its own training centres and the college system (Walsh, 1993). CERT, through the National Tourism Certification Board (NTCB), which again brings together the voices of the industry and educational sectors, coordinates the certification of tourism employees trained in a variety of situations and also offers opportunities for APL. CERT is also responsible for the provision of in-company and short-course training on behalf of tourism industry businesses on a commercial basis. The Irish model is unique in that it provides by far the most comprehensive approach to coordinating the inputs of education and the tourism industry into a unified system and, through CERT, operates through total coordination and the identification of training and development needs at both macro and micro levels. We will consider CERT's role in relation to manpower planning at a national level in Chapter 9.

## Management education, training and development

Thus far, the focus of discussion on partnerships between education/training interests and the tourism industry in various European countries has, in fact if not in intent, focused on training and development at a level which is normally described as craft, skilled trade or apprenticeship. The issue of meeting the training and development needs of future and existing managers for tourism in Europe has not been addressed except in so far as it is covered by in-company provision. The management environment also provides a diversity of approaches within and between national systems. Holloway (1993) points to a definitional problem which, while applicable at all levels, creates particular difficulties at university-level education. He notes that:

> The variety of definitions (of tourism) within Europe leads to different approaches to course curriculum design which add to the difficulties in seeking mutual recognition of qualifications between the European partners. For example, in the Netherlands recreation is seen as integral with travel and tourism, and in France, too, the terms 'leisure' and 'tourism' are used synonymously – at least, in terms of curriculum development. Germany has not yet recognized the need for vocational education or training for leisure and recreation, while (at the management level) Britain has chosen to develop distinct curricula for leisure and tourism, despite significant areas of overlap in knowledge and skills.     (Holloway, 1993, pp. 101–2)

In many ways, these problems of definition arise through historical accident within universities and other providers of management education. The location, scope and even the existence or not of specialist provision in the tourism area is frequently linked to the origins of initiatives of this kind. In Britain, the study of tourism in a wider context has frequently originated within specialist hotel and catering studies faculties – two of the earliest examples, at the Universities of Strathclyde and Surrey, have followed this model. This has greatly influenced programme structure and content as well as the professional as opposed to academic focus of courses. Other European models have seen the study of tourism develop rather more independently – at the Free University of Brussels in Belgium, for example. Belgian programmes in tourism 'are strongly influenced, in their design and emphasis, by the department in which they are located, which may be social sciences, economics or psychology' (Van Langenhove and Lowyck, 1993, p. 122). Likewise the Academy of Economic Studies of the National University in Bucharest, Romania, offers courses in tourism which have no vocational application and focus on macro concerns relating to the international tourism system.

Interestingly, Romania had no provision for the training and development of tourism sector managers until 1994, when initial courses were offered in the National Institute for Tourism Management and Training. Prior to 1989, managers were political appointments and, following the revolution, most hotel and other tourism managers were elected by fellow workers without any necessary qualifications for the post. Airey (1994) also notes a similar historical absence of management and business education for the industry in Poland.

The issue, in many respects, relates to the balance between practical vocational, professional business and academic theoretical inputs into the curriculum and the confusion which use of differing nomenclature can cause. For example, the Swiss Hotel Management Diploma, offered by many private institutions after two years' study, admits students who generally would not qualify for university-level education elsewhere in Europe. They undertake a highly practical, vocational course with twelve months in class and twelve months on work placement in the Swiss industry, undertaking entry-level work, primarily in the food and beverage area. Skull (1991) provides a very useful analysis of the system which produces graduates who, frequently, obtain entry-level positions within the hotel industry despite the completion of a 'management' qualification. The compelling necessity of describing the programmes as 'management' is market-driven in that courses would not recruit if they were described otherwise. It is a term frequently used within the tourism sector to describe education and training at a level where it would not be applicable or admissable in other economic sectors. This is one of the attractions of the sector and reasons for its over-subscription by applicants.

In Britain, the growth in provision in specifically tourism (as opposed to hotel, leisure or recreation) studies has been phenomenal in recent years. The Tourism Society (1993) note that 'at the beginning of the 1993/4 academic year ... a total of 36 institutions, mostly universities, were offering a total of 53 courses of which 27 led to bachelor degrees and 26 to postgraduate qualifications' (p. 7). These are very substantial increases over the equivalent 1992 figures. There is no evidence that the employment market justifies expansion in this sector but universities are responding to strong market forces within education as well as to the clearly generic nature of the business and vocational education received within programmes which provide for careers outside of the specific tourism and hospitality sector.

One of the management-level issues which forms the kernel of much debate within the European tourism and hospitality industry relates to achieving the appropriate balance between the vocational and professional on the one hand and academic or intellectual on the other. It is a debate which generates considerable passion from supporters of both extremes. On the one hand, the important concern of vocational relevance is used as a guiding benchmark within those systems which are aiming to ensure that their graduates can fit into the opportunities provided by the industry and undertake those tasks demanded of them immediately. This model has particular strength within the hotel and catering subsector and is at the root of the German apprenticeship scheme, which is the start of the long route to management. As Skull (1991) shows, Swiss hotel management education also draws upon the premise that the start of a career which aspires towards the management of a hotel must be well grounded in practical, vocationally relevent and, preferably, food and beverage skills. Within these systems, more complex and less practical skills and requirements are met at a later stage in the educational and training process.

The alternative extreme places the main emphasis of preparation for a management career within the tourism and hospitality industry in the context of a general university-level education. This provides the intellectual development and training upon which the specific demands of the tourism and hospitality sector can be grafted, either through postgraduate conversion programmes in universities and colleges or within workplace training and development. This route is rather more akin to some vocational traditions in the United States – for example, American legal training only commences when a college or university graduate enters specialist law school. It is also a view that has some support within sectors of the tourism and hospitality industry where recruitment focuses upon generic as opposed to specific skills and competencies (Baum, 1990; Baum, 1991b).

The reality, given the diversity that is the European tourism and hospitality industry, is that the ideal model, if such a concept exists, lies somewhere between the two extremes and that there is a place and need for programmes which place greater emphasis in both directions. However, our discussion in Chapter 6 pointed to the problems of image and lack of perceived professional status which the tourism and hospitality industry faces in Europe. One contribution to overcoming this problem could lie in the nature of qualifying education that is provided at higher levels. A review of curricula, learning resources and teaching methods employed within many tourism and hospitality management education programmes in Europe suggests that the emphasis on vocationalism has important consequences for the level of academic and intellectual demands that are made on students. By comparision with colleagues studying in areas such as psychology or the sciences, the benefits of vocational relevance appear to be gained at a cost to conceptual demands and academic rigour. This cannot be in the long-term career interests of those participating in such programmes.

Riley's weak internal labour market model highlights multiple ports of entry and a lack of formal progression criteria as characteristic of some subsectors within the tourism and hospitality industry. In practice, this means that the industry's managers have a wide range of backgrounds and training and that formal and specific academic or vocational training routes offer only one option among many to those aspiring to manage in the industry. At the same time, issues of status and professionalism as well as wider moves to place greater emphasis on formally recognized qualifications point to the need to ensure that those in management can point to equivalence in terms of their capabilities, whether gained in the workplace or in college. Thus formally recognized progression routes for those entering the industry at whatever level and for those already working in it becomes an important issue. In the United Kingdom, this need is being addressed through National Vocational Qualifications (and their Scottish equivalents) which provide for recognition of skills and capabilities acquired in both the educational and workplace setting from basic skills (Levels 1 and 2) through graduate and postgraduate management levels (4 and 5). The theory of the system, when fully established, is that it will provide full portability between work and education and allow managers and others, as their careers progress, to acquire additional recognition for what they are doing at work or learning in college.

Portability is also the theory behind moves to establish equivalent courses and qualifications for tourism and hospitality within the European Union. With established harmonization and recognition between training routes and courses, it should be easier for tourism and hospitality sector employees to avail themselves of opportunities in different countries of the Union. The work of CEDEFOP, as the EU's vocational training agency, has been important in establishing the framework for vocational harmonization within the twelve member states (for example, CEDEFOP, 1991). However, it is fair to say that the impact of CEDEFOP's efforts has been rather limited in an industry that, in general, does not place great credence upon formal qualifications and where, as we saw in Chapter 7, there is already a well established tradition of mobility within Europe.

Other initiatives include attempts by tourism and hospitality institutions and industry organizations to establish agreement and accreditation for programmes in different countries as equivalent and eligible for a common qualification. This route has had mixed success. A promising idea for a European Diploma in the hospitality area, EURODIP, foundered on different perceptions of equivalence between participating agencies. Northern European members were happy to interpret this in a fairly broad and general manner by accrediting existing and different programmes, thus allowing local interpretation of curricula and structure, while other participants, mainly from the south, sought the development of a truly common programme, identical in its content and delivery. More successful have been local arrangements between consortia of institutions in Europe, providing similar programmes leading to the award of common or joint certificates or those offered jointly by institutions, with students spending periods of time on all participating campuses. An example of such a programme is the BA(Hons) Management and European Tourism offered collaboratively by the Catholic University of Lille (France) and the Universities of Humberside (UK), Cadiz (Spain) and Vantaa (Finland). A further option has involved the UK-based Hotel, Catering and Institutional Management Association (HCIMA) offering professional recognition to programmes on a Europe-wide basis and thus establishing an alternative route to comparability and harmonization.

Education for tourism and hospitality in Europe, especially at management level, is going through a period of significant change. This is true not only in Western European countries but is even more applicable in the east, where major reforms are required to enable institutions and the industry to modernize the management and operation of businesses in all subsectors. The main imperative for change, however, is likely to be the continuing process of globalization within the industry, and the pressure that this will apply on institutions to ensure that courses and qualifications meet the needs of both individual graduates and the major employing companies.

REVIEW AND DISCUSSION QUESTIONS

1. How important is the education versus training debate? Has it surfaced at any point in your own school, college or working career?
2. Identify jobs and tasks which have changed significantly within your own lifetime and that of your parents (not only in the tourism and hospitality industry). What development needs resulted from such changes?
3. How can providers of education and training prepare students to be responsive to change?
4. If the main needs of tourism and hospitality employers are for staff with good interpersonal, communication and guest handling skills, should colleges and universities dispense with practical and vocational skills development and just concentrate on these areas?
5. Consider **three** situations where you participated in a specific training or development programme (in college, university or the workplace). Place each of these within the 'contextual map' (Table 8.1) against each of the categories specified. How could the programmes have been effectively varied through use of alternatives within the 'map'?
6. In what ways do the characteristics of the tourism and hospitality internal labour market affect the nature of vocational education and training it requires?
7. What are the main distinctions between the macro models of education and training for tourism and hospitality that are considered in this chapter?
8. How can the industry–education partnership operate more effectively in the tourism and hospitality sector?

# Planning to meet the human resource needs of the European tourism and hospitality industry

## 9

## INTRODUCTION

In this chapter, we return to one of the central tenets of sustainability in human resource terms and that is the need to institute effective strategic and operational planning mechanisms in order to cater for human resource requirements within tourism and hospitality at a micro and macro level. It is one of the main criticisms of the traditional human resource model within tourism and hospitality that planning is based on contingency and the attainment of short-term objectives.

Such 'short-termism' is common at different levels within the tourism and hospitality industry. It is characteristic at unit level, where it is common to witness recruitment and redundancy closely tracking cyclical and seasonal changes in demand without any apparent sense of anticipation or planning. The instability and uncertainty which such policies engender impacts upon the ability of the business to deliver the product and service which the customer is entitled to expect. Such practice puts the short-term profitability of the company before the delivery of quality service to the customer, in itself a major factor in ensuring long-term competitiveness. At the corporate level, performance demands on individual business units are frequently such as to ensure the short-termist approach outlined above. There is also a danger at corporate level that human resource decisions are made without reference to the needs of the individual business unit. In some hotel companies, for example, it has been traditional practice to rotate general managers on the basis of a two-year cycle of duty and to judge their performance on, primarily, financial outcomes over that short period. The consequence at unit level of this policy is an environment in which planning becomes almost nonexistent and human resource practices focus almost exclusively on attributes from the traditional paradigm to the neglect of sustainable practices. To those involved, sustainability is only seen to be of relevance in the context of two-year outcomes. The two-year rotation, while it has not entirely disappeared, is much less common in major companies than it was in the 1970s and early 1980s. Finally, short-termism is commonplace at the macro level of the region or the country, where planning is deficient in order to meet the long-term needs of the tourism and hospitality industry as a whole. However, probably of greater significance at this level is the absence of coordination between a plethora of government and private sector agencies within the human resource area, with an inevitable impact on the planning process.

In this chapter, we shall address human resource planning (or man-power planning as it is frequently known) at these three levels. Particularly emphasis will be given to the final dimension, that of the macro, and the case of one European country, the Republic of Ireland, will be examined in some detail in order to illustrate planning and coordination processes at work. Consideration of the planning process has deliberately been left to the latter part of this book because of its dependence on other aspects which have been considered in earlier chapters, notably the historical antecedents, characteristics and structure of the tourism and hospitality industry in Europe (Chapters 2 and 3) the labour markets within the sector (Chapter 4) the role of human resources in the delivery of quality service (Chapter 5) and the role of education and training (Chapter 8).

The principles of human resource planning have strong similarities at whatever level is being considered. The process is by no means new although its emergence in Europe as an identified field of activity and expertise cannot be traced much further back than the 1960s. Bramham (1983) attributes this focus to the social and economic climate of the period which increased the complexity of management. Technological and economic change imposed new constraints on management's freedom of action while labour shortages, especially in key skills areas, focused attention on the competitive nature of the labour market in a manner that had not really been experienced in the past. Subsequently, the need for a focused process of planning has been strengthened by pressure on companies to derive greater efficiency and productivity from their human resources, processes frequently accompanied by significant reduction in the number and status of staff employed. Within this changing environment, planning of human resources becomes an essential process.

A number of definitions of human resource planning exist:

> The systematic analysis of human resources in the future, directed to minimize uncertainty and surprise and to eliminating mistakes and wastage. (Lester, 1960, in Donald, 1974, p. 14)

> A strategy for the acquisition, utilization, improvement and preservation of an enterprise's human resources.
> (Department of Employment and Productivity, 1968)

> Manpower planning aims to maintain and improve the ability of the organization to achieve corporate objectives, through the development of strategies designed to enhance the contribution of manpower at all times in the foreseeable future. (Stainer, 1971, p. 3)

Two of these definitions are focused primarily on the needs of the organization; only Lester goes beyond that in order to imply the need to plan human resources at a macro level as well.

Bramham (1982) identifies three central concerns which apply to human resource planning at whatever scale it operates:

1. What sort of information about the external and internal environment is required?
2. To what uses will such information be put, particularly with respect to planning?
3. What techniques and methods of manpower planning should be utilized?

Bramham developed a framework for the planning process which incorporates all three areas (Figure 9.1). This provides a model at the level of the company which can be compared to that proposed for planning at the macro level later in this chapter (Figure 9.3). However, in many of its components, the framework does have applicability in the wider context as well. In many ways, Bramham's framework, in its relationship to the external environment in particular, takes us back to the earlier consideration of the tourism and hospitality labour market in Chapter 4.

## HUMAN RESOURCE PLANNING AT THE BUSINESS UNIT LEVEL

Bramham's framework provides an ideal mechanism through which to plan human resource requirements at the level of the business unit. The fragmented nature of the tourism and hospitality industry and the small business structure of many enterprises within the sector in Europe mean that, in reality, such planning (along with many other aspects of business planning and forecasting) is comparatively infrequent and unsophisticated in its application. Much managemnent practice – and that in the human resource area is no exception – is based on traditional practice (i.e. staffing levels are based on custom and practice with some shedding of numbers in response to changes in performance) and a relatively crude evaluation of needs. This process is mainly driven by seasonality and other cyclical factors which impact upon tourism and hospitality businesses. Thus hotels and attractions in locations such as Rhodes in Greece and Donegal in Ireland plan their staffing needs around the seasonality factor. Staff are recruited or return when the businesses reopen in the spring and are released again in the autumn when many seasonal businesses close. In terms of fluctuations in demand within the day or the week, planning revolves round the utilization of part-time or casual support staff to the main core establishment. The situation at the corporate level, as we shall see, can be somewhat different.

And yet, given the high cost of labour in most Western European countries, this aspect of planning is one that few small tourism and hospitality businesses can afford to neglect.

Bramham suggests that within his first stage, that of information collection or what he calls the investigation stage, there are four main areas that require consideration. The first of these is the business plan, which provides detailed information on a company's projected sales and financial targets as well as objectives with respect to new products or markets. This process will apply both to the independent small business and to the single business unit within a larger company. In the latter case, a local business plan may be prepared within the context of corporate objectives and both sources will require consideration within the human resource planning process. The business plan may impact

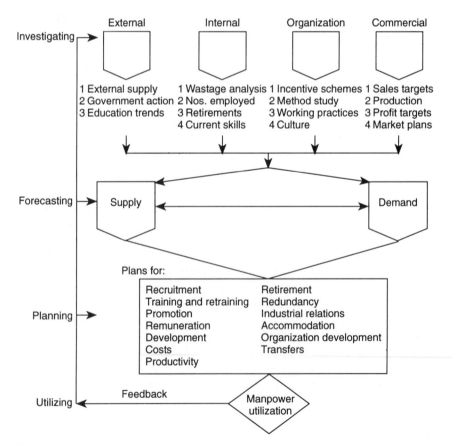

**Figure 9.1** A framework for manpower planning. (Source: Bramham, 1982.)

on human resource requirements in a number of ways. For example, a hotel may project increased business as a result of a new arrangement with a tour operator or may plan a special low-season promotion to increase business at that time of the year. Thus, an equestrian centre could target new overseas markets in Germany or Japan, supported by special multilingual promotional material. Such changes, and a wide range of others, will all impact on the number of employees required at specific times of the year as well as upon the specific skills that will be needed to cater for changes in business activity. In the example above, enhancing the language skills of existing or new staff may well be a necessary response to planned activity within the business plan.

The second component in the investigation stage is that of the organization. Consideration of the existing structure and management within the business or business unit as well as in the wider corporate context will influence the level and type of human resource provision that is required. For example, the process of centralization or decentralization of functions impacts on the range of functional responsibilities that are retained within an individual unit of a company. Many hotel companies have demonstrated both processes at the same time in recent times. While some functions such as marketing and sales have been centralized as a result of enhanced technology, a contrary move to greater unit autonomy in some companies has resulted in an increased and more complex range of tasks executed at unit level. Other organizational changes, such as moves towards the standardization of certain brands and products, for example Accor's Ibis hotels or the Posthouses within Forte's portfolio, also impact on both the level and skills of staffing that are required within individual units as well as corporately. Distancing strategies, such as those already discussed in Chapter 4, are also examples of organizational change which impact upon the human resources that a business unit will require in order to perform its functions – the elimination of an in-house laundry or the franchising of the restaurant are good examples from hotels, while the contracting out of maintenance functions by an airline represents the same process at work in a different subsector of the industry. Thus, human resource planning can only be carried out in a successful manner if organizational features are fully analysed and changes since previous planning activities are recognized.

Our analysis of factors which influence the tourism and hospitality labour market in Chapter 4 pointed to a wide range of external environmental forces which will influence the internal human resource climate. Likewise, the external environment must be considered when undertaking human resource planning at all levels. Legislative factors, local market trends, local employment features and changes in local training provision are examples of the kind of external considerations which a tourism or hospitality business must include in a preparatory analysis prior to human resource planning. The opening of competition to the beach bar, windsurfing school or heritage centre previously in a monopoly position are examples of information vital to the human resource planning process.

The final dimension within Bramham's investigation stage focuses on internal human resources, in other words an analysis of the existing staffing situation within the business unit or company. This analysis may include consideration of productivity levels, skills deficiencies and the reasons for high levels of staff turnover (collected by, for example, exit interviews). In addition, consideration of the age, gender and ethnic profile of the workforce can be important within the planning context, especially if reference is made to preparation for promotion as well as easing the responsibilities of some members of staff prior to retirement. This aspect of the information collection process requires regular attention, especially in those subsectors of the tourism and hospitality industry where staff turnover levels are particularly high. The information generated with respect to staff turnover in specific departments or within certain age groups can assist in the recruitment and staff retention planning process. Traditional dependence on transitory student labour, for example, may be reduced by looking at alternative sources of labour, such as mature women returning to the workforce, where turnover is not such a problem. This move, however, may require planning for changes in shifts and in the support facilities available for staff. Indeed, the gradual movement away from split shifts in hotels in Britain may reflect the increasing level of part-time female employment in the industry, at lower levels.

Bramham's second consideration, that of utilizing the information collected, is at the heart of the human resource planning process. This is the stage where the range of information collected is analysed and its implications translated into planning, both specifically in human resource terms and in the wider strategic context of the business unit. Thus human resource inputs may warrant a separate 'compartment' within the overall plan, but it is important to ensure that this compartment is not isolated from what are frequently seen as the mainstream concerns of product and marketing. There is a symbiotic relationship between all areas of the business, with total mutual dependency. It is a common problem, particularly in the small business sector of the European tourism and hospitality industry, that plans for the development of new products or new markets are made in total isolation of what these plans mean for the area of human resources. When, finally, HR considerations are addressed, it is frequently too late to intervene in a way that allows opportunities to be met and problems to be overcome in a sustainable manner. A hotel, for example, committed to catering for a new Far Eastern market may well only commence language and customs classes for existing personnel or seek to recruit staff with necessary language skills when the first group of guests are already in place. Such lack of foresight in planning can easily undermine the efforts put in in terms of marketing and product development. Likewise, declining hotel occupancy or airline load factors may stimulate a marketing response within the strategic planning process. However, reference to the human resource 'compartment' could have identified accelerating staff turnover and consequent deterioration in service as a possible contributory cause of the problem.

According to Bramham's model, human resource planning is, broadly, utilized in four main respects. The first purpose is that of forecasting human resource requirements. In the tourism and hospitality industry, business levels can be difficult to predict because demand is cyclical and is also very vulnerable to external influence. Thus the Gulf crisis in 1990 and 1991 closely followed by recession reduced the level of both business and leisure travel within and to Europe by a very large factor. These events could not be fully anticipated, although contingency plans could be and were implemented in order to reduce the impact of loss of traditional business sources. Many London hotels, for example, reacted by altering their market focus and, at the same time, reducing their staffing levels in a fairly draconian manner. However, many businesses in the tourism and hospitality industry claim that seasonality and cyclical demand within the week, for example, make the accurate forecasting of human resource requirements close to impossible. Provided that appropriate management information systems – especially yield management – are in place giving detailed information on the demand cycle and other factors which will influence the need for human resources in the short-, medium- and long-term, the relatively accurate forecasting of human resource requirements should be achievable.

The forecasting of human resource needs is not purely a quantitative process designed to enumerate the requirement for labour within the business unit. It is common to estimate the number of employees that are needed without giving consideration to factors such as the experience and skills requirements as well as the training inputs that will be necessary to meet these requirements. These qualitative aspects are of equal importance to those in the quantitative domain. It must also be recognized that forecasting beyond the short to medium term can be highly unreliable and subject to the influence of a variety of factors which cannot be predicted. Thus forecasting of human resource requirements can rarely be undertaken, with any accuracy, beyond a two- to three-year period. Anything beyond that is purely indicative and responsive to major external trends, such as computerization or the coming on stream of a new training college, rather than local factors.

Bramham provides a useful structure for identifying the different elements of human resource forecasting based on timescales ranging from the short term to five years. Figure 9.2 reproduces this timescale model.

For the small tourism and hospitality business, forecasting of human resource needs presents a number of problems.

- Predicting any future events at the macro or micro level is difficult and uncertain.

| | Basis of requirement | Basis of availability | Possible actions |
|---|---|---|---|
| 0 – 6 months | Current budget | Current manpower | Contractors Overtime Recruitment Redundancy |
| 6 – 18 months | Forward budget | Current manpower less projected leavers | Promotion Transfer Recruitment |
| 18 months – 5 years | Forward budgets and plans | Projected current manpower plus those completing training | Recruitment Planned rundown Training programmes |
| More than 5 years | Predicted market and technological changes | Expected labour market and education system supplies | Organization development and job restructuring Management development programmes |

**Figure 9.2** Timescale of forecasts and plans. (Source: Bramham, 1983, p. 150.)

- There is a temptation to extrapolate from historical data in an uncritical manner without modification in response to the present situation and anticipated future.
- For many businesses, insufficient information about past workload, productivity and skills levels has been retained. Effective human resource planning is an ongoing process and the system takes a number of years of record-keeping and experience to operate to maximum effect.
- The bases for the assumptions that are essential to planning are often difficult to establish, whether they relate to market factors or the impact of changes in a company's product profile.
- There is a lack of effective corporate or business planning. Discussion of the need for human resource forecasting has assumed that effective strategic and business planning takes place and that the forecasts will be inputted into this process – this is by no means always the case in the small, family-owned tourism and hospitality operations that dominate the European industry. In the absence of wider planning, it is difficult to forecast human resource needs with any accuracy or meaning. Where such planning is in place, it is often difficult to integrate human resource forecasts into the main planning process.
- The main techniques involved in human resource forecasting are statistical and extrapolative. Such reliance on the quantitative can give a spurious impression of precision and can also readily lead to the ignoring of important qualitative considerations.

- The processes involved in making accurate and useful forecasts of human resource needs are time-consuming and expensive and require skills that are not always available within the small business context. Units that belong to a larger corporate structure may be able to seek the support and guidance of the parent company but such services are not available to the small business and these problems frequently lead to the neglect of the process altogether.

Forecasting the supply of human resources is the second purpose identified by Bramham to which information obtained within the investigation stage can be put. The objective of effective human resource planning is to match demand with supply. Ensuring this actually occurs requires that a company has as full knowledge as possible about its internal and external sources of human resources. Thus supply forecasting is based on the analysis of a number of sources of information, including the following.

- The profile of the existing workforce, according to age, gender, home location, skills, qualifications and related factors. This will allow planning to cater for retirement, likely attrition for other reasons, potential for promotion within the existing workforce and similar projections. Many tourism and hospitality businesses faced with high turnover rates and the effects of seasonality may feel that such effort is not really worthwhile. However, identifying demographic, skills and related characteristics of employees can be a useful starting point towards reducing staff turnover and also in establishing some annual stability within the core of the seasonal workforce. For example, balancing a predominantly student, non-local workforce with some local, more mature personnel, who can be offered work again the next year, may give the opportunity of starting the next season with some of the required skills in place, thus benefiting the product and service standards during the early part of the season. Such strategies cannot be planned or implemented without the requisite information. Many tourism and hospitality businesses in Europe are actively involved in supporting the growing mobility of labour within the EU, especially among young people, through formal schemes and on an *ad hoc* basis. By its nature, this supply of labour is unstable and a business will benefit from introducing some means to balance and stabilize the overall workforce, such as utilizing a local core group. The hotel industry in Switzerland operates with a very high level of temporary labour, primarily foreign students who are on six month *stage* placements in the establishment and are replaced by other students when they complete their time. This approach can only work if allied to a strong and permanent supply of local operational and supervisory skills, equipped to work with the temporary employees. However, one example of a restuarant in Geneva, staffed only by *stagiers*, even at supervisory level, certainly does not follow this recommendation. Operating in these conditions depends on full management knowledge of their permanent employees and their characteristics.

- An analysis of leaving rates and the reasons that staff are choosing to move to other positions is also an important step in forecasting supply requirements and will influence future recruitment practices. People can leave for a variety of reasons – voluntary resignation to move to another job or out of the workforce (for example, to college or the home) redundancy, retirement, dismissal, completion of contract (at the end of the season, for example) and death. Businesses can benefit from understanding the reasons why people leave as one step towards reducing its impact – catering for recruitment, training and development can be time-consuming and expensive and it is in the company's interest to reduce but not totally eliminate staff turnover. People leaving of their own volition is the most significant cause of staff turnover and an understanding of the reasons why they leave (gained through exit interviews and similar techniques) may lead to changes within the working environment but may also result in alterations in recruitment strategies through targeting groups who are less likely to leave. Thus if a tourism and hospitality business located in a remote area consistently loses young employees because of factors such as the absence of local nightlife and homesickness, it may be beneficial to concentrate recruitment more on the local workforce and, possibly, to invest more in training and development in order to upgrade local skills, as opposed to selecting those from further away who may already have the requisite skills profile. This kind of change in recruiting cannot be undertaken effectively without forecasting and planning for its consequences.

- Strategies to influence the external labour supply environment in response to current and projected skills requirements. In particular, such strategies can focus on local and possibly national education and training provision. Thus if an analysis of existing skills requirements and those offered by education and training providers shows significant gaps or disparity, managers and owners of tourism and hospitality businesses may attempt to influence change at the level of the providers or to look to alternative sources of skilled labour, either through in-house training or turning to providers elsewhere. Colleges and universities in most European countries are keen to involve local tourism and hospitality representatives in an advisory capacity, and this is one legitimate strategy through which to address any such problems. On a larger scale, the *Hospitality Partnership* in the UK is intended to act as a forum for businesses and education to share experience and views while, at the same time, stating a commitment to good practice in the workplace and education by both parties.

The third contribution that a total picture of the human resource environment in which a company is located can make is to the area of forecasting needs with respect to skills and management development as well as career planning. Planning to meet these needs, both from a company and an individual point of view, is the logical consequence of such forecasts. This process depends heavily on careful identification of both company and individual skills and other needs and the ability to match the requirements of the organization with those of the individual. This is by no means always possible, especially within the small and family-owned tourism and hospitality businesses which characterize European tourism. However great the potential of a young employee, there are times when opportunities for promotion and enhancement do not exist within the organization, often because other individuals have been in post for a long time or because certain responsibilities are earmarked for family members. The options in this situation include recognition that it is possible to outgrow a company and to assist that person to move elsewhere with good grace. This is not always forthcoming and tourism and hospitality employers have been known to go to considerable lengths to block opportunities for mobility in order to benefit their own short-term requirements.

Alternatively, it may be possible to take a longer view and to anticipate opportunities in the future. A number of hoteliers in Ireland, for example, have developed the practice of encouraging promising young employees to take positions in Switzerland, Germany and the United States in order to further their experience and skills in a way that would not be possible in the 'home' hotel and have assisted them to find appropriate positions. Such placements are designed to tie into anticipated opportunities in the original company when the employee returns. Of course, they may never return but that is a risk to be taken.

Developing an effective career planning structure within a small company is never easy and, clearly, business units that are part of a larger national or multinational group have the distinct advantage of being able to link into the wider corporate environment, both to provide opportunities for their own staff and to recruit talent from elsewhere in the organization. However, small businesses cannot afford to neglect the needs and aspirations of their staff because they are likely to become disgruntled and to work with less commitment and interest, thus adversely affecting the quality of product and service on offer. They will also, probably, leave in any case but on a sour and negative note. Those that do not have ambitions or aspirations for promotion will remain behind and become 'thick-skinned' to customer needs and, in all probabilty, a liability as a result. Thus, close monitoring of individual staff performance, ambition and needs is an important contribution to ensuring continued motivation and commitment.

Managing skills and career development has a company as well as an individual focus. Planning development needs in response to or anticipation of identified skills shortages (due to growth in demand or anticipated retirement, for example) or changes in product or service requirements ensures the smooth passage of change rather than major disruption and dislocation. Thus a business can derive considerable benefit from investing in training and development well in advance of the expected need that transition or change can be as seamless as possible in so far as customers and fellow employees are concerned.

The final input that human resource planning can make is to the wider company policy formulation and planning process. At a budgeting level, forecasts with respect to the costs of recruitment, training and development and expected remuneration packages are central to both short- and longer-term cost management and will impact on the ability of the company to develop in other areas, notably on the product and marketing sides. However, the contribution of human resource planning goes beyond solely budgetary considerations. An underlying thesis of this book, most clearly represented in Chapter 5 but evident throughout, is that people within a tourism and hospitality organization are crucial to its success. Without good and empowered staff, quality in terms of product and service cannot be delivered, and without quality, business levels and consequently profitability will decline. Acceptance of this position places human resource planning at the forefront of the wider company planning process and not as the peripheral agenda item which it all too frequently is.

Human resource planning for the tourism and hospitality industry is more than the sum of the information that is collected and the use to which such data is put. Human resource planning is a frame of mind within the company environment, and thus in its most effective form integrates consideration of all aspects of the management of human resources into the company's planning process. The situation outlined in Table 1.4 in Chapter 1 illustrates the range of human resource considerations which contributed to the planning of a Taj Gateway hotel in Chiplun, India. Effective human resource planning is also central to the theme of sustainability which we introduced in Chapter 1. A consideration of Table 1.2 will demonstrate that a significant number of the practices within the sustainable paradigm relate to the planning process, the recognition that human resources cannot be seen as a purely short-term, immediate concern but require similar forethought to any other aspect of the operation of the business. In this context, it is also worth reflecting on the impact of Riley's concept of the weak internal labour market (discussed in Chapter 4) upon human resource planning within the tourism and hospitality industry in Europe. Such reflection may lead to the conclusion that a number of the problems which such planning faces and the barriers to its effective implementation can be directly attributed to the characteristics of the labour market within which the industry exists. Clearly these considerations apply beyond the level of the individual business unit at corporate and macro levels as well.

## HUMAN RESOURCE PLANNING AT THE CORPORATE LEVEL

In essence, human resource planning at the corporate level where a company operates in a number of locations is the same process and operates to the same constraints as that applicable in the context of the individual business. While clearly the scale is likely to be much larger, the objectives and process are largely the same. However, there are a number of factors which need to be taken into consideration at the corporate level which represent a difference in emphasis to that of the small company or individual business unit. Some of the factors make the process of human resource planning easier while others require additional skills and responses. These differences do not all necessarily exist between small and multi-location businesses in the manufacturing sector. They are in part influenced by the characteristics of the tourism and hospitality industry as part of the service sector which we have already considered in Chapter 5. These factors include the following:

- The fragmented nature of the business units within the company, whether they are hotels, travel agents, restaurants or airline stations in a large number of locations, may result in wide dispersion not only within a country but also on a transnational or transcontinental basis. As a consequence, companies may opt to plan on a national or regional basis but this, in itself, has certain drawbacks in maximizing the full benefits of planning in that important information may not be shared corporately as a result.
- This fragmentation impacts on the techniques of data collection that are employed at the investigation stage. There is likely to be greater emphasis on quantitative techniques in response to scale, and more qualitative assessments of needs and resources may be neglected as a result. Considerable care is required in assembling information at a corporate level so as not to lose important local dimensions and requirements.
- Fragmentation also means that individual units may well be operating in different customer and demand cycle (seasonality) environments. Responding to different customer expectations may require variation in the human resource provision, both in terms of numbers and skills, that are in place within units. Thus universal formulae for staffing levels may be totally inappropriate within all units of a company and the planning process needs to acknowledge this. One response to different market requirements has been branding within the hotel industry. This seeks to match broad customer requirements with respect to price, facilities and service to general specifications which are applied throughout the brand. Examples within the Accor group, for example, include their Formulae 1, Ibis, Novotel and Sofitel products. Branding is designed to standardize customer expectations so that an educated marketplace will know what to expect

from a particular hotel type and, therefore, will not be disappointed at what is on offer. Between each brand, different human resource planning criteria will apply, although common practice will normally operate universally within the brand. Forte's flexible contract (already discussed in Chapter 4) represents a common approach to all its United Kingdom hotels across brands. However, even within the parameters provided by branding, it may be difficult to respond fully to the range of customer requirements across a large number of hotels and to provide staffing levels and skills to meet these demands.

As we have already seen in Chapter 4, Johnston (1991) argues that the process of labour globalization will see companies harmonizing human resource policies and practices on a global in addition to national basis, with the notion of a single set of workplace standards inevitable as companies seek to standardize both production and delivery of goods and services. Branding is one step in this direction but the counter-argument, which is much more compatible with the sustainability model, is set out below.

- Despite Johnston's argument, fragmentation further implies that individual units operate within diverse labour markets and human resource planning must be sensitive to these variations. Differences in labour market characteristics can be found between operations within the same city as well as on a larger national or international plane. Such variety is the result of cultural, social, economic and political factors and will impact on a range of human resource concerns, including
  - the application of employment legislation;
  - the effects of competition within the labour market from other businesses in tourism and hospitality as well as other sectors;
  - the impact of local attitudes to employment within tourism and hospitality;
  - remuneration rates which are payable locally;
  - recruitment strategies that will be necessary;
  - training and development requirements;
  - as well as the framework of conditions, benefits and services applied to staff (relating to areas such as shift work, provision of meals, housing and creche facilities).
- Scale, however, provides companies with the facility to overcome some of the problems which small businesses face in planning human resource requirements. By operating a number of units, companies can adopt a level of flexibility between them in order to cater for variation in demand and the timing of demand between different business units. Thus key staff can be deployed to seasonal businesses as demand requires and then withdrawn to units with less seasonality when they are no longer needed. Likewise companies can operate effective promotion and development strategies at a corporate level, moving staff between units in order to fill vacancies or to meet the identified needs of individual staff members. As we have seen in

Chapter 4, Guerrier and Lockwood (1989b) suggest that in the hotel industry such planning only operates within the company core of managers and trainee managers but there is no reason why similar practices should not operate on a more local basis between units within a common area. The deployment of expatriate staff within many multinational hotel groups seems to go beyond what Guerrier and Lockwood envisage as the company core and frequently include skilled technical and operational staff in all departments of the hotel. Such practices are certainly common among foreign hotel companies opening properties in Eastern Europe.

- Linking to the above, companies are able to offer genuine career ladders within technical and managerial fields and thus are more likely to retain good staff than the independent business. Companies can also plan the career paths and promotion opportunities of key personnel, based on complete information about impending vacancies and changes in skills requirements, and so prepare individuals for their next move within the company. This process is known as succession planning and in a company such as Hilton International operates with the assistance of a company-wide computerized database.

It is clear that effective human resource planning is essential at the corporate level as it is in smaller businesses. Sustainability demands local flexibility within this planning and its application. Trends and projections suggest that such flexibility is not a priority among major tourism and hospitality companies which are geared towards increasing standardization in product, service and working environment.

## HUMAN RESOURCE PLANNING AT THE COMMUNITY, REGIONAL, NATIONAL AND TRANSNATIONAL LEVEL

### A planning model

The final approach to human resource planning for tourism and hospitality, and the one most neglected in the literature, is that at the macro level, whether involving a community, region, country or at a transnational level. The principles and parameters involved have much in common with small business and corporate planning but a number of factors differentiate the macro process from that within a single company. These factors include the following.

- The scale of operation is frequently much larger than that within a company although, given the size of some multinational tourism and hospitality companies, this is not a necessary distinction.
- The multi-sector nature of the industry needs to be considered, which can include all subsectors of the tourism and hospitality industry.

- There is a substantial involvement of public sector interests, both as employers within tourism and hospitality and as contributing partners within the human resource management process.
- There is multi-company and organization involvement, both in the public and private sectors, and therefore the attendant problems of obtaining data from such a range of sources within the investigation stage.
- There is a frequent lack of a single coordinating authority, at local, regional, national or transnational level, with responsibility for the planning of human resource matters within hospitality and tourism. At the same time, the management and development of human resources for tourism and hospitality may fall within the remit of a wide range of public and private sector companies and agencies. Examples of bodies whose brief may include a significant human resource component with respect to tourism and hospitality include:

  - local, regional and national tourism organizations;
  - ministries with specific responsibility for tourism;
  - other ministries and agencies responsible for the delivery of aspects of the tourism product (for example, ministries of agriculture, the environment, culture);
  - security and home affairs ministries with responsibility for police, immigration and customs, all of whom may have significant visitor contact;
  - national or regional education ministries, perhaps with a divide between responsibility for tertiary, vocational and university-level provision;
  - labour/employment/manpower ministries;
  - schools, colleges and universities in both the public and private sector;
  - public sector bodies responsible for the funding of education and training within the educational system and in industry;
  - specialist tourism and hospitality training agencies and consultancies;
  - public and private sector tourism enterprises and companies;
  - tourism and hospitality industry representative associations; and
  - transnational public organizations within the European Union and other geographical regions. (Source: Baum, 1994b.)

All these bodies have a legitimate interest in the planning process for human resources in tourism and hospitality on whatever scale is involved. Such planning cannot operate effectively without the co-operation and input of these interests. There are few examples world-wide of really inclusive and effective human resource planning within one industry sector at the scale implied here. The model that comes closest to it in Europe is that which operates in the Republic of Ireland and we shall consider that in greater detail later in this chapter. It is interesting to note that the World Tourism Organization's comprehensive guide to *National and Regional Tourism Planning* (1994c) includes only the briefest of references to human resource requirements in this field and the argument for an integrated approach – and one that includes human resources as a mainstream consideration in wider tourism planning – is all but neglected. The focus of the book is almost exclusively on policy and strategic development with respect to structure, sustainability, economic and cultural considerations, implementation and control, monitoring and market planning. One manpower case study is included in the book relating to Oman, but this clearly places the area at the fringes of mainstream tourism policy development.

In order to undertake effective human resource planning for tourism at a macro level, it is necessary to pursue a process comparable to that proposed by Bramham in Figure 9.1, especially in addressing the information gathering or investigation stage. Elsewhere, I have developed a conceptual framework which is designed to contribute to the development of an integrated human resource environment for tourism and hospitality at a macro level (Baum, 1993c). This framework is designed as a flexible and responsive approach to human resource planning in the context we have been discussing and is:

- comprehensive, in that it includes all sectors of the tourism and hospitality industry, all relevent aspects of human resource development, all levels of training and development, and is sustainable in that it reflects the demands of local cultures, traditions and tourism and hospitality markets;
- integrated, in that all components in the framework have clear and identifiable links to other elements and contribute to, or are beneficiaries of, other parts of the framework; and
- cohesive, in that the total framework, the overall outcome of the process, has a logic and applicability in its own right almost independent of its individual parts.

The framework is intended as a mechanism to support the coordination of human resource policy formulation and planning for tourism and hospitality at a macro level. It has the benefit of breadth in that the approach is designed to incorporate as many as possible of the diverse influences and considerations which affect effective human resource planning on this scale. It is non-evaluatory in that no assessment is implied of the relative importance of the various components. The framework focuses on five main areas, consideration of which comprises the investigation stage in Bramham's terms in relation to whatever is being addressed (local, regional, national or transnational).

1. The tourism and hospitality industry environment, its features and products, structure, markets and the impact of tourism in economic, social, cultural and political terms.

2. The tourism and hospitality industry and the labour market, relating to considerations such as features of the wider labour market; public employment and labour market-related policy; education and training policies; the application of official occupational classification schemes to tourism and hospitality occupations; as well as available statistical information about the labour market in tourism and hospitality and competing industrial sectors.
3. Tourism, hospitality and the community, giving focus to matters such as public attitudes to tourism and tourists; awareness of the industry and its economic/employment significance and related perceptual/awareness considerations.
4. Tourism, hospitality and the education system, covering the administration and funding of public and private education for tourism and hospitality; assessment and quality management; tourism and hospitality studies within the school curriculum at vocational and management levels; the education of teachers for tourism and hospitality; the outcomes of education programmes – destination of graduates, attrition from the industry; and tourism and hospitality industry attitudes and commitment to education and its providers.
5. Human resource development in the tourism and hospitality industry, giving consideration to matters such as in-company training policies and practices; financing and investment in human resource development from private and public sources (tax concessions, levy schemes); the role of industry in the education and training process (apprenticeship schemes, work placement/*stages*); recognition of training and skills development towards national qualifications and by the education system.

This conceptual framework is shown in summary diagrammatic form in Figure 9.3. A more detailed breakdown of each of the main elements within the framework can be found in Baum (1993c).

The framework provides the information base from which competent authorities in the public or private sector can develop policies and specific plans with respect to human resources in tourism and hospitality. It does not, of course, address what or who such competent authorities are and this question is not as readily answered as it might be at the individual business or corporate level. At national level, for example, few countries allocate responsibility for the development and implementation of human resource policies for tourism and hospitality to a unitary body. Rather, inputs are fragmented and may be duplicated between government ministries, national tourism organizations, education and training providers, as well as the public sector itself (Baum, 1994c). At transnational level, such coordination becomes even more fragmented, despite the best efforts of the Commission of the European Union. In information terms, the EU is largely dependent on inputs from national sources, and these are not necessarily derived from comparable bases or similar sources.

A *The tourism environment*
- Features and products of tourism
- Structure of the industry
- Tourism industry markets
- The impact of tourism

B *Tourism and the labour market*
- The national and/or local labour market environment
- Public labour market/ employment/industrial relations policies
- Educational and training policies
- Quantitative and qualitative information about human resources in tourism

C *Tourism in the community*
- National commitment to tourism
- Public attitudes to/ awareness of tourism
- Attitudes to and awareness of tourism as an employer
- Tourism within education
- Tourism and the media
- Careers awareness

THE HUMAN RESOURCES
ENVIRONMENT IN TOURISM

D *Tourism and education*
- The administration and management of public sector tourism education
- The funding of public sector tourism education
- Quality standards and qualifications equivalences in tourism education
- National assessment, examinations and awards
- Education for tourism at secondary school level
- Vocational skills education for tourism at craft level
- Supervisory and management education for tourism
- Centres of excellence in tourism education
- National recruitment and selection of entrants to programmes of study in tourism
- Teacher training for tourism
- Curriculum development centre for tourism

E *Human resource development in the tourism industry*
- Financing and investment in human resource development
- In-company training policies and practices
- Recognition of industry-based training within local and national education and training provision
- Role of industry in education

**Figure 9.3** An integrated human resource development framework for tourism and hospitality. (Source: Baum, 1993c, p. 241.)

In human resource planning terms, one of the most significant sources of information to the process is accurate statistical data about the quantity of employment and the attendant skills profile of the tourism and hospitality industry, as well as the means to estimate and project future employment and skills trends. Such information is not readily available in a form that is designed specifically for application within tourism and hospitality. In the United Kingdom, for example, it is necessary to combine data from a number of categories within the Standard Occupational Classification (HMSO, 1990) in order to aggregate total tourism employment, and even this is by no means inclusive – a number of occupational areas are omitted as they are included within broader, non-tourism/hospitality categories and cannot be isolated. Similar problems are found when employing the International Standard Classification of Occupations (ILO, 1988). Definitional problems are further compounded by the overlap in terms of demand and consumption between tourists and non-tourists of many goods and services and the problems inherent in isolating the employment impact of one from the other.

Essentially, there are four basic approaches to the quantitative measurement of tourism employment, although only one of them gives any depth of qualitative information. These are:

1. input–output analysis;
2. direct survey of the tourism industry;
3. the proportional method; and
4. the application of macro-economic methods.

*Input–output analysis*

This method makes use of the multiplier concept in order to derive estimates of aggregate employment within the tourism sector. According to Fletcher:

> The multiplier concept is based upon the nature of production and the purchase of intermediate goods and services within the production process. Each sector of the economy will, to varying degrees, employ labour in order to produce its output. If the number of persons employed by a firm is divided by the total output of that firm, labour/output coefficients (or ratios) can be calculated which show a crude relationship between the level of output and the number of people that would have to be employed in order to produce that output. (Fletcher, 1993, p. 78)

The multiplier effect can be extrapolated to a macro scale so that estimates of employment at community, regional, national and trans-national levels can be derived. Input–output analysis produces estimates of employment at three levels. These are direct employment derived from actual tourism expenditure and its employment creation impact; the indirect effect relating to the employment impact of secondary purchases by, for example, hotels and airlines which are necessary in order to cater for their customers, as well as building work, provision of electricity and a host of other goods and services; and, finally, the induced effect relating to employment which is generated because tourism and hospitality employees spend part of their own wages on goods and services and this expenditure, in turn, generates further employment.

Input–output analysis can derive the employment effect of these three forms of multipliers through analysis of 'out-of-state' tourist expenditure based on the normal assumptions on which such calculating tables are constructed. The analysis is based on a 'transactions' matrix which summarizes the entire structure of the economy and allows a complete analysis of the relationships between its various sectors. In other words, we can look at the way each sector engages in transactions with other sectors and with final demand.

Although allowing a rigorous analysis to be made of the economy, the technique is not without weaknesses. There are basic difficulties in dealing with domestic tourism by this method and, in most European countries, this is a severe delimiter as the domestic tourism economies of countries such as France, the UK and Ireland make a major contribution to the overall level of activity within the sector. Also, the length of time taken to develop input–output tables limits their usefulness; in the Irish context, for example, the most recent official tables are in respect of 1975 and, although Bord Failte Eireann updated these in 1985, the usefulness of even these is debatable. Such lack of currency is a major drawback and is one that does not allow this method to make a serious contribution to pragmatic human resource planning within the tourism and hospitality industry.

*The direct survey method*

If conducted on anything like a significant scale, this method is the most expensive information collection technique but is likely to give relatively comprehensive direct employment statistics. The method's contribution with respect to indirect employment is, of course, minimal. The approach normally involves conducting a survey of a sample of businesses involved in tourism activity. Respondents may be asked to give details of their total employment figures and to estimate the proportion of these associated directly with tourism *per se*.

As well as its limitations with respect to indirect employment, this method is vulnerable to allegations of subjectivity, especially in the allocation of business activity to tourism or non-tourism sources. However, the undoubted merits of the approach lie in the quality, depth and variety of data that can be collected within a survey. The impact of changes in employment structure, training opportunities, subsectoral variance and seasonality, to identify but a few significant factors, may all be estimated, albeit with the same caveat for subjectivity.

In the context of this discussion, perhaps the most significant benefit of this approach lies in its predictive value – this dimension can be incorporated into the survey and can be usefully employed to anticipate and plan for labour and skills changes within the industry. The direct survey method is one that can readily be updated on a regular basis – with appropriate resources, biannually is not unrealistic. Experience with this method in Ireland and Singapore, for example, suggests that there are further, extraneous benefits to be derived from the close contact and feeling of involvement/commitment within the industry which can result from participation in such studies.

*The proportional method*

This is the method used in, for example, British Tourist Authority studies, and it employs a simple theoretical approach. It estimates the proportion of total expenditure in each sector which is derived from tourism and then applies this proportion to total employment in the relevant sectors. In this way, tourism-related direct employment is estimated. Indirect tourism-related employment estimates are obtained by using the relationship of intermediate demand to total output in the economy as an indicator. For direct employment estimates, this approach has the very practical benefit that it can use current annual data such as the breakdown of personal consumer expenditure from the national accounts as well as relevant employment statistics. Some predictive estimates can also be obtained.

There are a number of theoretical difficulties with this approach and estimates with respect to factors such as regional variation and job/skills differentiation are only as good as the source segmentation that is available. Thus the practical value of this approach to those planning the labour and skills needs of the tourism and hospitality industry may be limited. That said, the method provides a feasible basis for annual estimation of tourism employment and one that can form the basis for selected in-depth studies.

*Macro-economic methods*

The three above methods provide point estimates of tourism employment. The use of a *macro-economic model* in the area of tourism and hospitality employment is designed to assess the marginal effect of increments in out-of-state tourism revenue. This is an attempt to use a behavioural model incorporating supply-side constraints to predict the employment effect of marginal changes in revenue.

As with all econometric models, a considerable degree of simplification is inherent in this approach and thus results have to be treated with some considerable caution. Judgement is required in deciding when to override the the model where necessary and a mere mechanical application could well result in erroneous conclusions.

The advantages of this approach lie in its conceptual neutrality which is lacking in varying degrees with respect to the other methods. Furthermore, it benefits from being a theoretical model in that it allows for the approximate prediction of the consequences of policy or environmental changes on employment. However, the local and fragmented nature of the tourism and hospitality industry cannot readily be acknowledged within this model and its value in planning and implementing local, regional and, in some cases, even national initiatives is severely limited.

*Summary*

One assumption that is implicit in three of the above methodologies, the direct survey method being the exception, is that employment and tourism expenditure and growth have a fixed association which is universally applicable to the whole tourism and hospitality industry. This may well not be the case as tangible evidence of growth, say through the building of a new hotel or the purchase of new aircraft, may well have very different employment effects relative to investment. The impact of similar developments will also vary greatly between different countries and companies. These variations are outlined in a WTO report:

> In broad terms, a four- or five-star hotel directly employs one person for every room. But, in addition, employment is created in other sectors of the tourism industry and it is estimated that this amounts to a further one and a half jobs for each hotel room. An investment of $95,000 for a hotel room therefore creates two and a half new jobs.
>
> The calculation of job creation in airline operations is more complicated and subject to substantial variations depending on the type of operation (long-haul or short-haul) and the efficiency and productivity of the airline concerned ... It can therefore be concluded that an investment of $150 million in a B747 will give employment to 400 people whereas an equal investment in hotels would give direct employment to over 1,500 people and total employment to 3,750 people. This is a major factor which governments must take into account when judging the merits of alternative policies.
>
> (WTO, 1994b, pp. 58–9)

What the WTO report fails to address within this conclusion is the issue of job quality and remuneration. Considerable disparity regarding these factors between airline and hotel industries in many European countries will partially reduce the gap in terms of the value of employment generated.

This methodological review is by no means exhaustive nor does it do full justice to the approaches described, either from a theoretical or a practical point of view. What it does do is to point out some of the potential difficulties in attempting to link employment predictions and planning too closely to the main research and analytical models that are available. As the following case study based on the planning process used with respect to the Irish tourism and hospitality industry will attempt to illustrate, an industry which is so complex and fragmented does not respond readily to generalization and classification – attempts to do so in too simplistic a form may have significant consequences for the planning process in the human resource area.

### The Republic of Ireland: a case study

The scope and significance of the tourism industry in the Republic of Ireland is well documented, both through official reports and plans (NESC, 1980; Stationery Office, 1985 and 1987; Fianna Fail, 1987; IHF, 1987; CERT, 1987) and through work that has been published elsewhere (Baum, 1989a; Walsh, 1993). As a tourist destination, Ireland is perceived to offer attractive and unspoiled scenery, an interesting cultural heritage, a friendly people and a good quality and standard of amenities. Current investment in tourism is relatively high by comparison with previous decades, spurred in part by positive and aggressive government support and incentives. This will have the effect of upgrading the standard and variety of facilities and of providing a stronger marketing and development base through which to promote the country's attributes as a tourist destination, particularly in the outdoor leisure and culture fields.

Membership of the European Union and the impact of the single market economy have the potential to adversely affect major areas of the Irish economy. Tourism, however, could be the net beneficiary from this environment. Investment through structural fund resources has already been significant in tourism and this continued until 1993 as a means of ameliorating other negative economic impacts. One report (Fitzpatrick, 1989) notes that funding from this source could rise to as high as 44% of total international tourism receipts in Ireland in the medium term, by a long way the most significant contribution through this source of investment within the Union and indicative of government commitment to the industry.

In terms of actual performance, Irish tourism is currently witnessing a period of development and sustained growth, in no small way due to this government support, but also reflecting more general business and financial optimism. Overall growth, in terms of foreign arrivals, domestic bednights and total expenditure by tourists has maintained steady growth since the late 1980s at a level that is very impressive in European terms – during the period 1987 to 1991, for example, a total growth in arrivals of 44%, or 10% per annum, was achieved. However, this growth must be treated with some caution. Irish tourism has consistently underperformed since peaking in the late 1960s. The value of Irish tourism has not grown to match that of other economies and the Republic's share of the overall world market has experienced a proportionate decline over this period, linked closely to political unrest in

Northern Ireland. We may be witnessing some partial redress of this long period of under-performance. However, shifts away from dependence on some traditional markets (the USA grew by only 1% in 1989) may indicate stronger and more sustainable trends within Irish tourism. Prospects for the short- to medium-term growth of Irish tourism appear to be relatively good and government predictions project further growth by 34% by 1997 over 1991 figures. This growth is supported by the maintenance of aggressive marketing, the continuation of transport deregulation and sustained investment in product development. Above all, government policy has given priority to tourism development since 1987, although Deegan and Dineen (1993) portray this attention to tourism almost as an act of desperation on the part of policy-makers following the failure of industrial policy in other sectors.

Before addressing the human resource issues in the Irish tourism and hospitality industry, some reference to the structure of the industry and its business environment is necessary. Tourism and hospitality in Ireland is characterized by diversity and dispersion; it is an industry 'of every parish' with particular impact on rural areas of the country where the effects of economic and social deprivation are most acute. A 1987 survey (CERT, 1987) estimated that 19 000 businesses were involved to a greater or lesser extent in tourism, enterprises that in turn may be classified into 45 discrete subsectors. These subsectors cover a wide range in terms of product, role and, above all, size, reflecting many of the components that are considered in Chapter 2. They include the one-person cottage industry or service as well as the 'giants' of Irish tourism in the form of the major hotel and transportation companies, and include businesses in the accommodation, leisure, food and beverage, transport and information/facilitation sectors. The key point – and one that cannot be overstressed in the context of human resource planning – is, on the one hand, this diversity and, on the other, the predominantly small, family-business structure of the industry. Outside the main cities, the tourism and hospitality industry is a highly seasonal activity in Ireland, particularly in the scenic west and south-west, and while the overall upturn in business has led to some season elongation, this has not impacted on all areas and tends to concentrate business in already overstreched destinations such as Dublin, Cork and Killarney.

Employment within the Irish tourism and hospitality industry reflects its business structure. The average operation has five employees, probably including part-time assistance and almost certainly with a major seasonal element, and is very likely to be built around a family structure. The use of temporary, seasonal and casual staff is extensive and, in some areas, constitutes a tradition in employment patterns that would be difficult to break. Even within the larger, more sophisticated sectors of Irish tourism, the majority of concerns are very small by the standards of almost any other industry or, indeed, Western European country. Of registered hotels 80% are 40 bedrooms in size or less bearing in mind the legal definition of a hotel in Ireland which excludes any establishment of less than 10 bedrooms); the impact of major hotel groups, while increasing, is relatively limited so that the vast majority of businesses are proprietor owned and managed.

Actual numbers in direct employment in 1987 totalled in excess of 152 000, these being the 'raw' figures which have not been adjusted to reflect part-time, seasonal or non-tourism related factors. This places tourism in second place within the Irish employment league, behind the declining agriculture sector and roughly on a par with manufacturing. Adjusted for part-time and seasonal working, these figures work out to a little over 110 000 full-time 'job equivalents' which, based on an average tourism dependency of 34%, translates into 38 500 'job equivalents' wholly dependent on tourism.

The reality of a tourism and hospitality environment such as that described above (and which in many of its aspects has major similarities to the industry in many other European countries) is that its fragmentation and the scale of its operations act as severe constraints on the application of tourism/hospitality business – employment impact models. Particular factors which blur the validity and practical use of such models include the following.

- The extent to which staff utilization and productivity are maximized within key tourism and hospitality industry sectors. In many cases, tourism is an 'anticipation' business in which staffing levels have to be judged on the basis of expected or possible business levels which may not always materialize. Thus, especially in small outfits, existing staff can cater for quite considerable increases in business volume without the requirement for personnel changes.
- Most tourism and hospitality sectors in Ireland involve considerable specialization and job demarcation. While multiskilling is certainly on the increase in Ireland, within a tight staff structure it is not necessarily feasible to staff up within each area to reflect business growth. Thus specialisms need to be prioritized and staff increases or restructuring may be out of line with business patterns.
- Competition, especially for skilled labour within very tight employment markets, may result in 'skills hoarding' by some employers in anticipation of business growth – this has the effect of limiting the impact of increases when they do occur and also of denying other companies access to these skilled personnel. Despite the second highest level of unemployment in the European Union, the tourism and hospitality industry still faces significant skills shortages and this leads to intense competition for labour.
- Within predominantly seasonal industries such as in Ireland, the impact of growth often results in season extension rather than increasing the number of tourists in resorts already working to capacity. Thus while actual numbers in employment may not increase, the period in work may be significantly longer – how such effects can be

evaluated in terms of raw job increase targets is difficult to ascertain. The alternative to this scenario is that high-season business goes elsewhere – if this is to another region within the same country (for example Kerry to Donegal) this is acceptable at a national if not a regional level. However, if the impact is to move tourists to another country (Switzerland to Austria or Ireland to Wales), no employment benefits can accrue.

- Economic or manpower planning models do not anticipate the possibility that available employment, even in times of high unemployment, may not be taken up. There are a variety of possible reasons for this, reflecting upon industry image, remuneration, geographical factors and the draw of employment elsewhere within an open labour market (such as the EU), to cite but a few. In Ireland, the haemorrhaging of skilled personnel is a major issue within the industry and, despite notions of reciprocal movement within the European Union (and the endeavours of organizations such as the Hotel and Restaurant Committee of the International Hotel Association (HOTREC) Ireland is by a very long way a net exporter of tourism and hospitality labour.
- Finally, key labour shortages and the areas of main demand within a growing tourism economy are frequently at a skilled level and thus offer opportunities not accessible to the untrained worker. In Ireland, for example, the key shortages are for chefs and management staff within hotels and restaurants. Thus investment in preparing these skills must parallel, indeed precede, initiatives in marketing and product development which will generate the extra tourism business.

Ireland provides an excellent example of a tourism and hospitality environment where a simple application of employment impact modelling will not necessarily provide an accurate picture of the real changes that occur in the labour market when the level of tourist arrivals increases. In this sense, tourism may not provide as simple an employment panacea as is frequently anticipated and considerable support investment through education and training, for example, may be required. How such support can operate forms the next stage in this discussion.

### The Republic of Ireland: Fine-tuning the employment implications of tourism growth

Thus far in this case study discussion we have reviewed some of the problems that arise when standard macro methodologies are employed to predict the employment impact of tourism growth. The issue is not the methods in themselves but rather in their inability to localize and sectorize with sufficient precision for the purposes of planning and development of appropriate strategies in education, training (pre-service and in-company) and other labour market measures. In other words, we may be able to predict that the tourism workforce will grow by $x$ thousand (in the Irish case the targets were 25 000 for the five-year period 1987–92 and a further 35 000 for 1995–2000) but that does not give much indication as to whether these jobs will be full-, part-time or seasonal, their level in terms of skills, whether they are 'new' jobs or extensions of existing ones, whether they represent more existing designations (as in the demand for more chefs in Ireland) or an entirely new breed of worker (as was the case in the Paris region with the opening of EuroDisneyland), or the geographical distribution of the new jobs by locality or region. In Ireland, the implementation of short-and medium-term strategies in order to cope with these factors falls within the ambit of CERT, the state training agency for tourism and an organization with the strength of position to take a broad national coordinating and development view of labour issues in Irish tourism. CERT's approach is designed to assist the industry to provide for changes within the manpower environment in tourism, whether these changes reflect retrenchment or boom. Some of these initiatives will be described and evaluated in terms of their impact in the context of what has already been said about tourism and the tourist industry in Ireland.

CERT's programme of research studies is at the centre of the information-gathering stage of national human resource planning for tourism and hospitality in Ireland. It is a major support platform for the development of both policy and practical interventions within Irish tourism. These programmes range from extensive and intensive manpower studies of the industry by main sector (and using broadly the methodology described previously as the direct survey approach) to specifically focused surveys and analytical studies which are designed to home in on particular areas of concern. The national manpower studies (CERT, 1992) go considerably beyond the basic estimation of actual employment. They focus on both the quantitative and qualitative detail relating to that employment, changes within the labour structure of businesses, the impact of manpower and training initiatives, predictions of manpower requirements, as well as regional and type of business variations (grade, size, etc.). The manpower studies have direct impact on the provision of education and training places by public sector authorities as well as on priority training categories and the attendant curricula required for their preparation. The specifically focused studies concentrate on the needs of specific sectors (for example leisure within hotels) as a means of providing rapid-response training for newly identified or emerging skills needs. They also look at the impact of technology in the industry and the implications of current Irish demographic trends for tourism into the next century.

Commitment to this programme of research ensured that CERT was able to respond fairly rapidly to the specific demands of government with respect to their tourism employment targets. The crucial need for skilled labour as opposed to untrained, semi- or unskilled personnel formed the main thrust of this response, which allowed the agency to map out and target human resource development priorities by category without further research. The inability of the existing education and training system to provide for these identified requirements is another issue and arguably one of the main weaknesses in overall government strategy for tourism.

Cost-effective and rapid-response training is a major platform within CERT's approach to meeting short- to medium-term skills requirements and has become a very significant component within the overall tourism training strategy in Ireland, largely because of the failure of existing institutions to meet demands in terms of quantity, hampered as they are by tight financial restrictions. This strategy involves the use of temporary training facilities during the down season, generally hotels, and the provision of mainstream school-leaver courses or programmes for the long-term unemployed without extensive capital investment or commitment.

This model is one which has wide applicability in other countries. An extension of this approach is the establishment of an increasing number of permanent training centres, operated under the auspices of CERT but established in short-lease premises frequently within industrial estates and designed to provide 'stop-gap' training places prior to investment in more permanent facilities within the Irish third-level college system. These centres are able to offer virtually year-round training and thus their output is considerably greater than is normally the case within mainstream education, where tradition and fixed agreements result in considerable under-utilization of facilities. One potential matter of concern in the establishment of such facilities is staffing, especially given the need to employ teachers with industry skills and experience when such attributes are in limited supply. The seasonal nature of the Irish industry means that the period of training in temporary training coincides with the down period in employment terms and the consequence is that there is a significant pool of seasonally under-employed personnel available for teaching posts. An added benefit of this process is that the temporary instructors return to industry with considerably enhanced training skills.

The design and implementation of curricula and programmes originate under the same roof as the research programmes which invariably precede them. This common responsibility within CERT means that there is a very close association between the interpretation of research findings and their translation into new educational and training initiatives within tourism. The facility to experiment and innovate (Baum, 1987) is also exercised and this allows for relatively localized or sector/subsector specific programmes to be implemented. This has resulted in a range of non-standard courses targeted closely to the identified needs within Irish tourism. Examples include:

- a multi-skills craft course designed to equip school-leavers with a range of skills appropriate to front-of-house situations in the small hotel or guesthouse;

- a tourist reception assistants course aimed at entrants who have basic commercial/secretarial skills and wish to retrain/gain additional skills for work within small tourism businesses, especially in the southwest of the country;
- an innovative tourist information officers course, designed in direct response to a request from the country's second tourism promotion agency, SFADCO;
- a distance learning management development course for young people studying as trainee managers (non-graduate) within the hotel industry and designed to enhance the level of their educational development as well as providing a credible counterbalance to the widespread emigration of college graduating young managers and the consequent shortage of middle managers within the industry;
- a range of different courses on offer within the secondary school system and designed as 'tasters' for various sectors of the tourism industry and with an increasing emphasis on the need to prepare young people to work for and within an international, particularly European, tourism market; and
- sector-specific and demand-anticipating short-course programmes for the Irish tourism and hospitality industry that ensure a very close link between identified training priorities and delivery to all levels of technical, supervisory and management staff.

These constitute but a sample of the range of initiatives that have been put in place as a result of the close tie-in between research and development within education/training for Irish tourism. This direct contribution to providing a relevant and responsive menu of educational and training programmes for Irish tourism is complemented by significant support activities which also link closely to research initiatives. These include national student recruitment for tourism and hospitality craft education, allowing CERT to monitor and manage the categories of tourism and hospitality staff trained for the industry and to maximize the utilization of scarce training places within the system. This is complemented by the centralized placement of graduates and work experience trainees, the effect of which is to go some way to ensuring a reasonably even distribution of trained personnel throughout outlets and regions. Training within colleges, centres and the industry is also enhanced by tailor-researched and developed resource materials, prepared because of the evident unsuitability of materials from outside of the country: CERT also acts as a 'clearing house' for work experience placements within Europe and beyond, designed to broaden the experience profile of tourism and hospitality students and young workers.

CERT's remit in undertaking this central coordinating role in all areas of human resource development within the Irish tourism and hospitality industry is to act in liaison with, and on behalf of, appropriate government departments to ensure the optimal use of state and European Union funds within the education and training of new entrants and experienced personnel and, at the same time, to work closely with the public and private sectors of the industry in order to ensure that training and skills development are in place to meet the specific needs of all businesses within all sectors of the industry. In this, CERT's human resource planning role is, probably, unique in Europe and is the model which provided the impetus to the development of the human resource management framework discussed earlier in this chapter.

## Transnational perspectives

We have considered the problems that are faced by attempts to manage the planning of human resource requirements for tourism and hospitality at a community, regional or national level. CERT provides a reasonably successful model by which to undertake such planning, but on the basis of highly interventionist and largely centralized public policy, which may not be politically acceptable within all European countries. Seeking an equivalent role at a trans-European level, therefore, presents even greater challenges and problems. The tourism and hospitality industry in Europe is, as we have seen in Chapter 2, very diverse in its product characteristics, its traditions and origins, the markets that it serves, the role that it plays in the national economies and, above all, the labour markets within which it exists (with regard to employment traditions, education and training systems, status of tourism and hospitality employment, among other considerations). If this transnational human resource planning process for tourism and hospitality is to be extended to Eastern Europe, its complexity is compounded because of the entirely different environment that pertains there and because of the rapid tourism and hospitality industry changes which are taking place at the present time.

Therefore it is not surprising that only limited contributions have been made to coordinated planning of human resource concerns on a pan-European basis. As we saw in Chapter 2, within the European Union, the closest that any initiative comes is through the 1991 *Action Plan to Assist Tourism* (CEC, 1991a), which proposes some limited measures in the human resource area, all to do with education and training. These are:

- identification of professional profiles of the sector;
- encouragement of the participation of tourism businesses in existing community action programmes for training;
- support for cooperation between universities and tourism schools and tourism professionals; and
- pilot actions for specific training in the sector: rural, social, cultural, environmental.

Such actions hardly consititute a comprehensive human resource plan for the tourism and hospitality industry. Even where specific actions have been undertaken, their impact to date has been limited.

Attempts to facilitate labour mobility within the Union by identifying job and qualification equivalencies under the auspices of the Union's vocational training agency CEDEFOP have produced requisite documentation but little or no actual use within the tourism and hospitality industry of the twelve member states. Despite the failure of human resource planning at a transnational level in Europe, there is a certain irony that the Union has been active in supporting regional development projects in the Caribbean, southeast Asia and, from 1994, in south Asia, which are designed to facilitate regional cooperation between participating countries in meeting their human resource development needs within the tourism and hospitality industry. Experience from this work suggests that some limited progress can be made towards applying the planning process beyond national boundaries.

REVIEW AND DISCUSSION QUESTIONS

1. What are the main purposes of human resource planning?
2. Outline the main features of Bramham's manpower planning framework and consider its applicability to the tourism and hospitality industry.
3. What are the main constraints to effective human resource planning at the individual business/business unit level in the tourism and hospitality industry?
4. What are the main benefits to the small tourism and hospitality business of human resource planning?
5. How does human resource planning at the corporate level differ from that at the individual business unit level?
6. What are the main constraints to effective human resource planning at the corporate level in the tourism and hospitality industry?
7. How can the integrated human resource development framework (Figure 9.3) be used to assist human resource planning at a national level?
8. What are the uses and deficiencies of the four measures of tourism employment that are considered in this chapter?
9. What are the main barriers to effective human resource planning at the macro level?
10. How might elements of CERT's approach to human resource planning be utilized in another country with which you are familiar?

# Sustainable human resource management – towards social responsibility in the European tourism and hospitality industry

# 10

This book opened by introducing the theme of sustainability in the context of the management of human resources within the European tourism and hospitality industry. In Table 1.3 the attributes of such sustainability were identified and contrasted with the features of what was described as traditional human resource practice. Subsequent discussion has returned to this theme of sustainability and attempted to link various dimensions of the management of human resources within the European tourism and hospitality industry to this underlying concept. At its heart, sustainable human resource management can be viewed from a number of perspectives.

## A MORAL DIMENSION

Sustainability by its nature has an underlying moral dimension in the humanist tradition which, at its simplest, argues that people respond postively to good treatment and negatively to malmanagement. This is an approach that contrasts markedly with that espoused by the narrow puritanism which has dominated much industrial development in Western Europe and is at the root of the old human resource model. The traditional approach is represented by the attitude that individuals are lazy, self-seeking and basically dishonest with the result that close supervision and punitive behaviour are seen as the only means by which to ensure productive and honest work. The implicit outcome of the implementation of sustainable human resource policies is one in which the employees are seen in positive terms as assets within a company and are treated, managed and rewarded accordingly.

What is argued for here reflects a rejection of the extremes of unsustainable human resource policies, as encapsulated by Orwell in the 1930s but still readily found in some sectors of the tourism and hospitality industry today. The origins of this argument, thus, have much in common with the objectives of some of the great nineteenth century industrial reformers, who looked to create alternatives to the existing working conditions in the 'dark satanic mills'. Practical reformers such as Robert Owen with his New Lanark Project, Lord Leverhulme and Port Sunlight, as well as the Cadbury, Rowntree and Wills families were motivated by religious and moral factors but at the same time did not neglect the business dimension of their projects. Their endeavours were not purely philanthropic but driven by a belief that it was possible and desirable to invest in people in order to increase their contribution to the enterprise and, thus, to enhance profitability. The concern of men such as Leverhulme and Owen was wider than the workplace alone. They saw the responsibilities of employers in paternalistic terms to include the total social and moral well-being of their employees and their families and thus their projects went considerably beyond the immediate workplace to include housing, educational, health, social, welfare and religious dimensions. They were, thus, sustainable in the context of community in that they recognized the links between a stable and contented wider community environment and efficient and profitable production in the workplace.

The moral force of good workplace practices in terms of conditions, remuneration and associated benefits has received the backing of the force of law in most European countries and the worst excesses, especially in relation to health and safety considerations, have been ameliorated. The most extreme practices are, inevitably, those associated with large manufacturing industries and conditions in the heavy plants in some parts of Eastern Europe still represent the unacceptable face of industrial exploitation. However, as we have seen in Chapter 6, the working environment in some subsectors of the European tourism and hospitality industry is far from exemplary. Exploitative remuneration and conditions, especially in relation to the use of female, youth and minorities labour, is relatively widespread and reflects the application of old human resource practices.

As has already been suggested with respect to the great nineteenth-century reformers, the underlying purpose of sustainability, in moral terms, is not solely altruistic. Provision of good working conditions and competitive remuneration, among other aspects of the total employment environment, are designed to provide long-term benefits to both employers and employees on the basis that a happy working environment is also a productive one. This analysis has additional force in the context of the tourism and hospitality industry because of the relationship between business profitability, the delivery of quality service and the role of low-skilled, front-line staff. This is the association that we explored in Chapter 5 and provides one of the most compelling arguments in favour of the provision of a workplace environment that is designed to meet employee needs and ensure their contentment and commitment to the company or business. This, in itself, is a major prerequisite before effective internal marketing can be introduced.

## COMMUNITY RESPONSIBILITY

A sense of community responsibility is a second perspective that derives from the sustainable model for human resource management in the tourism and hospitality industry. Community responsibility emanates from the notion that an employer, large or small, derives profits and a livelihood on the basis of the skills and toil of local labour and that such benefit must be balanced by a sense of responsibility and loyalty to that community. This notion of community responsibility is a commitment that has weakened greatly in manufacturing as the structure and ownership of the great industrial companies has shifted from the individual or family to the faceless conglomerate. In particular, such changes have heralded moves from individual entrepreneurship to corporate ownership; large multinational conglomerates have taken over from individual enterprises; technological substitution has reduced dependency on high levels of unskilled labour; and the perspectives provided by globalization enable companies to base their activity in the most profitable location worldwide, with little regard to local considerations. Cannon (1992) puts the argument like this.

> Breaking the bond between entrepreneurs and their workforce often coincided with the process of severing links with a community. This 'local' connection was once a key feature in the character and identity of the enterprise. Lever Bros in the north west, Imperial Group in Nottingham and Bristol, Rowntree in York symbolised the bond between a firm and a locality. Growth, relocation and acquisition have eroded this relationship.
>
> (Cannon, 1992, p. 3)

The sense of community identity between manufacturing companies and specific locations extends beyond these British examples and includes similar geographical associations throughout Europe, Japan and North America. Ford, traditionally associated with Detroit, now plans its production capacity on a global basis, involving manufacturing plants in the Americas, Europe and Australasia. Volkswagen's investments in Seat of Spain and Skoda in the Czech Republic provide the German company with the potential to move production from its high cost base in Germany to cheaper locations if necessary and, indeed, this implicit threat has facilitated significant changes to working practices in Volkswagen's German plants.

However, there are fewer such clear links between major service companies and the communities within which they are located. The Littlewoods leisure and retail empire, based in Liverpool, is one exception, with roots deep in that community. However, frequently where some level of connection and dependency has developed the links are much more fragile and vulnerable to changes in the business and technological environment. The nature of business in most subsectors of the tourism and hospitality industry is such that little long-term corporate identity with a specific location can be seen. By its nature, the industry is one of dispersal and not concentration, where production and service cannot be centralized. It is, as we have said earlier, an industry of every parish. There are some partial exceptions. Major airlines tend to concentrate their operations in one or, at most, a small number of locations. Thus, a very high proportion of the 30 000 workforce of British Airways is based at or close to Heathrow Airport, London, but increasingly some functions are being sited elsewhere in more cost-effective locations. For example, BA's central reservations now operate from outside Newcastle in the northeast of England. Likewise, 'honeypot' theme parks such as Disney require a level of investment so that local presence is not realistic. Even Disney, however, has dispersed to four major world locations (two in the USA, one in Japan and one in France) and has developed a policy of local retail outlets which both merchandise Disney brands and provide dispersed promotion and access to its products in support of the main locations.

While the scale of many tourism and hospitality businesses is such that a widely recognized identity between one company and its community is not that common, in another sense the very smallness of most tourism and hospitality enterprises necessitates a local focus which may be absent in larger firms. A high level of family involvement in the operation and management of many concerns implies a local commitment and such businesses will generally supplement their skills requirememts from within the local labour pool – they are unlikely to have the resources to look more widely for expertise. Furthermore, the seasonal nature of many such businesses means that long-term employment commitments to those from outside of the locality are unlikely. In this sense, therefore, the growing strength of multiple unit tourism and hospitality businesses on a national and transnational level, combined with the market power provided by centralized computer reservations and information systems, are likely to weaken the local community connection of the industry.

In addition, moves towards standardization in the delivery of product and service in larger corporately owned operations has significant implications for the role that a local labour market has to play in meeting the skills demands of such businesses. On the one hand, there is likely to be a reduction in the overall skills levels required in response to automation and standardization, while on the other opportunities for local entrepreneurship will also be reduced and management requirements met from within a central planning process. Such changes will, ultimately, have the potential to undermine the sustainability of the industry in human resource terms especially as demographic pressures increase the competitiveness of the labour market for semi- and unskilled labour, unless the corporate tourism and hospitality sector recognizes the importance of its community links.

There is a sense beyond the individual business in which the tourism and hospitality industry does have a strong community link and identity and that is as a collective entity. Many locations within Europe are identified as tourism destinations, whether we are talking about the great cities of Paris, Rome or St Petersburg, the Greek islands, the Swiss ski resorts or touring and sporting terrain such as west Cork in Ireland. In these locations, the tourism and hospitality industry, if it does exist as a collective body, has strong community associations. In economic terms such destinations, to a greater or lesser degree, depend upon tourism and hospitality for their livelihood and any significant downturn in business will affect the prosperity of the communities concerned. Tourism and hospitality also can provide the basis and rationale for investment in infrastructure such as utilities and transportation, which are of direct community benefit and can contribute to the preservation of local historic and cultural resources as well as providing new ones, such as the branch of the Tate Gallery in St Ives, Cornwall. In this sense, tourism, as Murphy (1985) rightly argues, is a community resource and also a community responsibility. This responsibility extends to ensuring the sustainability of human resource policies and practices that operate within it. Sustainability, in this context, applies to the manner in which local tourism and hospitality employers relate to the local labour market, the extent to which they actively encourage local people to work within the industry or, by way of contrast, seek to recruit from possibly cheaper labour pools elsewhere. It also relates to the extent to which the tourism and hospitality industry and their public representatives ensure that there is educational and training provision locally which is designed to cater for the skills requirements of employers in that resort community, thus enhancing the local skills base and reducing the imperative to attract trained personnel from elsewhere to meet specific needs. The coordinated efforts of the tourism and hospitality industry and local political interests in Kerry, Ireland can be given considerable credit in the establishment of specific training courses for the industry at the Tralee Regional Technical College during the late 1980s, thus providing educational and training opportunities within the community as well as meeting skills shortages within the local industry.

## A BELIEF IN THE SUPERIORITY OF INTRINSIC OVER EXTRINSIC MOTIVATION IN THE WORKPLACE

The sustainable model also has implications for the way in which managers in the tourism and hospitality industry perceive their employees and understand how they are motivated and what provides satisfaction in the workplace. This perception, in part, derives from the sense of loyalty to a community but also reflects a perspective on the individual that is different from the old model, with its emphasis upon short-term results and externally driven rewards and punishments. Traditional human resource management views people as an immediate and dispensable resource, from which maximum productivity must be extracted with the overall objective of enhancing profitability in the short- to medium-term. This view can be traced back to Adam Smith and the notion of rational individuality in all things within the economic sphere. Smith's perspective leads to the notion that people will only perform to their optimum through extrinsic motivation, primarily through the allocation or withdrawl of financial rewards or other such benefits. The concept that people may be motivated by other forces than extrinsic reward does not figure within Smith and is a view that re-emerged strongly, through New Right thinking, in Western Europe during the 1980s.

Smith's economic individualism gained support from Darwin's thesis that all species, including humans, adapt to the environment which they face and that those which adapt best survive while those which fail to change become extinct. Applied to the individual and to the economic world, this leads to the notion of the survival of the fittest in a competitive world, where only those companies and those individuals best equipped to succeed will actually do so and those that fail do so as part of the natural order of things. There are also implications of a meritocracy, where all individuals start with an equal chance of success and those that are fittest attract the accolades associated with achievement while those without the necessary attributes will remain stationary or may indeed be cast aside.

The logical outcome of a 'marriage' between Smith and Darwin is a working environment that is designed to maximize profitability while, at the same time, rewarding those individuals who contribute most to the achievement of this objective. At the same time, those unable to make the required level of contribution do not benefit from the company's success or, indeed, may be penalized for their failure to contribute. This approach leads to short-term perspectives on employment, whereby staff are seen as an expendable resource that only have a role to play for as long as their contribution is one towards profitability. The notion of a right to employment on a continued basis which, until recently, formed the backbone of Japanese business practice cannot reside comfortably alongside Smith's free market labour environment or the survival of the fittest in business Darwinism.

This combination of Smith and Darwin has a third dimension within the old human resource model and that is the underlying puritanism to which we have referred earlier. This combines the notion of primarily extrinsic motivating factors in the workplace with competitiveness based on survival, and adds the belief 'that Man was a self-seeking, greedy person whose skills, abilities and miseries at work were to be dealt with as commodities to be supervised, checked, evaluated and traded' (Mahesh, 1994, p. 27).

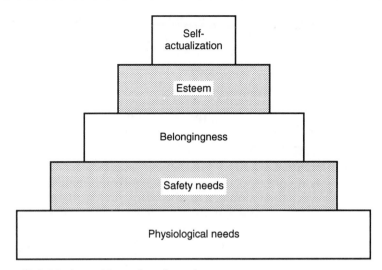

**Figure 10.1** Maslow's hierarchy of needs.

The traditional human resource management model can also be linked to the Maslowian model of human motivation. As Figure 10.1 shows, this model postulates that behaviour is determined in response to a hierarchy of needs. On the basis of this hierarchy, people will only be motivated by a particular level provided that needs with respect to all levels below have been met. As Maslow himself put it:

> For our chronically and extremely hungry man, Utopia can be defined simply as a place where there is plenty of food. He tends to think that, if only he is guaranteed food for the rest of his life, he will be perfectly happy and will never want anything more. Life tends to be defined in terms of eating. Anything else will be defined as unimportant. Freedom, love, community feeling, respect, philosophy, may all be waved aside as fripperies that are useless, since they fail to fill the stomach. Such a man may fairly be said to live by bread alone.    (Maslow, 1943, quoted in Mahesh, 1994, pp. 36–7)

In many respects, the old, non-sustainable model of human resource management is based upon assumptions that an employee's prime motivators at work are those at the base of the Maslow hierarchy, with particular emphasis upon the physiological and safety dimensions. Rewards in this context are primarily extrinsic, tangible and immediate and can readily be equated with an economic return for labour provided. This perspective must be seen in its historical and social context. Mahesh rightly points out that the systemization of work, which is attributed to the thinking of men such as Frederick William Taylor and Henry Ford, occurred at a time when labour in the United States was in considerable surplus and a prime motivator for many immigrant families was the ability to provide food and a home. Rewards beyond these levels on the Maslow hierarchy were, by comparison, relatively unimportant and employees were willing to accept repetitive and demeaning work routines as their only source of income. Such conditions no longer pertain in Western Europe although they have to some extent re-emerged in Eastern Europe.

In an environment where absolute poverty and destitution is not a widespread problem, employee expectations bypass lower, primarily extrinsically motivated needs in the Maslow hierarchy and look to the satisfaction of personal requirements in terms of the intrinsic, that is belongingness, esteem and self-actualization. Mahesh (1994) reports a number of empirical studies which amply demonstrate that intrinsic motivation has greater force and leads to more permanent modifications in behaviour than is the case with primarily extrinsic motivators located at the base of Maslow's hierarchy. The traditional human resource management model is mainly extrinsic in its motivation and, therefore, cannot cater fully for more complex human aspirations.

By contrast, the new paradigm seeks to cater for such needs. The sustainable human resource approach requires that both employers and employees take a long-term view of their relationship in the mutual interests of both parties, of their customers and, ultimately, of company profitability. It is a perspective which recognizes that quality service, a key contributor to competitive advantage in the tourism and hospitality industry, depends for its delivery on committed, well trained, well rewarded and, above all, empowered front-line staff. Empowered behaviour, the key to quality service, cannot be developed on the basis of extrinsic rewards alone. Its achievement depends upon management commitment, from the top, in the form of trust and faith in the capacity of all employees to deliver the desired service and a willingness to invest, through training and development of the individual, in the long-term objective of its attainment. The corollary with respect to employees is a long-term commitment to the company and its objectives and a rejection of mobility for the sake of short-term benefit.

The role in the delivery of service and customer care that is implied by empowerment certainly takes the notion of motivation within the Maslow hierarchy into the realms of belongingness and esteem if not into that of self-actualization. Employees must, within the empowerment model, have a true sense of belonging to the company for whom they work and this sense can be generated both by the faith and trust which employers and management bestow upon their staff and from the implementation of effective internal marketing practices. The rewards are those of esteem in the eyes not only of the employer but also of the customer. The notion of servility and inferiority which dogs so many service encounters in the tourism and hospitality industry is much less likely to occur in an environment of true empowerment, where front-line employees have both pride in what they are doing and the authority to relate to their guests as equals. The Ritz Carlton approach, to which reference has already been made earlier in this book, represents a good example of service on the basis of equal status but different needs and roles in the service encounter.

## A FAITH IN THE CAPACITY OF THE INDIVIDUAL

Sustainability goes beyond a perspective on the factors which motivate employees in the workplace and reflects upon the way in which managers and supervisors view the potential for development and the capacity for growth of those with whom they are working. The traditional human resource model sees people in the specific context of the job that needs to be done. Thus recruitment and training strategies are designed to enable a business to meet its immediate skills requirements, to 'plug a gap' in the workforce which results from attrition by a previous post-holder or as a result in growth in demand. This view rarely looks beyond the immediacy of the specific vacancy in question and thus the individual who applies for the job is evaluated in terms of their ability to fill that gap here and now. It is rare to find companies that take this view, giving consideration to their existing human resources for the vacancy in question unless the personnel profile of individuals who are available exactly fit the requirements of the vacancy.

Sustainability in human resource terms, by contrast, means taking a longer-term perspective and considering the potential of the individual to grow within that job towards greater responsibility or skills demands. It also implies recognition that what an individual actually achieves in a job is closely related to the expectations that significant others have of him or her. In the work context, this means managers or supervisors. The consequences of what is known as the Pygmalion effect mean that, in simple terms, low expectations deliver poor performance while high expectations enable individuals to excel. In other words, individual and group performance is significantly affected, in both positive and negative terms, by the expectations that others have for that individual or group. A number of empirical studies have demonstrated the relevance of this proposition to the process of learning and to achievement in the workplace. Mahesh refers to the conclusions of Goddard (1985) who reviewed some 300 Pygmalion effect studies. These are

1. What managers expect of their subordinates and the way they treat them largely determine their performance and career progress;
2. A unique characteristic of superior managers is their ability to create high performance expectations that subordinates can fulfil;
3. Less effective managers fail to develop similar expectations and, as a consequence, the productivity of their subordinates suffers;
4. Subordinates, more often than not, appear to do what they believe is expected of them; and

5. The highest output is achieved by jobholders whose supervisors expect – and insist upon – high performance.

(Mahesh, 1994, pp. 64–5)

This argument that people in the workplace perform according to the expectations that are held about them is of considerable importance in the context of the tourism and hospitality industry. We have seen in earlier chapters that the industry in Europe remains one of high labour intensity, with only limited potential for technology substitution and that much of this labour is inputted at a low skills level. We have also reviewed the role of front-line staff in the delivery of service within most tourism and hospitality businesses noting that these staff are frequently the members of the organization with the lowest level of skills and, in terms of remuneration and status, perceived to be the least valued. These staff also deliver the vast majority of an organization's 'moments of truth' to the customer and, in doing so, play a major role in the relationship marketing effort of the company. This delivery of service generally takes place without supervision or direct control.

Yet it is true to say that, within the traditional human resource management model in tourism and hospitality, companies have relatively limited expectations of their front-line staff. They are readily dispensable at times of reduced demand and are the last to benefit from enhanced rewards and benefits when the company is performing well. It is a widely held expectation that front-line staff will exhibit limited loyalty to the company and will move elsewhere without compunction. Training and development are frequently seen as a wasted investment for this group, as staff will in all probability use their new found skills as bargaining tools in the search for better employment elsewhere. Recruitment is based on short-term expectations and in order to meet immediate requirements. All in all, employers have what they would describe as 'realistic' expectations of staff in this category and base their relationship with individuals upon such expectations. The logic of Pygmalion is that front-line staff, faced with such expectations, will deliver precisely what is anticipated, certainly no more and possibly less. As a result, a vicious circle of limited expectations and limited performance is established. The consequences of this scenario, from the employer's perspective, are those which characterize the old human resource model in Table 1.3 and are manifest in terms of:

- limited vision in recruitment;
- a failure to identify the real potential of those who are selected;
- a total lack of, or at best low investment in, training and development;
- a lack of nurturing for future growth and enhancement;
- a disinclination to delegate or give responsibility to front-line staff; and
- expectations of limited capability, low company loyalty and rapid staff turnover.

From the point of view of the front-line employees, this scenario results in attitudes and behaviour such as:

- a low sense of loyalty to a company that appears to place limited value in the individual;
- a frustration at the lack of opportunity for growth or enhancement;
- a reluctance on the part of the highly motivated and ambitious to apply for jobs within the company;
- limited motivation to perform better or to raise productivity or service standards;
- a disinclination to accept delegated responsibility; and
- high levels of staff turnover.

Within the sustainable paradigm, this negative expectation cycle is broken. Expectations in this context are not driven by the notion that individuals have limitless potential and that all members of staff or new recruits can become a chief executive, an award-winning chef or a top equestrian instructor. Rather it is a perspective which treats each individual on his or her merits, recognizes their individuality and seeks to nurture and develop the potential that exists to its maximum level. It is an approach which does not make generalized assumptions about people based on current employment status/level, gender, race, physical disability, educational background or the level of the post that is currently held. Above all, it is an approach that demands openmindedness and the ability to recognize the potential for growth in all individuals. From an employer's point of view, recognizing the power of the Pygmalion effect has a number of important consequences which are implicit in the sustainable paradigm. These include:

- recruitment that considers the longer-term needs of the company rather than just filling an immediate gap and thus looks at individuals from the point of view of their potential as well as their existing skills/experience profile;
- recruitment that looks at existing staff and their potential when appointing to positions of responsibility before turning to outside sources of labour;
- management attitudes and style that support individuals in their aspirations for growth and enhancement within the company and, if need be, elsewhere;
- encouragement for staff to participate in training and development in order to meet personal and company needs and objectives;
- management and supervision that seeks to pass responsibility to front-line staff through delegation and empowerment;
- rewards and benefits that encourage performance, loyalty and long service; and
- provision of clear and public criteria for promotion and access to development which do not discriminate on the basis of gender, race, physical disability or any other factor.

By the same token, the Pygmalion effect within the sustainable paradigm has a number of implications from the perspective of the employee. These include:

- viewing employment as a process which provides opportunities for growth, development and enhancement for those that have the skills and aspirations in that direction, but also acknowledging that there may be some delimitors on this process within a specific company;
- recognizing that growth, development and enhancement are earned over a period of time and are not a right bestowed on the basis of specific training or qualifications;
- being realistic in the workplace and recognizing the personal limitations that exist in terms of potential and achievement, or what Mahesh (1994) calls the concept of 'threshold limitations';
- demonstrating commitment and participating in training and development opportunities in the workplace even though immediate enhancement and rewards may not follow; and
- accepting that managers and supervisors make employment decisions in good faith and without prejudice or discrimination on the basis of gender, race, physical disability or other factors.

Therefore this perspective on sustainability implies a focus on the individual and recognition of the potential for growth and development that exists, to differing levels and in various ways, in each individual. In the absence of this faith, true empowerment is impossible and, as a consequence, genuinely effective service quality cannot be achieved in the tourism and hospitality industry.

## A LONG-TERM VIEW OF HUMAN RESOURCE MANAGEMENT

Sustainability in human resource terms implies a commitment to the individual and his or her potential for growth and development. This, by its very nature, necessitates a long-term perspective with respect to the organization's human resource requirements. The old human resource model in Table 1.3 points to widespread practice in the tourism and hospitality industry of giving priority to short-term objectives and to viewing people as a readily adjustable resource which can be manipulated in response to market changes, especially on the demand side. This problem is well illustrated by companies in a number of subsectors which invest heavily in the development of physical plant and in attendant marketing prior to the opening of a new or expanded tourism and hospitality facility but only give last-minute attention to meeting the skills requirements of the project. This is true at a regional or national level as well as within individual projects. Tourism and hospitality schools and colleges are typically built in response to a human resource crisis within a fledgling industry rather than in parallel, or indeed in advance of them. The consequences of a lack of planning in this domain can be considerably in terms of, for example, poor service delivery or the need to draft in expertise from outside of the community, region or even country in order to meet new skills demands. Likewise, traditional deficiencies, especially the lack of human resource planning at times of growth, may necessitate a company to recruit from outside in order to fill positions of responsibility in the organization rather than investing in the planned development of existing staff in anticipation of change.

I have argued elsewhere (Baum, 1993a), that the human resource development lead time in tourism and hospitality is generally considerably greater than is the case with respect to the product or marketing development of a project or area. The sustainable human resource paradigm within tourism and hospitality focuses upon the planning needs in this area at all levels, whether relating to a small company expanding or diversifying its markets or to a city or region planning to reorientate its economic and employment structure in the direction of tourism and hospitality from other, possibly declining, areas of activity. A number of industrial cities in Britain, such as Bradford, Glasgow and Liverpool, are examples of locations where such transition has taken place in recent years. Planning of this nature may be required at the company level or within a wider context and, therefore, frequently will involve a number of agencies and providers, including those within the industry itself as well as among education and training organizations and support funding agencies. The application of integrated planning mechanisms, such as those discussed in Chapter 9, become an important contributor to sustainability in this area.

Sustainable human resource planning is also an important factor in ensuring that a community's true potential, in terms of the skills and related attributes that it has to offer, are fully recognized. This has important implications in terms of the discussion in Chapters 6 and 7 about recognizing the potential of all sections of the community and overcoming the limited representation of women and ethnic minorities among senior positions in the industry. We have already discussed the dangers inherent in underestimating the potential of the individual for growth and development. The same principle is true at a community and, indeed, a national level. The long-standing practice of employing expatriate management and technical staff in the major hotels of many developing countries in Asia, Africa and the Caribbean is justified on the grounds that local skills do not exist to take on such responsibilities. Such an assessment may well have been true at the onset when no tourism and hospitality tradition existed in the area and when little or no local training was available. However, such an argument loses its potency in locations such as Hong Kong and Singapore where the skills exist to operate every other kind of complex industrial and service industry, including world-rated airlines, but hotels still preserve their expatriate connection.

Unless the growth and development potential of the local community is fully recognized and acted upon, the original analysis will become self-fulfilling and, indeed, local expertise will not be recognized. Furthermore, senior positions in hotels will become seen as the preserve of expatriates and ambitious and able young people from the local community will not opt for the industry in their career choices. In the European context, this particular issue has much salience with respect to new and increasing investment in the developing tourism and hospitality industry of the east. There is a clear danger that, in the absence of investment in education and training, major tourism and hospitality companies will fail to recognize and develop local potential to the highest levels and perpetuate many of the problems expatriate management faced in the developing world.

At a more local level, assumptions are readily made about the ability of a community to respond to changes in the economic structure and provide the required expertise for the tourism and hospitality industry after the decline of other, traditional industries. On the basis of such assumptions, companies may neglect to test local potential and look elsewhere for the necessary skills. Such assumptions become self-fulfilling as members of the local community see that quality opportunities and those offering scope for development and enhancement are taken by outsiders.

## McDONALDIZATION AND SUSTAINABILITY

In this book we have encountered a number of conundrums and their satisfactory resolution has only in part been addressed. One of the more important of these is that of how to reconcile two seemingly incompatible trends within the European tourism and hospitality industry. On the one hand, the service revolution has established quality in this domain as a prime market demand, and differentiation in terms of service has increasingly been shown to be a major factor in consumer choice (Balmer and Baum, 1993). This in turn has led to articulation of the concepts of internal marketing and staff empowerment, essential ingredients in the really effective delivery of quality service in the tourism and hospitality industry. Internal marketing and empowerment in turn are concepts that have close associations with the application of sustainable human resource policies and practices.

The counter-balancing weight on the scales of this conundrum is that of McDonaldization or the rational standardization of product and service delivery within the tourism and hospitality industry. McDonaldization, a term which Ritzer (1993) introduces to the vocabulary and so clearly articulates, is a natural development from earlier Taylorism and Fordism in the manufacturing context. However, according to Ritzer's thesis, McDonaldization represents a process which has impacted upon the wider social domain beyond the workplace and created a culture which cherishes speed and convenience of delivery, labour-saving attributes and the certainty and confidence provided to the consumer by the standardization of product and service delivery.

The logical consequences of McDonaldization in human resource terms involve the deskilling of many jobs in the European tourism and hospitality industry. The process of standardization in terms of product and service delivery, combined with the implementation of computerization in accounting, control, sales and marketing and a host of related areas, means that the nature of work is changing in most sectors of tourism and hospitality, especially in those operations affiliated to the larger, multinational companies. This impact applies at all operational and management levels and reduces the pre-entry and qualification levels required by the company. It also limits the investment that companies need to make in order to prepare new entrants as well as in anticipation of promotion or change.

As a result of these changes and their impact, McDonaldization contributes towards the perpetuation of a low-wage and low-status environment in the tourism and hospitality industry and this is a trend that is likely to be maintained despite demographic pressures in the labour market. At a national level, deskilling and attendant processes are, in part, reflected in the restructuring of the United Kingdom's economy since 1980, with the majority of new jobs created being in the low-paid, low-skills service sectors, including the McDonaldized areas of tourism and hospitality. The issue of low versus high wage economic development is at the heart of much of the disagreement between Britain and its European partners and is closely linked to the effects of McDonaldization.

McDonaldization does not sit comfortably with the concept of sustainable human resource development in the European tourism and hospitality industry. It reduces the skills requirements of work thus contributing to a lessening of the overall skills base within a community and eliminates from the industry at a local level many of the more qualified, professionally-focused positions within the workforce which tend to offer higher remuneration and better career prospects. McDonaldization also has an in-built acceptance of some of what have been described as the negative dimensions of the old human resource model, notably high labour turnover and a lack of opportunities for enhancement and development. McDonaldization views labour as a transitory resource, readily replaced, and because of the low skills and training requirement, such turnover has little impact on the delivery of product or service. Because labour is transitory, there is little need to avoid repetitive and demotivating routines in the workplace because tolerance will not be tested in the relatively short period of time that most individuals will spend in the job. Employees, in turn, accept the parameters of the jobs that they are undertaking and do not look for anything beyond short-term outcomes from their work and the satisfaction of lower order motivational needs. This short-termism, in turn, contributes to the overall image of the industry as an employer and deters many of the potentially more able among school and college leavers from applying for other than temporary and transitory positions. Little by way of a long-term commitment is made or stake taken within the local labour market by companies which have focused on standardization, and this is the antithesis of the sustainable paradigm. The alternative and undoubtedly much more expensive focus of investing in the individual and in the community is of long-term benefit to both the company and the people it works with, and through this process to the quality of product and service that is delivered to the consumer. It is only with long-term commitment to the individual and, through him or her, to the community, that true empowerment can be achieved which, in turn, allows employees to obtain more than lower levels of motivational benefits from the workplace.

At the end of the day, there is no clear resolution to the McDonaldization–sustainability conundrum. While considering the impact of standardization in the European tourism and hospitality industry and its growing importance at a macro level, it is important not to forget that the majority of small businesses in the industry remain inured from its immediate effects. However, the not inconsiderable effects of budget hotels upon traditional small town establishments in France and Britain as well as the consequences of fast-food restaurants on more traditional competition point to some of the areas of potentially significant impact which cannot be ignored. The eventual outcome with respect to this conundrum may be a wide and growing gulf between those operations on the one hand which focus upon depersonalized systems and the delivery of low-cost products and services with a minimal skills input, and those on the other which focus on high-cost, premium service delivery in a personalized, customized format, with an emphasis on quality and empowered front-line staff and management.

## SUSTAINABILITY AND SOCIAL RESPONSIBILITY

We commenced this chapter with a consideration of sustainability in the context of its moral dimension from a largely humanist perspective. The morality of the argument is also entirely compatible with the teaching of most mainstream religions and, indeed, with common sense. Its only possible source of conflict comes in relation to the short-term cost of sustainable policies and the impact that such approaches have on the somewhat blinkered judgement of financial investors particularly in Western Europe. There is no doubt that the human resource practices which sustainability implies can be costly to implement and maintain in the short-term and there remains a reluctance on the part of stock market investors to view investment in people as a worthwhile risk. Indeed, pressures have been inexorable in the other direction in recent years with plaudits awarded to those companies which have succeded in reducing the labour requirement and downsizing their workforce. It is the argument in this book that such strategies cannot work in the long-term within those sectors of the European tourism and hospitality industry which seek to maintain a quality product and service, and that investment in human capital is the only viable and profitable strategy that companies in this market can adopt.

This argument draws much of its strength from the wider debate about the social and corporate responsibility of business in general and how industry and late twentieth-century capitalism in general relate to the wider physical, social, economic, cultural and political environment in which they exist. Much of the discussion in this debate has focused primarily on physical and ecological concerns and the sustainability of industry in the context of finite natural resources and the degradation of the environment. However, similar arguments in terms of social and corporate responsibility go beyond this dimension and impact upon how companies and the corporate sector in general relate to their host communities and the responsibilities and loyalties that they have at that level. The record of many major companies, in this respect, has not been particularly good in recent years. The relationship of the corporate sector to people in the workplace and in the community is a central aspect of the social responsibility of the business sector. This theme emerges as important in the discussion of writers in this area such as Schumacher (1975) Cannon (1992) Sorell and Hendry (1994) and, indeed, Mahesh (1994), to whom considerable reference has already been made in this chapter.

Ethical human resource policies are sustainable human resource policies. Their implementation requires commitment and, above all, a vision of the future within European tourism and hospitality which recognizes the increasingly competitive global environment with which the industry is faced. The human resource vision that will support the competitive position of European tourism and hospitality is derived from the sustainable paradigm as the main tenets of the traditional model have increasingly been shown to be flawed. Connock (1991) articulates the need for vision in this respect when he argues as follows:

> Developing the HR vision is about articulating the long-term HR goals, core values, key behaviour and underlying philosophy which derive from, support and complement the business mission and strategies. It will be realistic yet visionary; specific enough to be meaningful yet general enough to be applicable in different parts of the business. It will appeal to staff at all levels by demonstrating a clear direction which captures the emotions. From the HR vision will come HR strategies, objectives, milestones, performance measures. All will be integrated and cohesive, deriving from the business mission and ultimately judged on the success of the business in fulfilling that mission. (Connock, 1991, p. 172)

If we transpose the corporate context which Connock considers to that of the wider European tourism and hospitality industry but apply the same principles, we have the arena for the sustainable human resource vision which this book has sought to address.

---

REVIEW AND DISCUSSION QUESTIONS

1. Are moral and ethical considerations unrealistic luxuries to employers in the highly competitive tourism and hospitality industry?
2. In what ways might tourism and hospitality companies have both a more detached and a closer relationship with the local community than a heavy manufacturing plant?
3. What strategies could a tourism and hospitality company employ in order to strengthen its community links?
4. Identify situations where the Pygmalion effect may have worked to the advantage or disadvantage of yourself or friends?
5. What steps can managers take to reduce the potentially negative impacts of Pygmalion?
6. How useful is Maslow's motivational model to understanding the needs and aspirations of staff at all levels in the tourism and hospitality industry?
7. What motivational levels will empowerment in the workplace satisfy?
8. Is sustainable human resource management incompatible with Ritzer's idea of McDonaldization?
9. How important is a sense of social responsibility to a tourism and hospitality company in formulating its human resource policies and practices?
10. Refering back to Table 1.3, how would you edit, revise or expand the sustainable paradigm in the light of reading this book?

# References

Aderhold, P., Teigland, J., Steene, A. and Koskinen, J. (1993) Tourism in Scandinavia, in *Tourism in Europe: Structures and Developments* (eds W. Pompl and P. Lavery), CABI, Wallingford, Oxford.

Airey, D. (1994) *Education for Tourism in Poland*. Proceedings of the EuroCHRIE Conference Hospitality Schools East-West, Vienna, April 1994.

Akehurst, G., Bland, N. and Nevin, M. (1993) Tourism policies in the European Community member states. *International Journal of Hospitality Management*, **12**(1), 33–66.

Albrecht, K. and Zemke, R. (1985) *Service America*, Dow Jones-Irwin, Homewood, Ill.

*An Action Strategy for Sustainable Tourism Development*. A publication of the Tourism Stream, Action Strategy Committee, Globe '90 Conference, Vancouver, British Columbia, March 1990.

Anon (1993) Novotel overhauls management culture. *Caterer and Hotelkeeper*, 19 August, p. 22.

Aslan, A.H. and Wood, R.C. (1993) Trade unions in the hotel and catering industry: the views of hotel managers. *Employee Relations*, **15**(2) 61–70.

Atkinson, J. (1985) *Flexibility, Uncertainty and Manpower Management*, Institute of Manpower Studies, Brighton.

Balmer, S. and Baum, T. (1993) Applying Herzberg's hygiene factors to the changing accommodation environment: the application of motivational theory to the field of guest satisfaction. *International Journal of Contemporary Hospitality Management*, **5**(2), 27–31.

Bar-On, R. (1989) *Travel and Tourism Data*, Euromonitor Publications, London.

Bartlett, N. (1993) Forte introduces flexible rosters. *Caterer and Hotelkeeper*, 19 August, p. 7.

Battersby, D. (1990) Lifting the barriers: employment and training in tourism and leisure. *Insights*, D7–1.

Baum, T. (1987) Introducing educational innovation in hospitality studies. *International Journal of Hospitality Management*, **6**(2), 97–102.

Baum, T. (1988) Towards a new definition of hotel management. *Cornell HRA Quarterly*, **29**(2), 36–40.

Baum, T. (1989a) Scope of the tourism industry and its employment impact in Ireland. *The Service Industries Journal*, **9**(1), 140–51.

Baum, T. (1989b) Managing hotels in Ireland: research and development for change. *International Journal of Hospitality Management*, **8**(2), 131–44.

Baum, T. (1990) Competencies for hotel management: industry expectations of education. *International Journal of Contemporary Hospitality Management*, **2**(4), 13–16.

Baum, T. (1991a) *Perceptions of Employment in the Tourism Industry.* Working Paper, School of Accounting, Business and Economics, University of Buckingham, Buckingham.

Baum, T. (1991b) The US and the UK – comparing the expectations of management trainees. *Cornell HRA Quarterly*, **32**(2), 79–84.

Baum, T. (1993a) Human resources in tourism: an introduction, in *Human Resource Issues in International Tourism* (ed. T. Baum), Butterworth-Heinemann, Oxford.

Baum, T. (1993b) Human resource concerns in European tourism: strategic response and the EC. *International Journal of Hospitality Management*, **12**(1), 77–88.

Baum, T. (1993c) Creating an integrated human resource environment for tourism, in *Human Resource Issues in International Tourism* (ed. T. Baum), Butterworth-Heinemann, Oxford.

Baum, T. (1994a) The development and implementation of national tourism policies. *Tourism Management*, **15**(3), 185–92.

Baum, T. (1994b) Managing the development and implementation of national human resource policies for tourism, in *Tourism: The State of the Art* (eds A.V. Seaton *et al.*) John Wiley and Sons, London.

Baum, T. (1994c) National tourism policies: implementing the human resource dimension. *Tourism Management*, **15**(4), 259–66.

Baum, T. and McLoughlin, L. (1984) Catering for lifeskills. *Irish Institute for Training and Development Journal*, October.

Baum, T. and Reid, P. (1986) Developing the ladder to professionalism. *Florida International Hospitality Review*, Fall, pp. 45–53.

Bemelmens, L. (1942) *Hotel Splendide*, Hamish Hamilton, London.

Berry, S. (1992) *The Impact of the British upon Seaside Resort Development in Europe.* Proceedings of the Tourism in Europe 1992 Conference, Durham.

Borer, M.C. (1972) *The British Hotel through the Ages*, Lutterworth Press, London.

Bramham, J. (1982) *Practical Manpower Planning*, 3rd edn, Institute of Personnel Management, London.

Bramham, J. (1983) Manpower planning, in *A Textbook of Techniques and Strategies in Personnel Management* (eds D. Guest and T. Kenny), Institute of Personnel Management, London.

Bramwell, W. and Lane, B. (1993) Sustainable tourism: an evolving global approach? *Journal of Sustainable Tourism*, **1**(1), 1–5.

Braverman, H. (1974) *Labor and Monopoly Capital*, Monthly Review Press, New York.

Bridgford, J. and Stirling, J. (1992) The European dimension: employee relations in Europe, in *The Handbook of Human Resource Management* (ed. B. Towers), Basil Blackwell, Oxford.

Brotherton, R. (1993) *Hospitality Management Education and Graduate Training in Britain and Europe*, Blackpool and the Fylde College.

Burton, R.C.J. (1994) Geographical patterns of tourism in Europe, in *Progress in Tourism, Recreation and Hospitality*, Volume 5 (eds C. Cooper and A. Lockwood), John Wiley and Sons, Chichester.

Buzzard, J. (1993) *The Beaten Track: European Tourism, Literature and the Ways to 'Culture', 1800–1918*, Clarendon Press, Oxford.

Byrne, D. (1986) *Waiting for Change? Working in Hotel and Catering*, Low Pay Unit, London.

Cannon, T. (1992) *Corporate Responsibility*, Financial Times/Pitman, London.

Carlzon, J. (1987) *Moments of Truth*, Ballinger, Cambridge, Mass.

CEDEFOP (1991) *Occupations in the Hotel Tourist Sector within the European Community: A Comparative Approach*, CEDEFOP, Berlin.

CERT (1987) *Scope of the Tourism Industry in Ireland*, CERT, Dublin.

CERT (1992) *Manpower Survey of the Hotel, Catering and Tourism Industry in Ireland*, CERT, Dublin.

Chaieb, K. (1994) Untitled presentation to the Proceedings of the EuroCHRIE Conference Hospitality Schools East–West, Vienna, April.

Christensen, J. (1987) Women in management: advice to recent graduates. *Cornell HRA Quarterly*, **28**(2).

Christopher, M., Payne, A. and Ballantyne, D. (1991) *Relationship Marketing*, Butterworth-Heinemann, Oxford.

Churchill, D. (1994) Time to upgrade, *The Sunday Times Style and Travel*, 22 May, p. 38.

Collis, R. (1994) Pros and cons of code-sharing. *Executive Travel*, September, pp. 36–8.

Commission of the European Communities (1990) *Social Europe: The Labour Market*, Supplement 3/90, CEC, Luxembourg.

Commission of the European Communities (1991a) *Community Action Plan to Assist Tourism*, Com (91) 97 final, CEC, Brussels.

Commission of the European Communities (1991b) *Social Europe: Immigration of citizens from third world countries into the southern Member States of the European Community*, Supplement 1/91, CEC, Luxembourg.

Commission on Industrial Relations (1971) *The Hotel and Catering Industry, Part 1: Hotels and Restaurants*, CIR Report No. 23, London.

Commission for Racial Equality (1991) *Working in Hotels: Report of a Formal Investigation into Recruitment and Selection*, CRE, London.

Conlin, M. and Baum, T. (1994) Comprehensive human resource planning: an essential key to sustainable tourism in island settings, in *Progress in Tourism, Recreation and Hospitality*, Volume 6 (eds C. Cooper and A. Lockwood), John Wiley and Sons, Chichester.

Connock, S. (1991) *HR Vision. Managing a Quality Workforce*, Institute of Personnel Management, London.

Cook Johnson, G. (1991) *How Service Leaders Empower their Employees*, Reacon, Toronto.

Cooper, C., Fletcher, J., Gilbert, D. and Wanhill, S. (1993) *Tourism: Principles and Practice*, Pitman, London.

Davidson, R. (1989) *Tourism*, Pitman, London.

Davidson, T.L. (1994) What are travel and tourism: are they really an industry? in *Global Tourism. The Next Decade* (ed. W. Theobald), Butterworth-Heinemann, Oxford.

Deegan, J. and Dineen, D. (1993) Irish tourism policy: targets, outcomes and environmental considerations, in *Tourism in Ireland: A Critical Analysis* (eds B. O'Connor and M. Cronin), Cork University Press, Cork.

Department of Employment and Productivity (1968) *Company Manpower Planning*, HMSO, London.

Dewey, J. (1916) *Democracy and Education*, Macmillan, London.

Donald, B.L. (1974) Manpower and a planned future, in *Planning for Human Resources* (eds C. Margerison and D. Ashton), Longman, London.

Dronfield, L. and Soto, P. (1982) *Hardship Hotel*, Counter Information Services, London.

Edwards, J. and Sampaio, F. (1993) Tourism in Portugal, in *Tourism in Europe: Structures and Developments* (eds W. Pompl and P. Lavery), CABI, Wallingford, Oxford.

EIESP (1991) *Education for Careers in European Travel and Tourism*, European Institute of Education and Social Policy, Paris.

Feiffer, M. (1985) *Going Places*, Macmillan, London.

Fianna Fail (1987) *Putting Growth Back into Tourism*, Fianna Fail, Dublin.

Fitzpatrick, J. (1989) *Travel and Tourism in the Single European Market*, EIU Special Report 2014, London.

Fletcher, J. (1993) Input–output analysis and employment multipliers, in *Human Resource Issues in International Tourism* (ed. T. Baum), Butterworth-Heinemann, Oxford.

Foster, K. (1991) Not just a job. *Management Service Quality*, May, pp. 223–7.

Fuller, J. (1971) *Chef's Manual of Kitchen Work*, Batsford, London.

Gabriel, Y. (1988) *Working Lives in Catering*, Routlege & Kegan Paul, London.

Gilg, A. (1991) Switzerland: structural change within stability, in *Tourism and Economic Development: Western European Experiences*, 2nd, edn (A. Williams and G. Shaw), Belhaven Press, London.

Goddard, R.W. (1985) The Pygmalion effect. *Personnel Journal*, June.

Goodstein, L. and Burke, W.W. (1991) Creating successful organizational change. *Organizational Dynamics*, **19**(4), 5–17.

Guerrier, Y. (1993) Bali, in *Human Resource Issues in International Tourism* (ed. T. Baum), Butterworth-Heinemann, Oxford.

Guerrier, Y. and Lockwood, A. (1989a) Managing flexible working in hotels. *The Service Industries Journal*, **9**(3), 406–19.

Guerrier, Y. and Lockwood, A. (1989b) Core and peripheral employees in hotel operations. *Personnel Review*, **18**(1), 9–15.

Hall, D. (1991) *Tourism and Economic Development in Eastern Europe and the Soviet Union*, Belhaven Press, London.

Hall, E.T. and Hall, M.R. (1990) *Understanding Cultural Differences*, Intercultural Press, Yarmouth, Mass.

Hallam, G. (1994) Why are hotels contracting out portions or all of their food and beverage operation? A comparison between the United Kingdom and North America. Unpublished MSc thesis, University of Buckingham.

Hicks, L. (1990) Excluded women: how can this happen in the hotel world? *The Service Industries Journal*, **10**(2), 34–41.

Hill, R. (1993) Tourism in Germany, in *Tourism in Europe: Structures and Developments* (eds W. Pompl and P. Lavery), CABI, Wallingford, Oxford.

HMSO (1990) *Standard Occupational Classification*, HMSO, London.

Hofstede, G. (1980) *Culture's Consequences: International Differences in Work-related Values*, Sage, Newbury Park, Calif.

Hofstede, G. (1985) The interaction between national organizational value systems. *Journal of Management Studies*, **22**(4), 347–57.

Holloway, C. (1993) Labour vocational education and training, in *Tourism in Europe: Structures and Development* (eds W. Pompl and P. Lavery), CABI, Wallingford, Oxford.

Hotel and Catering Industry Training Board (1981) *Image of Hotel and Catering Work*, HCITB, Wembley, London.

Hotel and Catering Industry Training Board (1984) *Manpower Flows in the Hotel and Catering Industry*, Research Report, HCITB, London.

International Labour Office (1988) *The International Standard Classification of Occupations*, ILO, Geneva.

International Labour Office (1989) *Conditions of work in the hotel, catering and tourism sector, such as hours of work, methods of remuneration, security of employment*, Hotel, Catering and Tourism Committee of the ILO, Geneva.

Irish Hotels Federation (1987) *Tourism Working for Ireland: A Plan for Growth*, IHF, Dublin.

Johnson, R. (1991) A strategy for service – Disney style. *Journal of Business Strategy*, **12**(5), 38–44.

Johnston, W.B. (1991) Global work force 2000: the new world labour market. *Harvard Business Review*, March–April, pp. 115–27.

Kanter, R.M. (1983) *The Change Masters: Innovation and Entrepreneurship in the American Corporation*, Simon & Schuster, New York.

Keiser, J. and Swinton, J. (1988) Professionalism and ethics in hospitality. *Florida International Hospitality Review*, **6**, 23–31.

King, R. (1991) Italy: multi-faceted tourism, in *Tourism and Economic Development: Western European Experiences*, 2nd edn (eds A. Williams and G. Shaw) Belhaven Press, London.

Knight, I. (1971) *Patterns of Labour Mobility in the Hotel and Catering Industry*, HCITB, Wembley, London.

Labich, K. (1990) America takes on the world. *Fortune*, **122**(7), 42–4.

Lane, B. (1992) *Sustainable Tourism: A Philosophy*. The Rural Tourism Unit, Department of Continuing Education, University of Bristol.

Lauermann, E. (1992) British Airways in Europe: a human resource viewpoint of development. *European Management Journal*, **10**(1), 85–6.

Lavery, P. (1993) Tourism in the United Kingdom, in *Tourism in Europe: Structures and Developments* (eds W. Pompl and P. Lavery), CABI, Wallingford, Oxford.

Leeds, C., Kirkbride, P. and Durcan, J. (1994) The cultural context of Europe: a tentative mapping, in *Human Resource Management in Europe: Perspectives for the 1990s* (ed. P. Kirkbride), Routledge, London.

Leiper, N. (1979) The framework of tourism. *Annals of Tourism Research*, **6**(4), 390–407.

Leiper, N. (1990) *Tourism Systems*, Occasional Paper 2, Department of Management Systems, Massey University, Auckland, New Zealand.

Lester, R.A. (1960) *Manpower Planning in a Free Society*, Princeton University Press, Princeton, NJ.

Lewis, R. and Chambers, R. (1989) *Marketing Leadership in Hospitality*, Van Nostrand Reinhold, New York.

Lewis, J. and Williams, A. (1991) Portugal: market segmentation and regional specialisation, in *Tourism and Economic Development: Western European Experiences*, 2nd edn (eds A. Williams and G. Shaw), Belhaven Press, London.

Linney, C. and Teare, R. (1991) Addressing the human resource challenges of the 1990s. *International Journal of Contemporary Hospitality Management*, 3(2).

Long, V. and Wall, G. (1995) Small-scale tourism development in Bali, Indonesia, in *Island Tourism: Management Principles and Practice* (eds M. Conlin and T. Baum), John Wiley and Sons, Chichester.

Low Pay Unit (1976) *Low Pay in Hotels and Catering*, LPU, London.

Lucas, R. (1993) The Social Charter – opportunity or threat to employment practice in the UK hospitality industry. *International Journal of Hospitality Management*, **12**(1), 89–100.

Macauley, I. and Wood, R.C. (1992) *Hard Cheese: A Study of Hotel and Catering Employment in Scotland*, Scottish Low Pay Unit, Glasgow.

McDonald, R. (1994) *The Nature of Tourism-related Employment in Urban Areas: The Liverpool Example*. Paper presented at Tourism: The State of the Art Conference, University of Strathclyde, Glasgow.

McIntosh, D. (1994) Following the Bass route to IIP. *Voice*, April, pp. 24–5.

Mahesh, V.S. (1988) Effective human resource management: key to excellence in service organizations. *Vikalpa*, **13**(4), 9–15.

Mahesh, V.S. (1993) Human resource planning and development: micro and macro models for effective growth in tourism, in *Human Resource Issues in International Tourism* (ed. T. Baum), Butterworth-Heinemann, Oxford.

Mahesh, V.S. (1994) *Thresholds of Motivation*, McGraw-Hill, New York.

Mansfield, S. (1990) Customer care in tourism and leisure. *Insights*, The English Tourist Board.

Mars, G. and Mitchell, P. (1976) *Room for Reform*, Open University Press, Milton Keynes.

Mathieson, A. and Wall, G. (1982) *Tourism: Economic, Physical and Social Impacts*, Longman, London.

Medlik, S. (1988) *What is Tourism?* Proceedings of the Teaching Tourism into the 1990s Conference, University of Surrey.

Mole, J. (1990) *Mind Your Manners: Managing Culture Clash in the Single European Market*, Industrial Society, London.

Murphy, P. (1985) *Tourism: A Community Approach*, Methuen, London.

National Economic and Social Council (1980) *Tourism Policy*, Stationery Office, Dublin.

Orwell, G. (1933; reprinted in 1986) *Down and Out in Paris and London*, Penguin, Harmondsworth.

Page, E. and Kingsford, P.W. (1971) *The Master Chefs: A History of Haute Cuisine*, Edward Arnold, London.

Parsons, D. (1990) Winning workers: rising to the demographic challenge. *Employment Gazette*, February.

Pieters, R. and Geevers, D. (1995) National tourism policy in Bonaire, in *Island Tourism Management: Principles and Practice* (eds M. Conlin and T. Baum), John Wiley and Sons, Chichester.

Pizam, A. (1982) Tourism manpower: the state of the art. *Journal of Travel Research*, **11**(2), 5–9.

Poetschke, B. (1995) Key success factors for public–private sector partnerships in tourism planning, in *Island Tourism: Management*

*Principles and Practice* (eds M. Conlin and T. Baum), John Wiley and Sons, Chichester.

Pompl, W. and Lavery, P. (1993) *Tourism in Europe: Structures and Developments*, CABI, Wallingford, Oxford.

Poon, A. (1993) *Tourism, Technology and Competitive Strategies*, CABI, Wallingford, Oxford.

Price, E. (1994) The limitations of the law in influencing employment practices in UK hotels and restaurants. *Employee Relations*, **15**(2), 16–24.

Quinn, F. (1990) *Crowning the Customer*, The O'Brien Press, Dublin.

Richards, G. (1992) *European Social Tourism: Welfare or Investment*. Proceedings of the Tourism in Europe 1992 Conference, Durham.

Riley, M. (1985) Some social and historical perspectives on unionization in the UK hotel industry. *International Journal of Hospitality Management*, **4**(3), 99–104.

Riley, M. (1991) *Human Resource Management: A Guide to Personnel Practice in the Hotel and Catering Industries*, Butterworth–Heinemman, Oxford.

Riley, M. (1993) Labour markets and vocational education, in *Human Resource Issues in International Tourism* (ed. T. Baum), Butterworth-Heinemann, Oxford.

Ritzer, G. (1993) *The McDonaldization of Society: An Investigation into the Changing Character of Contemporary Social Life*, Pine Forge Press, Thousand Oaks, Calif.

Robinson, G. (1993) Tourism and tourism policy in the European Community: an overview. *International Journal of Hospitality Management*, **12**(1), 7–20.

Robinson, O. and Wallace, J. (1983) Employment trends in the hotel and catering industry in Great Britain. *The Service Industries Journal*, **3**(3), 260–78.

Robson, J. (1993) Soaring to new heights. *Managing Service Quality*, January, pp. 465–8.

Russell, B. (1926 – 7th impression 1960) *On Education*, Unwin, London.

Saunders, K. C. (1981) *Social Stigma of Occupations: The Lower Grade Worker in Service Organisations*, Gower, London.

Sheldon, P. (1989) Professionalism in tourism and hospitality. *Annals of Tourism Research*, **16**(4), 492–503.

Schlesinger, L. and Heskett, J. L. (1991) The service-driven company. *Harvard Business Review*, September–October, pp. 71–81.

Schumacher, E. F. (1975) *Small is Beautiful*, Harper & Row, London.

Skull, A. (1991) Swiss hotel management education. Unpublished MBA dissertation, Brunel University.

Sorell T. and Hendry, J. (1994) *Business Ethics*, Butterworth-Heinemann, Oxford.

Sparrowe, R. (1994) Empowerment in the hospitality industry: an exploration of antecedents and outcomes. *Hospitality Research Journal*, **17**(3), 51–74.

Stainer, G. (1971) *Manpower Planning: The Management of Human Resources*, Heinemann, London.

Stationery Office (1985) *White Paper on Tourism Policy*, Stationery Office, Dublin.

Stationery Office (1987) *Improving the Performance of Irish Tourism*, Stationery Office, Dublin.

Steinecke, A. (1993) The historical development of tourism in Europe, in *Tourism in Europe: Structures and Developments* (eds W. Pompl and P. Lavery), CABI, Wallingford, Oxford.

Tanke, M. (1990) *Human Resources Management for the Hospitality Industry*, Delmar, Albany, NY.

Taylor, R., Airey, D. and Kotas, R. (1983) Rates of pay in the British hotel and catering industry. *International Journal of Hospitality Management*, **2**(3), 157–9.

Toffler, A. (1985) *The Adaptive Corporation*, McGraw-Hill, London.

Tourism Society, The (1993) *The Profile of Tourism Studies Degree Courses in The UK 1993*, The Tourism Society, London.

Towner, J. (1985) The history of the grand tour. *Annals of Tourism Research*, **12**(3), 310–16.

Turner, L. and Ash, J. (1975) *The Golden Hordes: Tourism and the Pleasure Periphery*, Constable, London.

Urry, J. (1994) Europe, tourism and the nation-state, in *Progress in Tourism, Recreation and Hospitality*, Volume 5 (eds C. Cooper and A. Lockwood), John Wiley and Sons, Chichester.

Valenzuela, M. (1991) Spain: the phenomenon of mass tourism, in *Tourism and Economic Development: Western European Experiences*, 2nd edn (eds A. Williams and G. Shaw), Belhaven Press, London.

Van Langenhove, L. and Lowyck, E. (1993) Belgium, in *Human Resource Issues in International Tourism* (ed. T. Baum), Butterworth-Heinemann, Oxford.

Vikhanski, O. and Puffer, S. (1993) Management education and employee training at Moscow McDonald's. *European Management Journal*, **11**(1), 102–7.

Walsh, M.E. (1993) Ireland, in *Human Resource Issues in International Tourism* (ed. T. Baum), Butterworth-Heinemann, Oxford.

Walsh, M.E. and McKenna, M. (1990) *Women: The Under-utilised Resource in Tourism Employment*. Proceedings of Tourism Research into the 1990s Conference, New College, Durham.

Walsh, T. (1991) 'Flexible' employment in the retail and hotel trades, in *Farewell to Flexibility?* (ed. A. Pollert), Basil Blackwell, Oxford.

Watson, P. (1988) Training for quality service. *Journal of European Industrial Training*, **12**(2), 20–3.

Williams, A. and Shaw, G. (1991) Western European tourism in Perspective, in *Tourism and Economic Development: Western European*

*Experiences*, 2nd edn (eds A. Williams and G. Shaw), Belhaven Press, London.

Witt, S. (1994) Opening of the Eastern bloc countries, in *Global Tourism. The Next Decade* (ed. W. Theobald), Butterworth-Heinemann, Oxford.

Wood, R.C. (1992a) *Working in Hotels and Catering*, Routledge, London.

Wood, R.C. (1992b) Hospitality industry labour trends. *Tourism Management*, **13**(3), 297–304.

Wood, R.C. (1993) Status and hotel and catering work: theoretical dimensions and practical implications. *Hospitality Research Journal*, **16**(3), 3–16.

World Tourism Organization (1994a) *Tourism in 1993 – Highlights*, WTO, Madrid.

World Tourism Organization (1994b) *Aviation and Tourism Policies: Balancing the Benefits*, Routledge, London.

World Tourism Organization (1994c) *National and Regional Tourism Planning: Methodologies and Case Studies*, Routledge, London.

Young, G. (1973) *Tourism: Blessing or Blight?*, Penguin, Harmondsworth.

# Author index

# Geographical index

# Subject index